SOCIAL CAPITAL IN HONG KONG

This book is on a burning issue. How can we apply the theory of social capital in practice and what can be learned from the practice of social capital for a further elaboration of its theory? Authors in this volume succeed in building a bridge between social science and social life, thereby offering ideas on how social capital in communities can be strengthened.

Professor Dr. Beate VOLKER
Department of Sociology/ICS
Utrecht University
The Netherlands

The present book provides a timely reflection on Hong Kong's initiatives of social capital development, along with a critical discussion of major connectivities of social capital and its relationship with social enterprise. This has been made possible by the coming together of scholars and practitioners with strong backgrounds in social science, health, and business. Their multi-disciplinary scholarship and practical experience should assure the wide appeal of the book.

Professor Siu-kai LAU
Head of the Central Policy Unit
The Government of Hong Kong SAR, China

Social Capital in Hong Kong
Connectivities and Social Enterprise

Edited by
Sik Hung NG
Stephen Yan-Leung CHEUNG
Brahm PRAKASH

City University of Hong Kong Press

First published 2010
Second printing 2011
Printed in Hong Kong

ISBN: 978-962-937-186-9

Published by
City University of Hong Kong Press
Tat Chee Avenue, Kowloon, Hong Kong

Website: www.cityu.edu.hk/upress
E-mail: upress@cityu.edu.hk

我們尋找社會中最失落最無助最頹廢的一群，用關愛重燃希望，發掘他們的潛能，重建他們的信心。激發他們的動力並扶持他們重上人生道路，引導他回饋社會服務他人。最關鍵的在回到我們的第一條信念：尊重他是一個獨立而有價值的人。度身分析他的困難和需要，貼身以建立互信。不離不棄耐性地支持他鼓勵他，直至自立上路而止。*

中華人民共和國香港特別行政區
社區投資共享基金委員會主席 (2002–2006)
鄔維庸醫生
*第三屆社區投資共享基金分享論壇暨計劃博覽會場刊 (第五頁)

We search for the most despondent and helpless within our community and re-ignite their hope with compassion; to rebuild their confidence by finding their potentials; and to re-energize their life journey, providing the channels for them to serve others. The crux is in returning to our first principle, in that we recognize and respect the intrinsic values of each person. We take time to understand their individual needs. We walk closely with them to rebuild mutual trust; and not to waver in our support until the person is firmly re-established.**

Dr Raymond Wu Wai-yung
Chairman of the Community Investment
and Inclusion Fund Committee (2002–2006)
Hong Kong SAR, China
**Source of English translation:
http://www.ciif.gov.hk/tc/msgfromchair/msg_Dr_WU_c.html

Table of Contents

Foreword

Professor LAU Siu-kai
Head of Central Policy Unit,
The Government of Hong Kong SAR

May I begin by sharing with you a story of an elder, Lady Ng, reported in a local newspaper. Lady Ng is a "full-time" senior volunteer who does 3,000 hours of voluntary work per year. She starts her voluntary work at 08:30 in the morning until 11:00 at night, seven days a week. Except for spending around 8 hours at home per day, all her time is devoted to voluntary work. Lady Ng serves different types of people including the mentally retarded, dementia patients, elders living in Homes for the Elderly, people being tried by courts, drug abusers, and wives of prisoners. To service recipients, be they old or young, male or female, ill or retarded, she never says "no." She gives up a leisurely life at home and has taken up such a challenging and rewarding task in her elderly years. Though Lady Ng is an experienced volunteer, she also has some difficulties in her voluntary services. Once she visited an elderly man at home. The old man was quite stubborn and rejected her, sending his fierce dog to threaten her. Lady Ng responded, "I am not afraid of dogs. I patiently talk to you. If you like this, then accept it. If not, I will go away. I come with the intention to show my concern to you." After listening to this, the old man softened his attitude and Lady Ng succeeded in talking to him for 8 minutes. After more contacts with her, his stubborn attitude was melted by her kindness and patience. Now, Lady Ng and this old man became very good friends. Reflecting upon her life as a volunteer, Lady Ng concluded, "Being a volunteer is happier than having my career in the past. In the past I had contact with upper class people, with conversations centring around making money, socialising and showing-off. However, being a volunteer, you can find the true meaning of genuine love, tolerance, acceptance and concern. The satisfaction and happiness that this brings is concrete and more real!"

Although Lady Ng's story may on the surface reflect only her volunteering experience, at a deeper level it has profound meanings for social capital and its diverse connectivities, and hence a fitting introduction to the present book.

Besides financial capital and human capital, social capital is another form of capital that is important for the smooth operation of the economy and society. Social capital has been one of the most widely discussed and researched upon sociological concepts in the last two decades. It attracts attention and arouses interests not only from sociologists, but also from economists, policy studies experts, policy-makers, social workers, as well as community leaders. Many issues and themes related to social capital have been discussed and written upon. Let me begin, however, with the Chinese classics and cite from Mencius, who says, "Respect the old members of my family and also those of other families. Protect my young and also other people's young." This is in line with Confucian philosophy: "Men did not love their parents only, nor treat as children only their own sons. A competent provision was secured for the aged till their death, employment for the able-bodied, and the means of growing up for the young. They showed kindness and compassion to widows, orphans, childless men, and those who were disabled by disease, so that all were sufficiently maintained." These Chinese teachings underpin the building of social capital and its connectivities in Chinese society. They have influenced the philosophy underpinning many charitable organisations in contemporary Hong Kong and represent a form of social capital that is still strong and visible. Although social capital exists in all societies, its level of availability varies. This varying level of social capital in different societies may take different forms as well as being embedded in different social institutions. For example, informal mutual aid in the neighbourhood might be prominent in 7-storey public rental housing estates in 1950s and 1960s Hong Kong, whereas nowadays we have more organised formal voluntary services provided by the government and NGOs, while informal mutual aid among neighbours has diminished compared to a few decades ago: some Hong Kong people may not even know their neighbours living on the same floor of their residence nowadays.

Putnam identified a general decline in levels of social capital in the contemporary society, with people spending much time in front of the television screen, thus having less time to sustain social networks. With growth in the use of internet, people in general, especially the younger generation, may be spending more time in front of a computer than in front of a TV in the 21st century. However, this does not necessarily imply the demise of social capital. Levels of social capital may still be sustained but take a new form, one being built in the cyber world; instead of having 'bowling clubs' as sustainers of social fabric, as suggested by Putnam, people may create and maintain social networks in, or resting on, the virtual world: for example, forming computer clubs, maintaining msn networks, etc. These forms of social networks are common among Hong Kong's younger generation. Such new forms of social network may extend beyond immediate social circles and national boundaries, adopting a global colour, for example, using the internet to establish global network to recruit volunteers and solicit donations for disaster rescues in particular parts of the world.

The Hong Kong SAR Government has long recognized the value of social capital that facilitates the development of a harmonious Hong Kong society. In his 2004 Policy Address, the Chief Executive made specific reference to the Government's initiative in setting up the Community Investment and Inclusion Fund to develop social capital and forge tripartite partnerships: "The social welfare sector has been encouraging volunteerism and has proposed many new ideas to involve the business community to participate in community affairs. In addition, we established the Community Investment and Inclusion Fund in 2002. These have sown seeds for a tripartite partnership between government, the business community and the third sector (not-for-profit sectors). I have asked the Secretary for Health, Welfare and Food to examine ways to develop this tripartite partnership and seek to inculcate this concept in the community to help it to take root."

The present book provides a timely reflection on Hong Kong's initiatives of social capital development such as the Community Investment and Inclusion Fund, along with a critical discussion of major connectivities of social capital and its relationship with social enterprise. This has been made possible by the coming together of scholars and practitioners with strong backgrounds in social science, health and business. Their multidisciplinary scholarship and practical experience should assure the wide appeal of the book.

Foreword

Mr. CHEUNG Kin-chung GBS JP
Secretary for Labour and Welfare, Labour and Welfare Bureau,
The Government of Hong Kong SAR

This special volume takes a collaborative cross-sector and cross-disciplinary approach to social capital development. Social capital fosters social harmony, a necessary condition for intergenerational social inclusion. It is considered by expert economic agents, such as the World Bank, and the Asian Development Bank, and by sociologists such as Robert Putnam, to be the essential social glue and cement that bind different communities together and strengthen the resilience of a community during times of major social and economic changes. It is regarded as the essential fourth capital, along with human, financial, and infra-structural, to achieve and enhance the social and economic outcomes. It does so by changing mindsets, building relationships and creating new opportunities through institutional collaboration.

The present volume is timely as social capital development and its strategic application are very relevant today, when innovative solutions are needed to address the downstream impact of the financial tsunami, or the financial meltdown as it's called in other parts of the world. Perhaps more so than it was in 2001, when social capital development was first systematically introduced into Hong Kong. Let me now provide a very brief context for the introduction of this policy initiative, which has been referred to by several authors of this volume.

At the turn of the new millennium, in the wake of the Asian financial crisis, Hong Kong, like most of its neighbours, was experiencing rapid, sometimes radical and often unprecedented changes that brought about new socio-economic challenges. The Hong Kong Government was committed to operating, funding and supporting what had been generally regarded as relatively comprehensive and increasingly sophisticated social welfare provisions. The new social and economic challenges, however, would suggest that traditional social welfare services alone were no longer adequate. There was an urgent need for different types of competence, adaptability, resilience and entrepreneurship at individual and community levels. Against this background, in his 2001 Policy Address, the then Chief Executive of the Hong Kong SAR, Mr. Tung Chee-hwa, announced the establishment of the Community Investment and Inclusion Fund (CIIF) as a new policy initiative, and I would say this also marked the beginning of a cultural revolution on the Hong Kong social welfare landscape. The HK$300 million fund seeks to promote the development of social capital in Hong Kong. More specifically, it provides seed funds to community projects helping build the capacity of the disadvantaged, encourage mutual support, and develop cross-strata neighbourhood networks as well as new social and economic opportunities through cross-sector relationships. A CIIF Committee was formed in 2002 and charged with the responsibility to manage the fund and advise the Government on social capital development. The first 12 projects they approved were launched in one of the most difficult times in Hong Kong history, on April 1, 2003, when Hong Kong was hard hit by the SARS epidemic. To make an impact in such circumstances was no easy task at all, but adopting the right strategies was already a move in the right direction.

The majority of Hong Kong people are housed in "vertical" communities stretching over 20 or 30 storeys. Vertical communities: as many as 10,000 people may be living in one multi-storey block. Such vertical communities call for different neighbourhood development strategies. I am delighted to note that indigenous models in social capital building are emerging, such as flexible neighbourhood-based, mutual-help after-school care. There are also volunteer floor stewards and estate mentors who form the core of neighbourhood support networks, particularly in public housing estates. Unique forms of "modern apprenticeship schemes" are made possible through tripartite relationships involving the government, NGOs, and the business sector.

I am also pleased to see that social capital development strategies are raising social and economic participation, especially among the disadvantaged, through enhancing their capacity and self-esteem with the help of cross-sector partnerships. Such participation is necessary for creating gainful employment and fostering community leadership. Organisational cultures are hard to change. It is most encouraging that the culture of cross-sector collaboration is also gradually taking root in Hong Kong. Over 4,700 partners, including businesses, NGOs, schools, professional groups, residents' associations, hospitals, district councils and government departments, are jointly implementing projects funded by the CIIF.

Within a relatively short time since the CIIF was established, its expected policy impact is clearly emerging. By now, we have accumulated a critical mass of social capital development initiatives, totalling over 200 projects that reach out to all the 18 districts in Hong Kong. Some 530,000 people from different age groups, different social strata and cultural or ethnic backgrounds are participating in these capacity-building, networks and community-building initiatives. This amounts to about 7.5% of Hong Kong's total population of seven million people. They involve communities at different stages of development, including new towns, older and redeveloped communities, where social and neighbourhood networks have to be built or rebuilt.

That the CIIF projects are able to mobilise the community in support of families is evident in a new town called Tin Shui Wai, a fast growing new town in the remote northern part of Hong Kong, bordering with Shenzhen in Mainland China. Tin Shui Wai in the past has been described rather unfairly by local media and by some people as a town of sadness, a dump town, because of its high unemployment rate, high crime rate and juvenile delinquency, multiple suicides, concentration of social security recipients and new arrivals from the Mainland. I totally disagree with this stereotyping of Tin Shui Wai. I recall vividly that on the 14th October, 2007, there was a multiple suicide, a mother threw her daughter out of a window from the 25th floor, followed by her son, and then she jumped to her death. The whole community was absolutely shocked. As a result, this prompted much community effort and community concern on this new town. I decided, in collaboration with my CIIF colleagues and with the support of the Chairman, that we must do something decisive and innovative about Tin Shui Wai, to turn it into a town of hope. As a result of concerted efforts, by the end of 2009 the CIIF has already supported 26 projects which cover over 80% of the public housing estates where most of Tin Shui Wai residents are living. We are now transforming this town into a town of hope. I was there some time ago to launch a project driven by female professionals – female doctors, lawyers, accountants, nurses and so on – who joined forces with a local female association to host a Christmas celebration for the kids and provide medical check-ups for middle-aged and elderly women. I was really deeply touched. Since the multiple suicides, I have revisited the town time and again, I can see the changes, always up but not down.

The above may give you a rough idea of what the CIIF has achieved, but actually we attach great importance to the scientific evaluation of the effectiveness of the CIIF's operation and the social capital development strategies that it seeks to promote. In 2004, we commissioned a consortium of seven research teams from five universities – in Hong Kong we only have eight universities – to undertake an independent evaluation of the overall effectiveness of the 56 projects supported by the CIIF at the time. These independent evaluation studies were completed in March 2006. Their findings were reported to, and generally acknowledged by, the Hong Kong Legislative Council. They are also publicly available at the CIIF website. Overall, both the academic evaluation and participants' reports have affirmed the effectiveness of the social capital building strategies promoted by the CIIF, namely, undoing negative labelling effects, transforming social roles, building the capacity of disadvantaged groups, and finally, empowering individuals to become self-reliant.

By the end of 2009, over 20,000 participants who might otherwise have remained passive recipients of welfare services and financial assistance have been turned into volunteers and project organisers – which, I would say, is a cultural revolution. It changes the role from recipients to givers, serving others in need, contributing actively to the development of their respective communities and increasing their own employability. Thanks to the hard work of the project teams and their supporters, neighbourhood relations have become closer and stronger. Over 440 mutual help networks have been established, connecting people from different ages, social backgrounds, and ethnicities in support of some 14,000 families. Such cross-strata networks serve to broaden peoples' perspectives and motivate them to change. The "us-versus-them" way of thinking is set to change.

The CIIF also encourages a different perspective on achieving sustainability. Initiatives such as mentoring, which build in-depth relationships are more instrumental than one-off programmes in fostering trust and reciprocity at times of need. The CIIF generally supports projects with funding for up to three years. Project teams are required to plan for sustainability from the very start to ensure that social capital outcomes such as positive changes to participants' attitudes, mutual help networks, shared ownership by collaborators and work opportunities, will become sustainable after the expiry of project funding. A number of successful projects do not require continued funding because of the support networks established, partnerships formed and changes entrenched. Let me give you an example, the Lok Kwan Home Repair Co-operative project. Lok Kwan is one of Hong Kong's largest trade units, the federation of trade units in Hong Kong, which is aimed at changing the mindset of a group of middle-aged and older unemployed trades people and home decorators. They are mostly from the building decorative industry, and re-engaging them with the community is difficult but can be achieved. CIIF funding for this project expired in 2006, but the project, having earned over $10 million Hong Kong in business turnover by the end of 2008, has continued to operate with over 250 members, and is self-managed and self-sustained. Also sustained are the many social outcomes achieved, including community partnerships, improved family relationships, and middle-aged husbands returning home dignified with their earnings to support their families. Restoration of self-esteem for the unemployed is very important, as well as the participants' commitment to serving others as volunteer mentors.

These are our initial successes and while this is encouraging, we need to achieve continual and vigilant enhancement. To this end, we are extending the CIIF's influence through a variety of strategies, including the recent successful launch of the Social Capital.Net, the sc.net. It is not a website, but a network of people who support the CIIF and are willing to help promote the concept of social capital to enable more people to benefit. Apart from consolidating successful experiences, this human platform also serves to proactively engage new partners with strong community networks and private companies. We will encourage the development of flagship projects to serve as models that inspire others. We will continue to host a unique type of CIIF learning platform that brings together project participants, business collaborators and policy makers to reflect on progress, achieve policy integration and envisage new initiatives and practice. Road shows and media engagement are in place for transferring knowledge to the general public and generating data and publications of relevance to university students and professors in support of social capital research and courses, both locally and abroad. We have also commissioned a second evaluation study to review the outcome indicators, assessing the impact of the projects on the community and identifying critical success factors in ensuring the sustainability of social capital outcomes. This will enable an evidence-based approach to facilitate the application of social capital concepts to regular welfare services or other policies where appropriate.

I am hopeful that the present volume will provide further insights and impetus for the development of social capital in Hong Kong, and other modern cities in Mainland China and elsewhere.

Acknowledgements

The inception of this volume was inspired by the late Dr. Raymond Wu Wai-yung, who cherished the vision of academics and practitioners coming together to jointly provide a critical analysis of social capital and its indigenous evolution and spread in Hong Kong SAR. We share his vision. Given the rapid pace at which Hong Kong SAR and other Asian economies are growing, and the global volatility that these societies are experiencing, social capital and its diverse connectivities can furnish useful anchoring to communities, neighbourhoods, local governments, and social protection networks.

Our writing project was supported by authors whose richly diverse backgrounds and firm commitment have ensured its success. Some of the chapters were presented at the 2008 International Conference on "Social capital and volunteering in modern cities: Building intergenerational inclusion," which was sponsored by the City University of Hong Kong and co-organised by the University of Macau, the University of Salford, and the Central Policy Unity of the Hong Kong SAR Government. These and other chapters have grown out of research programmes, professional practice, and innovative government initiatives.

At various stages of editing this volume, we have received gratefully funding support from the City University of Hong Kong, through its Department of Economics and Finance and the Department of Applied Social Studies. Our sincere appreciation also goes to Professor Siu-kai LAU and Mr. Matthew CHEUNG Kin-chung, whose substantive forewords have enriched this volume.

Sik Hung NG
Stephen Yan-Leung CHEUNG
Brahm PRAKASH

Notes on Editors and Contributors

Editors

Sik Hung NG, PhD, FRS(New Zealand), is Chair Professor of Social Psychology, City University of Hong Kong, and a Member of the Provisional Minimum Wage Commission, Hong Kong SAR Government.

Stephen Yan-Leung CHEUNG, PhD, is Chair Professor of Finance and Dean of the School of Business, Hong Kong Baptist University, Advisory Professor of Fudan University, and Adjunct Professor of the Management School of Shanghai Jiao Tong University.

Brahm PRAKASH, PhD, is Adjunct Faculty, Asian Institute of Management (Manila). He was a former Director, Poverty Reduction and Social Development, Regional and Sustainable Development of the Asian Development Bank, and Senior Fellow (Equivalent to Full Professor) and Head, Educational Planning, National University of Educational Planning and Administration (NUEPA, formerly National Institute of Educational Planning and Management), New Delhi.

Authors

Kevin AU, PhD, is Associate Professor and Associate Director of MBA Programmes, Centre for Entrepreneurship and Department of Management, Chinese University of Hong Kong, Hong Kong SAR.

Thomas A. BIRTCH, PhD, is Senior Research Fellow, Centre for Economics and Policy, University of Cambridge, England.

Alice Ming Lin CHONG, PhD, is Associate Professor in the Department of Applied Social Studies, City University of Hong Kong, Hong Kong SAR.

Wai-Sing CHUNG is Chief Officer (Education), The Mental Health Association of Hong Kong.

Adelaide Pui Ki HUNG, M.Phil, was Senior Research Fellow, City University of Hong Kong, Hong Kong SAR.

Martin JOHNSON, PhD, is Professor in Nursing, University of Salford, England.

Albert LEE, MBBS, FRCP, FRACGP, FFPH, is Head of Division of Health Improvement and Director of Centre for Health Education and Health Promotion, School of Public Health; Professor (Family Medicine), Department of Community and Family Medicine, The Chinese University of Hong Kong, Hong Kong SAR.

Joe Cho Bun LEUNG, PhD, is Professor in Social Work and Social Administration, The University of Hong Kong, Hong Kong SAR.

Kwan Kwok LEUNG, PhD, is Associate Professor in Sociology, City University of Hong Kong, Hong Kong SAR.

Tit Wing LO, PhD, is Professor in Criminology, City University of Hong Kong, Hong Kong SAR.

Grace Fung-Mo NG, MPP, was Project Manager, Community Investment and Inclusion Fund, Hong Kong SAR Government.

Tina L. ROCHELLE, PhD, is Assistant Professor in the Department of Applied Social Studies, City University of Hong Kong, Hong Kong SAR.

Julia RYAN, is Senior Lecturer in Older Adult Nursing, University of Salford, England.

Steven M. SHARDLOW, PhD, Doc. Soc. Sci. (h.c.) is Professor of Social Work (Foundation holder of the Chair), University of Salford, England.

Wai-fong TING, PhD, is Associate Professor in Social Work, Hong Kong Polytechnic University, Hong Kong SAR.

Edward TSE, PhD, is senior partner of Booz & Company and Chairman for Greater China (Shanghai, Beijing, Hong Kong and Taipei), and a member of the Consultative Editorial Board of Harvard Business Review Chinese Edition.

Barbara WALMSLEY, CQSW, MA, is a Teaching Fellow at the University of Keele, England.

Social Capital in Hong Kong

Connectivities and Social Enterprise

1

Social Capital – An Introduction

Brahm PRAKASH

How can the same thread pass through such diversity?

David R. Streeter
Seventh Letter
A journal of a Zen mountain dweller

ᚽᚾᚽᚾᚽᚾᚽᚾᚽᚾᚽᚾᚽᚾᚽᚾᚽᚾᚽᚾᚽᚾᚽᚾᚽᚾᚽᚾᚽᚾᚽᚾ

I. Introduction

Social capital is one of those concepts that have risen spectacularly during the last few decades. The concept broadly relates to the role of social relations vis-à-vis economic development and their mutual dynamics. Although sentiments underscoring a broad relationship between social relations and economic progress can be traced through earlier times, social capital has lately developed into a popular social science concept with diverse applications. A lot of new literature has been generated with a parade of protagonists of the concept, as well as critics. Those in favour say that they have found the "missing" piece (see Grootaert 1997; also Harris and Renzio 1997) and that the concept would help us understand the good or indifferent economic performance of societies or groups. The critics, on the other hand, point out that the concept of social capital is amorphous, hence, not appropriate for serving as an unambiguous determinant of economic development. In a rapidly changing and prolific environment, social capital has come to mean different things to different people – as such, consensus as to its

1

contents, its varied emphases and measurement methods is hardly shared uniformly among analysts, scholars and commentators. Sobel (2002) reflected this well when he titled his review article as: "Can we trust social capital?"

This chapter contains a short introductory write-up capturing some of the strands of the concept. The write-up follows an inter-disciplinary approach, and is written from the perspective of a development practitioner. The major objective is to be able to capture the scope of the subject and bring out its multifaceted nature. Given the interest the concept has aroused in such a short time,[1] our objective is fulfilled if readers could be made aware of its limitations. At the same time, simply because social capital cannot be measured precisely, the concept itself should not be dismissed as nonsense. With this modest goal, and hoping that we are able to provide some flavour of the debate, we proceed further, notwithstanding the hazards.

The chapter is divided into six sections. Section II describes different concepts and approaches that have been used to describe social capital. It is followed by a brief section (III) that looks at the concept historically. Section IV then describes the methods that have been used to conduct empirical studies in social capital or measure the impact of social capital on income and development. Section V provides a brief appraisal of this discussion by way of wrapping up the overview. It is followed by Section VI which gives an overview of the contributions in this volume.

II. What Is Meant by Social Capital?

Social capital is defined as "those social relationships that help people to get along with each other and act more effectively than

---

1 For example, see ". . . the number of journal articles listing social capital as a key word before 1981 totalled 20, and between 1991 and 1995 it rose to 109. Between 1996 and March 1999 the total was 1,003 and the growth shows no sign of abating." (Harper 2001:6 quoted in Field 2003:4). This flow continues unabated in recent years. A more recent count shows the number to have more than doubled to 2277 (Smart 2008).

they could as isolated individuals" (Carroll 2001, p. 1). The significant term in the definition is "relationships". In our view, it constitutes the core of the social capital concept, while recognising that relationships can take varied forms. Serageldin (1996) describes social capital as a "glue that holds societies together". A more comprehensive definition is provided in Serageldin and Grootaert (2000, p. 44)

> (Social capital is) generally recognised as necessary to a functioning social order, along with a certain degree of common cultural identifications, a sense of "belonging" and shared behavioural norms. This internal coherence helps to define social capital. Without it, society at large would collapse, and there could be no talk of economic growth, environmental sustainability, or human well-being . . .

The driving forces behind such social relationships are "trust, mutuality and reciprocity" which characterise these social relations and their *inter se* interactions (Fukuyama, 1995). Trust, in particular, lies at the heart of social capital. Uphoff (2000, p. 222) cites the etymology of the word "social" to imply that some characteristics such as "personal attachment, cooperation, solidarity, mutual respect, and sense of common interest" are inherent to the adjective itself. This points out to the value-based view of social capital. We note that similar observations about the significance of the role of social processes in economic development are made by a number of traditional, as well as contemporary authors including Smith (1910), Weber (1964) Solo (2000), Heilbronner (1985), Sen (2000) and Lucas (2002).

Unfolding Scope

The precise form social capital takes varies as per its context, its configuration and specific profile. In this sense, the empirical manifestation of the concept is, to a large extent, determined by "a varying function of the action of the others" (Weber, 1964, p. 23). its context including the size of the group. It is this varying empirical context that brings in different influences, forms and concepts.

These perceptions in turn provide to analysts a basis to differ and debate. The size of the group matters for social capital. A small-sized group could be more tightly knit and could have more solidarity, like a family, a club or an ethnic group. On the other hand, the bigger groups that maintain such relationship could reap larger gains, insofar as the scale does not erode the attributes of trust, mutuality and reciprocity. However, in a large, varied and anonymous situation, it is often hard to keep these attributes to the fore. In this sense, as one moves from small to large groups "connectivity and linkages" emerge as important determinants of the scale and scope of social relations. Going by the nature of the relationships, these social relations could also be characterised as vertical or horizontal linkages, as is often done in the business management literature (Carroll 2001, 1p. 7).

Networking as such emerges as the generic concept underlying social capital.[2] One talks of intra-group "bonding" and inter-group "bridging" also termed "internal" and "external" relations, respectively. Although different in nature, both are important components of social capital, with bonding strengthening the cohesiveness, and bridging widening the outreach. In the context of bonding and bridging, one also hears of "thin" and "thick" connections. These refer to the intrinsic flexibility and open-ness in a relationship that is ascribed more to "thin" than the "thick" connections. The latter often refer to drug cartels, criminal gangs and other similar groups where relationships may neither permit the freedom to disagree nor walk away without some risks. Thin relations, in contrast, imply open-ended relations which one may or may not utilise without substantively damaging the underlying relationship. As such one could have multiple thin and overlapping relationships.

With the growth of information and communication technologies (ICT) during the last two decades, connectivity has spread rapidly so that the forms and frequency of networking have gained visibility. An immediate consequence is that opportunities for

---

2 See Schneider (2006); also see Campbell (2007, p. 532 on centrality of "networks" in Schneider's analysis of social capital.

interaction have proliferated hugely. Networking has become more tangible and has acquired a certain degree of visibility and recognition.[3] However, not all of these enhanced interactions contribute to the "bonding" or "bridging" capital. What they indicate is that the potential for networking has increased considerably and all sorts of "communities" of practitioners are developing and interacting within, and without. The information revolution is actualising the role of social capital in a manner that had not been foreseen when the concept was taking root.[4]

The inter-personal relationships to which social capital has been generally attributed often relate to some similarity in values which are long established and command allegiance. These are "accretionary" in nature, and traditionally, these have been in the making for a long time before they start serving as the foundation for social capital (Uphoff, 2000, p. 227). Pay-off from social values takes place over a long period; and in the context of a situation evolving over the long term, we have the possibility of social capital being perceived in structural form. On the other side, social capital can be seen in several informal arrangements, stretching all the way to the cognitive domain of individuals. The spectrum of social capital, from cognitive domain to its structural form, reflects the manner in which the underlying values are subscribed and how these are coalesced and interfaced with public policy. Uphoff (2000, p. 219) invokes the role of expectations to broker an interaction between the structural and cognitive social capitals. Carroll (2001, p. 7) modifying this schema describes the interaction as the dynamic aspect of social capital. An obvious point to recognise is that one can engineer all kinds of different perspectives on the analysis of social capital depending on the purpose of the enquiry and the situation at hand.

Social capital can also be thought of at different spatial levels, say, the micro, the meso and the macro. Given its proximity and directness, it is easy to perceive the roles of trust, relationship and

---

3 See Brown and Duguid (2000, p. 142) "Networks of this sort are notable for their reach – a reach now extended and fortified by information technology."

4 For further extension of social capital as networking in the context of supply chain management see Min, Kim and Chen (2008).

rules in getting things done at the micro level. As we go to the higher levels of spatial aggregations, some of these features get folded-in, with some other patterns starting to appear more prominently at the macro level. For example, at the highest level, many of these could become more systematic and formal. Institutions could assume a public role, and compliance could be more automatic and mandatory rather than consensual. With the aggregation of the relationship at the societal level, the overall character of the relationships may assume new forms and undergo changes for good or bad. It is obvious that the aggregation of these relations is not linear; instead, they add up somewhat differently. Nor can these be measured with a degree of certitude. Several attempts are currently being made to model, measure and estimate social capital quantitatively (Durlauf and Fafchamp, 2004).

In some cases, social capital tends to acquire some of the characteristics of public goods with their traditional characteristics of non-rival and non-exclusive consumption. Such public goods tend to be underprovided when left to the markets alone, and often need to be supplemented by public policy. As such, civil society and the public institutions end up prompting the right motives and values (or holding the negative values in check) to encourage citizens to pursue their interests and welfare more effectively. This, of course, suggests that social capital can be created and augmented in a society – a view towards which not everyone may be favourably disposed. In the context of a multi-layered supply chain, or a multi-layered government, social capital is embedded and nested throughout the myriad links whether these be publicly so identified or not. The currently unfolding global financial crisis and its contagion in the real economy and wider society reveals the functioning of these channels.

Trust, mutuality and reciprocity are identified as prominent attributes in most formulations of social capital; and these are also viewed as important pre-requisites for the smooth compliance of legal contracts. Looking at social capital from the perspective of adhering to the "rules of the game" reveals its interface with the institutional approach in which the central focus is on "human cooperation" and coordination (North, 1990, p. vii; Bowles, 2004). For social capital, trust is overriding and reciprocity is a characteristic of normality. For sustainable development, the "rules of the game" have to be commonly understood, owned, and routinely subscribed to by the group as a whole. Such a behaviour is crucially linked with governance and growth overtime, and is now an important aspect of the development discourse.

The issue of trust especially requires careful handling as it interfaces with the assumption of rationality in economic analysis. In the past, the role of the state (hence bureaucracy) and the scope of markets was limited. Thus, much of the social transactions were governed by social sanctions, values and culture, whether explicitly or implicitly; and mutual trust played an important role in the old and settled societies. With the prominence of exchange-based relations, the need for invoking rationality was imminent, and to that extent dependence on trust could be underplayed. However, mutual familiarity generated by the marketplace also engendered trust among fellow investors, financiers and traders.[5] This trust was a product of markets in the commercially leading regions a la Adam Smith. The practice of traders, for example, jewellers, diamond-dealers or merchants, signifies this kind of trust across the world. Thus, when it comes to trust and market economies, one comes across two opposite kinds of development vis-à-vis trust. On the one hand, the onset of market-exchange reduced exclusive reliance on traditional trust; on the other hand, frequent interaction in a market-place created a new kind of trust among operators. An interesting article by Getz (2008) examines the role of social capital in the context of agrarian change and development in the case of Mexico. It focuses on the "complex ways in which social capital can shape the relationship between the market linkages and development outcomes" (Getz, 2008, p. 556).

The issue of trust and its relationship with social capital has invoked many contributions in the literature. For example, Bruni and Sugden (1999), in their article entitled "Moral canals: Trust and social capital in the work of Hume, Smith and Genovese", trace the changing concept of trust through time, and describe how its scope

---

5   This relationship lies behind the concept of customer loyalty, such as in the case of the incentives programmes of airlines, hotels etc.

has been narrowed down to "individual actions". They point out when and how trust can be rational, and also spell out the conditions under which economic and social institutions can generate trust. They describe Genovese viewing trust as a precondition of market development in the developing regions.[6] The way the railways were financed in the United States in the nineteenth century illustrates an important point about trust and goodwill (Eichengreen, 1996). In those days, when little financial market related information was available, much infrastructural investment was attracted and made through word of mouth or informal contacts; often, going by the values of the financial houses involved in the enterprise serving as the basis. Financial houses that were known to be honest and reputed, succeeded in raising funds even for far-flung places which the investors had never heard of themselves, leave alone visited or known.[7] The role of social capital in financial development is now well-known, especially in the field of microfinance (Bastelaer (2002) for microfinance; and see Guiso, Sapienza and Zingales (2000) for finance in general, also Woodworth (2008), and Dakhli and De Clercq (2003, p. 23)). The breakdown of trust in the present financial crisis and ensuing credit crunch is a reminder of the crucial invisible role the trust plays in normal times.

A Variation on the Theme of Capital?

Economists customarily see all relations – whether physical, financial, or human – through the prism of prices and within the rational choice theory framework. The concept of social capital seemingly further stretches the notion of capital to social relations.

---

6   In a seeming inversion of process, what was earlier considered an outcome of the market-led economic development in the case of the industrialised western countries, has now become in governance literature a precondition of development and development assistance for developing countries in the post-industrialised world; for an interesting critique of "development as history", see Rist (2002).

7   Eichengreen quotes Johnson and Supple (1967, p. 338) saying that investment "tended to be a cumulative social process in an environment lacking an impersonal, national money market".

This provoked many scholars, and has drawn fire from all sides. Nobel laureate Arrow (2000, p. 4) says: "I would urge abandonment of the metaphor of capital and the term, 'social capital." Another Nobel laureate Solow (2000, p. 6) asked: "Why social *capital?* . . . an attempt to gain conviction from a bad analogy."[8] Since then hundreds of followers have felt free to join the fray. The critique was especially relevant for the methodological weaknesses of the concept and difficulties involved in its measurement.[9] The rational choice theory framework was also constricting as social capital differed from a purely atomistic assessment of individual phenomenon that forms the foundation of economic analysis. Instead, social capital is based more on the "generalised morality" or "we-rationality" as opposed to "individual rationality."[10] Beyond economics, this variation on the theme of capital has also caused disagreements among sociology and political science academics who felt that an essentially social concept was being unnecessarily pushed towards economics by hitching it to capital. Thus, instead of broadening the scope of economics, the metaphor was essentially seen as endorsing the primacy of capital – irrespective of its form – whether physical, financial, human or social.

Notwithstanding, other Nobel laureate economists like Coase, North, and Sen, have been engaged in broadening the scope of economic analysis. For them the role of social relations in facilitating economic exchange and enabling better coordination is quite persuasive. They looked at social relationships assisting transactions, contracts and markets, and determined that stable and dependable relationships are important for economic development as these help reduce transaction costs (Coase, 1988 and Ostrom 2000). Positive social relations means contracts get settled smoothly

---

8 Italics in the original.

9 In some sense, this was in keeping with the tradition. Even in mainstream economics, capital measurement has aroused strong emotions and caused serious controversies, see Harcourt(1972).

10 From a management perspective, the application of social capital at firm level in the context of the old and new economies is illustrated in Van Buren (2008).

with minimal recourse to outside interventions, and render markets more efficient.[11] In brief, these economists saw, among other things, social relationships as an instrument for making markets work better.[12] Thus perceived, social capital is an important adjunct to the core economic instruments. It creates space for a goal-oriented interaction between state, market and society, especially over a longer-stretch of time. This longer time perspective is an important feature of any investment or capital[13] (see North, 1994; also Bastelaer, 2002, p. 255).

Social capital has, in fact, turned out to be a tremendous attraction for multilateral development institutions like the World Bank.[14] The idea of factoring social features originally surfaced in 1980s, when similar development projects were performing unevenly across societies. This drew attention to the underlying social factors and institutions. The recognition of social capital also enabled the World Bank to move away from the narrowly based Washington consensus (Bhattacharyya 2004, pp. 19–21). It allowed international financial institutions to focus on poverty reduction and the provision of social services for the poor, including the launching of the millennium development goals[15] at the turn of the millennium. Social capital drew the attention of the decision-makers to the targeted social contexts of the needy groups. These concerns also contributed to evaluating investments from the point of view of

---

11 On the dynamics of people's knowledge and experience, see North (1990, p. 76): "People's perception that the structure of rules of the system is fair and just reduces costs; equally, their perception that the system is unjust raises the costs of contracting (given the costliness of measurement and enforcements of contracts)."

12 Nobel laureate Sen (2000, p. 116) also underscores the role of the "complementarity between different institutions – in particular between non-market organisations and the market".

13 On the use of the metaphor of investment as related to social capital, see Uphoff (2000, p. 223 also pp. 227–228).

14 On how the World Bank managed to meld together Bourdieu's and Putnam's perspective together see Schneider (2008, p. 426); also see Smart (2008, p. 412).

15 For a review and an update of the millennium development goals in the Asia Pacific region see UNESCAP (2005).

outcomes rather than just outputs.[16] Thus, in the development discourse, social capital has been associated with significant re-orientation.

In the 'nineties the emergence of transition economies provided an opportunity for introspection and questioning the practices of the former communist countries. In many of these established societies, social capital was ravaged and trampled, ironically, in the name of freedom from the clutches of the market-led hedonistic pursuits. In the context of the post-Soviet Union environment, the concept of social capital fitted well with the emerging debate on the different types of capitalisms in the world. Some of these events help to understand the environment in which the concept of social capital was born, although surrounded with much controversy.

Notwithstanding, not all economists accept the legitimacy of this view of social capital – not even as an auxiliary to economic systems. They question its lack of rigour and find it incompatibility with the assumptions and methods of economic analysis. One of the methodological critiques of social capital from an economist's point of view was advanced by Durlauf and Fafchamps (2004). They found the formulation of social capital "unsatisfactory", "tautological and not falsifiable". In particular, they proceeded to demonstrate their reservations by examining the empirical works in the area and note ". . . how functional notions of social capital are inconsistent with rigorous theorising of the type mainstream economists pursue" (2004, p. 26)[17] It is not that Durlauf and Fafchamps do not see social capital as significant, but that they do they not find its methodology defensible.[18]

---

16 Among the international financial institutions, this practice is known as the results-based management.

17 For a brief but clear statement on the methodology of the economic theory, especially the neo-classical paradigm, see Silberberg and Suen (2000, 1–24).

18 "The bottom line, however, is clear: without some form of voluntary acceptance by the public, government efforts to provide public goods are likely to fail, social capital is thus probably essential for public good delivery. But the forms it may take are likely to vary depending on local conditions, i.e., from generalised trust in government and formal institutions to interpersonal trust mobilised via clubs and networks." (Durlauf and Fafchamps 2004, p. 14)

While upholding the need for a rigorous and consistent methodology, we note that this methodological concern varies from discipline to discipline, especially when it comes to a multi-dimensional concepts like social capital which can be found wanting from all sides. Even among economists there are differences on this issue.[19] We return to some of these again towards the end of the chapter.

III. Social Capital through History

Whatever the merits of the concept of social capital, it is interesting to note that its birth and arrival on the scene have not been easy. Despite hundreds of papers being written about social capital, the concept is still struggling for recognition and identity. In contrast, in layman's terms, it has been for long a part of the received wisdom that one has a greater obligation to friends, people from one's own community and neighbourhood, and members of one's own family.[20] As one moves from a total stranger to friends and immediate family members, the consideration towards them increases. Durlauf and Fafchamp (2004, p. 1) open their survey of social capital with a quote from Aristotle's *Nicomachean Ethics* (Book VIII, 9.61) which observes, "It is more shocking, e.g., to rob a companion of money than to rob a fellow citizen, to fail to help a brother than a stranger, and to strike one's father than anyone else".

In more recent times, Tocquevillian description of the 19th century American scene captures the humming of associational activities there. At the macro level, Marx, in his critique of capitalism, developed his distinctive views on the role of social

---

19 It is instructive to see how Nobel laureate Ronald Coase (1988, 3) sarcastically summarises his views on economic orthodoxy: "We have consumers without humanity, firms without organisations, and even exchange without markets."

20 See Sen (2000, pp. 261–262). "Different persons may have very different ways of interpreting ethical ideas including those of social justice. . . . But basic ideas of justice are not alien to social beings, who worry about their own interests but are also able to think about family members, neighbours, fellow citizens and about other people in the world."

structures in facilitating market-led evolution. In the 20th century, Durkheim articulated the underpinning of social relationship as "a source of meaning and order" (Field 2000, p. 5). Weber is well-known for identifying the role of certain social ethical norms and values for achieving progress and development. Thus, throughout history, one comes across a range of facets being identified as facilitating economic change, lending it meaning, or rationalising its evolution. It would seem that social capital had been manifesting itself in multiple forms and threatening to break out on the scene for a long time.

The Main Architects

Three of the principal contributors – Bordieu, Coleman and Putnam – who are generally credited with having made seminal contributions to social capital, each took different lines in advancing the concept and its use. Bordieu essentially followed the Marxian analytical framework, viewed social capital in the broader historical context and emphasised the process of social evolution, especially for developing an alternative to capitalism.[21] Coleman, meanwhile, has attempted to smoothen the ground between sociology and economics, and developed the concept as a natural continuum of capital in the social domain. His application involving the role of parents in the school management is based on extensive survey data and its analysis. Putnam (1993) in his *Making Democracy Work: Civic Traditions in Modern Italy* studied decentralisation of development and the emergence of local communities in Italy. The formation of social capital is seen in this study as explaining the unequal levels of economic development in the northern and southern Italy. Putnam's later work, *Bowling Alone* (2000), dramatically put the concept of social capital right at the top and contributed immensely towards its popularity.

---

21 Given his predilections, due to which Bordieu was seeking an alternative to capitalism, see Navarro (2008).

IV. Applications, Measurement and Methods

Its long past and recent prolific growth have bequeathed social capital with a variety of applications, methods and measurement techniques. Methods ranging from simple anecdotal accounts and large-scale, especially conducted surveys, to secondary data with sophisticated statistical analyses, have been all used to measure social capital. To some extent, it is this multifacetedness of the concept, as described above, that is responsible for the deployment of an extraordinarily wide set of tools and techniques. These studies have taken place in the context of many disciplines, most of them in sociology, political science, and economics. Some are interdisciplinary in nature, and are undertaken as case studies or poverty surveys, or in a problem-solving mode. These applications have taken place all around the world – in Africa, Latin America, Asia, Europe and North America – although the motives and the themes change with the place. Most of these have been carried out within the last two decades because of a keen interest in the concept and the curiosity to see whether it helps to explain something over and above what was earlier known. Thus, one comes across both a wide disciplinary nature as well as spatial distribution of applications.[22]

Investigators with different disciplinary backgrounds have not only taken interest in different aspects of the social capital, but have also brought their favourite techniques to unravel the mysteries they are attempting to resolve.[23] Given the plethora of literature, it is not possible to describe a substantial survey in such a short note. Hence, in this section we briefly recount some of the more well-known and recent social capital works and their methods, so as to make readers aware of the possible variations in applications with a view to set the stage for discussing the contributions included in this volume.

---

22 Some of the early instances of different applications of social capital are enumerated in Carroll (2001) and Dasgupta and Serageldin (2000).

23 For a comprehensive overview of the use of quantitative analytical techniques in social capital measurements, especially in the context of the World Bank's Social Capital Assessment Tools (SOCAT), see Gootaert (2002, 41–84). For examples on the applications of qualitative methods, see Reid and Salmen (2002, 85–107).

Preferred Sectors of Application

After starting from simple participatory development exercises with or without a poverty reduction focus at the micro and village levels, social capital applications have covered swathes of rural areas under the influence of any of the following: irrigation systems, watershed management, or agricultural productivity, agricultural marketing and rural credit programmes. Some of these applications have also included microfinance activities, either as stand-alone or along with other activities. Forestry and environment management have also been contiguous applications.[24] Most of these sectors have had a mixed history in the sense that despite huge amounts of resources, implementation efforts were not often successful. In this sense, these were really difficult cases that needed to respond to the peculiarities of the ground conditions and required a closer understanding of the clientele and their environment. Similarly, applications have been carried out in urban development, especially where water and sanitation services in the poor neighbourhoods and slums areas are concerned. In all these applications, the key has supposedly been to involve the stakeholders in determining, designing and implementing development schemes. Uphoff study (1996) is a good example applying the concept to the domain of agriculture in Sri Lanka and describing how both structural as well as cognitive social capital contribute to the enhanced welfare of the population. The author underscores the need for methodological rigour to identify the concept of social capital more accurately.

Rising above the field studies, applications have also been conducted at the meso and macro levels where these have addressed the federated organisations, be they rural or urban. Occasionally, studies like the Putnam's Italian study have compared subnational regions. The major thrust of such studies is to inform the policymaking bodies in the higher echelons about the need to factor in the peculiarities of the clients more painstakingly. Applications

---

24 Some of these interventions have been supported by the World Bank, the Asian Development Bank and other regional development banks. Some critics view the World Bank's adoption of social capital to be "acontextual and ahistorical" (Bhattacharyya et al., 2004, p. 21).

have ranged across workers and work situations, productivity, industrial development and the financial sectors. Here, too, the micro level studies have been supported ultimately by the evidence generated at the macro level, on the role of social capital in determining income and economic development. In addition, there are economy-wide or system-wide studies empirically measuring the contribution of social capital to economic growth.

Data

Social capital studies have utilised all kinds of data. Sometimes, these have been used to measure the contribution of social capital, whether directly or indirectly, via proxy variables supposedly capturing the social capital effects. Both primary and secondary data have been used. The World Bank, which conducted some special surveys for this purpose, developed an entire methodology for collecting social capital data under its Social Capital Initiative. Using the survey methodology in Tanzania, Narayan and her colleagues measured the social capital at the community level. A special household survey was designed and used to collect data, among others, on three aspects: households' membership in groups, the characteristics of those groups, and the individuals' values and attitudes (Narayan 1997, and Narayan and Princhett, 2000). The analysis of the resulting data was then undertaken with the help of both quantitative and qualitative techniques to understand what facilitated collective action by community groups.

Sometimes, scholars have found it useful to access already existing survey data and culled out certain variables to test the contributions of social capital. The World Value Survey is one such survey that has been used quite often. Secondary data sources, on the other hand, have been used more frequently than primary data when undertaking studies at the country or macro level. We will discuss issues related to this type of use below when we review statistical modelling for social capital.

Social Capital Modelling

Notwithstanding the reservations of economists, particularly those of a neo-classical persuasion, had about social capital, there have been some important attempts at understanding the social capital within the methodology of the mainstream models of economic analysis. Among others, the works of Glaesar (2000), Bartolini (2004) and Keele (2004) are illustrative of this approach. Glaesar (2000) makes the point that while there is much that is written in the literature about the theoretical aspects of social capital, and that some evidence also exists as to its possible impact and benefits, there is little that one knows about the connections between the two, how this transmission mechanism works and under what conditions.[25] To fill this void, Glaesar (2000) proposed and empirically tested "a model of optimal individual investment decisions" (like the human capital models of Becker (1993)) touching on a series of characteristics of an individual such as life-cycle, mobility, occupation, home ownership, travels, and patience.[26]

Meanwhile, Knight and Yueh (2002) apply individual level modelling of social capital to the urban labour market and treat *guanxi* as a variant of social capital in China. They focus on three measures of social capital, viz., the size of a worker's social network, his membership and that of his parents in the Communist party. Knight and Yueh have studied both the administered labour markets, as well as the emerging open labour-market segments. They have found evidence of positive gains to workers in terms of their social network and party membership. A more recent application of multivariate analysis in China is found in Chen and Lu (2007) that focuses on the presence of social capital in the urban areas. The data for the study was collected through a survey in 2004.

At the aggregate level, there is the Bartolini and Bonatti (2004) study which extends the Ramsey-Solow type growth model.[27] In the study of Bartolini and Bonatti, social capital is entered into the

---

25 See also Miguel, Gertler and Levine (2003, 1) ". . . the process of social capital creation and destruction remains poorly understood".

26 Following the human capital, one can focus on the expertise residing in social relationships as an important determinant of social capital, see Cornwell and Cornwell (2008).

27 For details on these models see Barro and Sala-i-Martin (2004, Chapter 3, 143–203).

production function, but the results generated are not in line with the a priori expectations. It determined that the presence of social capital is not production augmenting. Whereas both Glaesar (2000), and Bartolini and Bonatti (2004) attempted to develop models of social capital within the economic framework, Keele (2004) developed a macro model of social capital which began with the premise that social capital is a predictor of social well-being. As such, he is interested in learning about changes in social capital over time. He focuses on two variables, i.e., civic engagement and interpersonal trust, and then goes on to develop a longitudinal model of change in levels of social capital over time, with the help of a specific time-series measure.

In viewing social capital within the economic development convergence hypothesis, Helliwell and Putnam used multivariate regression analysis. Their key variables included a composite measure of civic community, institutional performance and citizen satisfaction in the model. With the help of a multivariate model, this Italian study revisits the comparison between northern and southern Italy, and the possible role of social capital in determining development outcomes. A more recent example of multivariate statistical analysis explaining observed income variations in terms of social capital factors is by Wim Groot, Henriette Maassen van den Brink and Bernard van Praag (2006). Renata Serra (2004), meanwhile, conducted an application of factor analysis on Indian state level data. The study attempted "to assess the role of measurable aspects of social capital in accounting for the observed differential performances across India" (2004, p. 290). Garip (2008) analyses migrant social capital presents in the context of Thailand and derives interesting results about the choices migrants make and their impact in light of their diverse information and experience.

A few observations on the multivariate modelling of social capital are in order here. Multivariate methodology is attractive because of its capacity to handle large data and to suggest plausible relationships across variables. An interesting example of recent application of multivariate models including the use of longitudinal data is Besser, Recker and Agnitsch (2008). However, in many applications, its core assumptions about the exogeneity of explanatory variables, their independence and the homoscedasticity of errors are critical. When these assumptions are violated, the estimates of coefficients generated by these models tend to be biased, in the sense that they capture some other effects or do not necessarily capture the right effects. Such estimates are misleading; and the investigators need to be aware of these limitations. Some remedial measures are available to fix these problems, but these measures are usually difficult and complex. The thrust of the criticism by Durlauf and Fafchamps (2004) relates to this kind of problem with social capital analysis and applications oblivious to the violation of the underlying assumptions.

An important issue is related to the comparison of different studies. The social capital concept is embedded in the wider context of societies and picks up these effects. One of the outcomes is that it is difficult to compare the findings straightaway, except indirectly. As a rule, developing economies tend to be diverse and more heterogeneous, thereby making it difficult to transplant learning without validating the key contextual features once again. In a sense, this heterogeneity impedes the portability of social capital results straightaway and of benefiting from them (Bhattacharyya et. al. 2004; also Prakash and Selle 2004). On the other hand, often the economic performance of East Asian countries, including Japan, Korea, Singapore, and the People's Republic of China, is attributed to their similar values and motivations. Japan has been a leading example of this type of growth and related social values (Morishima, 1982; Sen, 2000, pp. 261–268).

V. Social Capital – A Perspective

We have fleetingly touched on the different aspects of the concept of social capital, instances through which one can recognise more closely the uses to which different institutions are putting the concept. This brief narration, we hope, has equipped us to start examining the concept with more familiarity. We choose to focus on only a few aspects, as given below.

First, the most important issue seems to be the concept of the sociological approach of viewing a person in relation to social institutions, as opposed to the self-interested economic human being who is atomistic and stripped of social relations. The idea of social capital takes off on this relationship of human beings with each other, and is thus fully rooted in their social perspective. We noted above that from the earlier times, certain social attributes have been seen to be a pre-condition for the smooth operation of markets, although mainstream economists find it difficult to come to terms with social capital, largely because of the incompatibility of their methodologies. It is only in the context of development economics, and in the search for a universal theory of growth that is applicable to the developing as well as the developed world, that the new approaches are emerging, e.g., the role of institutions and human capital in the hands of Lucas (2002), North (1990), Stiglitz (2000) and Williamson (1996), among others. Lucas (2002, 38) considers even human capital accumulation a "social activity, involving a group of people in a way that has no counterpart in the accumulation of physical capital".

We noted that among the classical writers, it was Adam Smith who played on the roles of customs, norms and acceptable behaviour in explaining the economic functioning of society; and in this sense he took these social attributes as givens. However, the recent, more rigorous and analytical formulations that are shorn of vague concepts would have nothing to do with social capital and actually object to the use of the very term "capital". Dasgupta (2000) recognises the disjointed nature of the domain of economists and sociologists vis-à-vis social capital when he says:

> Social capital is in a different category from these because it has its greatest impact on the economy precisely in those areas of transaction in which markets are missing (Dasgupta 2000, 398).

In addition to the differences in the analytical and philosophical perspectives, the real problem lies in the methodology of estimating social capital's contributions to economic growth. Obviously, the concept is far too complex and varied to be measured in an unambiguous manner, and for all to agree – despite the fact that some rigorous field-based studies have yielded evidence in favour of social capital (Krishna, 2000, Narayan, 2000, Putnam, 2000, Grootaert and van Bastelaer 2002). Lucas (2002, p. 56) notes that measurement of even the physical capital is not straightforward: "The fiction of 'counting machines' is helpful in certain abstract contexts but is not at all operational or useful in actual economies – even primitive ones."

Moreover, mere analytical discussion is hardly adequate to understanding, addressing and resolving the concerns regarding the practice of social capital. One needs to have a much more detailed and rigorous understanding of the way development is happening on the ground, to be able to understand the contribution (whether positive or negative) of social capital more concretely. We need to ascertain how some of the significant interactions at the community level, in terms of education, health, sanitation, neighbourhood activities, are carried out, financed and valued. Detailed case studies can help understand how certain groups or communities are able to use opportunities, while others might not. In a multiplayer government situation, it is also important to see how these groups and communities are embedded in the system, and how effectively they are supported through a hierarchical system. Krishna (2000, p. 89), who has undertaken an extensive rural study in a western state in India, observes: "In cases in which behaving in a coordinated manner assumes a high degree of legitimacy, we find that high social capital is in evidence." Emphasising the social nature of this coordination, he observes, "Behaviour coordinated by custom, by a norm of appropriateness, is a better guarantee of sustained cooperation, than is behaviour backed by individual calculation".

In this context, the role of knowledge and information emerges as an important feature. Depending upon one's access to information, the nature of interactions among people and the sustainability of coordination are determined. Even for the same level of physical capital, societies are able to galvanise and release different amounts of social force and determine outcomes. These are more easily seen when social interactions are scaled up and large masses of groups gather and create synergies. It is in this sense that social capital essentially functions as a collateral resource that helps societies draw more out of a given situation.

Finally, through the instrumentality of interaction, social capital helps to bring the broader relationship among business, government and society into the domain of public policy. Business focuses on market relations and improvises on them. Government provides and maintains a regulatory environment for business to conduct its activities and the society to be humming in a healthy mode. And society, through its institutions, keeps both business and government in consonance with its perspective and vision. This, perhaps, is the most aggregate and meta view of social capital manifestation. Many economists, classical as well as modern, have underscored the need for a more inclusive and cohesive concept of development. This is especially relevant in modern times, given the growing pace of globalisation. In the current crisis, it is being realised that the era of unbridled market-led developments is over, and that markets need to be regulated and subjected to oversight.

To conclude, we note that in real life, most of the activities and interactions are not purely economic nor purely social, etc., but are a combination of several strands. Development draws upon economic, social and psychological features, etc., in a cohesive manner. Development practice is concerned with addressing any of these features when it becomes a constraint to development. Social capital contributes to this process and facilitates development, as economic governance requires both rational actions as well as trust, especially when investments are on the cutting edge.

Empirically, it is much easier to see social capital in action in activities at the community level. For example, those engaged in the Community Investment and Inclusion Fund (CIIF), a major initiative in building social capital among groups in Hong Kong SAR, know much more about it as they have experienced how social capital contributes to the welfare and development of the groups involved. NGOs, civil society organisations and other action groups have a crucial role to play in this regard.[28] At times of economic crises, their role becomes especially important. For example, when severe economic restructuring takes place and people experience dislocations, it is important to put in place a safety-net below which people are not allowed to fall, and to protect the niche areas of long-term concerns such as health and education. Doing so helps preserve resilience in the community and society, and gives them the

---

28 See also Wong (2007) and Holliday and Tam (2001).

courage to rise again when the outlook changes. Given the current phase of globalisation, uncertainty and volatility, it is important to reinforce mutual interactions and support.

Notwithstanding the real significance of social capital on the level of practitioners, there are many unresolved concerns at the theoretical and methodological levels. There are also issues related to estimating the contributions of social capital. Although much progress is being registered on both the analytical and estimation fronts, the issues are far from being resolved. However, it is also useful to keep in view the fact that social capital is not the only concept with outstanding issues. Rather, it also holds true for many other aspects, especially on the measurement of capital in general.

VI. An Overview of Themes and Contributions

Let us now turn to the practice of social capital and briefly examine what kind of evidence we find in the studies gathered in this volume. The collection addresses both theoretical and empirical aspects of social capital generally in the context of developing Asian countries, and particularly in relation to Hong Kong SAR. Contributions have been grouped under three broad categories, namely, social capital practice and development, connectivities of social capital, and social enterprises. The contributions constitute a multidisciplinary group and come from both the developed and the developing countries. A brief overview of each chapter follows.

This introductory chapter is followed by a contribution by Ting on the "Praxis of Social Capital". The chapter introduces the essential concepts of social capital. It goes on to differentiate between the emphasis laid on individual interactions in the social context, and on the role of institutions in the creation of social capital. These are respectively identified as the contributions emerging from the Anglo-Saxon and the Scandinavian countries. Outside of these familiar cases, the author point out that Hong Kong SAR presents a unique blend that could be termed as the third or the alternative middle. She goes on to explain how the Hong Kong case embodies elements of both the system and serves as an example of the middle way. It is in this context that the author describes the practice of social capital and links it with the discipline of social work as practiced by professional social workers. Ting makes an interesting point by asserting that it is the professional social worker who in fact is engendering social capital, at least in the case of Hong Kong SAR.

The next chapter by Chong (a social gerontologist and social work practitioner) and Ng (a policy analyst and the director of CIIF) focuses primarily on one kind of social capital, i.e., bridging social capital. The essential motivation for the authors' focus on this is the potential contribution to development that bridging social capital is capable of making. Using results from some of the empirical studies under the CIIF project as evidence authors build their case for promoting bridging capital. However, they plead for a greater emphasis on community led bridging capital including youth and elderly with a view to build a "stronger social networks, social connectivity, improved individual and community health and community-business engagement".

Hung, Leung and Ng in their contribution situate the concept of social capital fully in the context of Hong Kong SAR. Focusing on the post-1997 period, the high point of their contribution is to relate the concept more tangibly to the situation in Hong Kong. As a result, social capital no longer seems anymore an abstract concept with some esoteric applications. Instead, it emerges as an important means of achieving policy objectives. In this sense, it is a continuation of the theme initiated by the foregoing chapters 2 and 3. Particularly noteworthy is their discussion of findings with regard to the measurement of the social capital in Hong Kong as evidenced in the government sponsored Community Involvement and Investment Fund.

Moving on to connectivities of social capital, chapter 5 by Joe Leung explores different aspects of social capital in the context of community and its capability to facilitate local area and neighbourhood development. The high point of this contribution is that it traces the evolution of growing community participation in Hong Kong over the last 30 years, and undertakes a comparative analysis in relation to China and Singapore. It delineates how the government in Hong Kong SAR gradually developed its understanding about the role the community could play, and how this eventually culminated in the setting up of the CIIF. All this analysis is carried out against the backdrop of developments in the UK with regard to community participation.

Chapter 6 by Dr. Lee suggests that social capital may influence the health behaviours of neighbourhood residents by promoting more rapid diffusion of health information, increasing the likelihood that healthy norms of behaviour are adopted, and exerting social control over deviant health-related behaviour. The notion of human capital and social capital begins to offer explanations why certain communities are unable to achieve better health than other communities despite their similar demography. Author seeks to improve our understanding of the determinants of health particularly the social, cultural and political aspects. It is believed that such understanding would help health services to benefit from organisations and institutions created and structured for other purposes, and thus, would put health services on a wider agenda. The "healthy setting" approach can build the capacity of individuals, families and communities to create strong human and social capitals.

Using the example of gangs, chapter 7, by Rochelle (health psychologist), Lo (criminologist) and Ng (social psychologist), illustrate some of the features of the social capital by looking specifically at the structural and cognitive aspects of social capital by and the behaviour of gangs. It illustrates both the negative and positive aspects of social capital in describing gangs behaviour. Most importantly, it highlights the need to analyse objectively the factors involved in the creation of social capital because ignoring it is hardly a solution. Social capital can also be used for rehabilitating old gang members.

The next contribution by Shardlow, Walmsley, Johnson and Ryan looks at social capital in the context of ageing and focuses on the social capital amongst the elderly. It applies the familiar social capital triumvirate of bonding, bridging and linking social capital triumvirate to the situations and anecdotes of the elderly and then derives some implications for the discussion about active ageing and about the social capital. Shardlow et al., bring out two aspects that are of special interest here in the context of East Asia. One, dealing with the rapid changes in the demographic structure of the region which is likely to see elderly growing in numbers, and two, the likely evolution of the traditional family culture in which the elderly are held in high respect, at least overtly.

In a skilfully argued chapter, Shardlow broaches the subject of a possible new paradigm for the social work – a paradigm that may be rooted in the wider conceptual framework of the social capital taking due cognizance of the role of networks in the lives of individuals. Tracing the antecedents of the social work, the author looks at the contemporary urban and city life, and draws parallels in support of inducting network analysis into the received social work analysis. Shardlow builds a fairly persuasive case for considering such a move. There is, of course, no reason to think that the new social work paradigm should be confined only to city lives. Shardlow's suggestion leads one to assert that networking within rural settings is even more functional, lasting and vital to one's life than living in the city where many of the things are intermediated through the market framework.

Coming to the last section on social enterprises, in chapter 10 Cheung and Chung provide a concrete example of social enterprises and social capital in action.[29] They present a case study of a social enterprise in Hong Kong SAR that assists people with disability (PWD). It describes how PWDs are trained and employed in a near commercial mode running a café, several convenience stores mostly located in hospitals and other businesses. It narrates the story of their success and tells how the enterprise grew from one café/store into a chain employing over a hundred PWDs and other persons in the retail outlets and in sheltered workshops. The case is also a good example of public-private partnership working together with a civil society organisation to take care of disadvantaged persons. The chapter also includes a transcript of a focal group interview and takeaways. It is certainly an excellent example of what can be done given the commitment to do good in the society.

Au and Birch from the Centre for Entrepreneurship at the Chinese University of Hong Kong SAR and the Centre for Economics and Policy of Cambridge University respectively, present

---

29 On the concept of social enterprises see Massetti (2008).

a well-argued case for linkages across social capital and social enterprises. They develop an analytical framework in chapter 11 and then apply it to draw appropriate implications for both the social capital and the social enterprises. The authors also spell out implications for public policy and assert how their individual independent components finally find an integrated home under this institution.

The final chapter in the volume (chapter 12) by Dr. Edward Tse approaches the topic of social capital from the point of view of corporate management. If any evidence was in fact needed, Dr. Tse makes a pitch for the potential contribution of social capital in the making of a successful corporation. The chapter focuses on the horizontal linkage across corporate social responsibility, the soft power of corporations and social capital, and goes on to show the relationship between the three. The key message of the chapter is that social capital helps to generate soft power, without which corporations can hardly project themselves as innovative, responsible and growing organisations. The myths, goodwill and legacy of a corporations stems from the social capital that is deeply embedded within it.

To conclude, there are some significant implications of this exercise insofar as the volume draws attention to several important aspects of social capital for Asia-Pacific region. Firstly, a number of contributions are rooted in the world city of Hong Kong. The CIIF experiments in Hong Kong SAR are replicable widely in other growing urban centres and cities, and as such social capital projects and activities should have a growing role to play in years to come. Second, despite the unprecedented growth rates during the last three decades, the Asia-Pacific region is still home to the largest number of poor in the world. So far development activities have by and large leant heavily on governments and markets to procure relief for these millions in poverty. The possibility now exists that additional interventions can be launched with the help of social capital and to that extent the future development efforts can be more broadly based, including the role of civil society, NGOs and the disadvantaged themselves. Social enterprises are a new vehicle for combining business efficiency with some social good and thus hold promise across a whole range of activities.

Finally, to move the old societies of the region into becoming the dynamic champions of democracy, and market-led inclusive growth it is important to go beyond the narrow development frameworks and develop a better understanding of their tradition, trust, culture and institutions. Recent development experience around the world shows that these deeper transformations tend to be integrated and need wholesale support. Economic development is more easily secured when it is aligned well with the underlying social mores, values and proclivities of a society. The ongoing global financial crisis has underscored many of the above messages, and it is sincerely hoped that the contributions in this volume will add their part in sustaining the faith in development – a development that is sustainable and harmonious for all.

Acknowledgements

The review has benefited much from, and draws upon the available works, among others, especially of Dasgupta and Serageldin (Eds, 2000), Carroll (2001), Grootaert and van Bastelaer (2002), and Field (2003); see References below. Earlier versions of the draft have benefited much from the comments and suggestions of Sik Hung Ng, Shiladitya Chatterjee, Steve Tabor, and N.V. Varghese; the usual caveat applies.

References

Aristotle (Edited by H. Rackham, 1934). *Nicomachean Ethics*, Book VIII, 9.61 http://www.perseus.tufts.edu/cgi-bin///ptext?lookup=Aristot.+Nic.+Eth.+1160a+1

Arrow, K. J. (2000) *Observations on Social Capital* in P. Dasgupta and I. Sergaldin (Eds) *Social Capital: A multifaceted perspective*, (pp. 3–5), Washington, DC: The World Bank.

Barro, R. J., and Sala-i-Martin, X. (2004) *Economic growth*. New Delhi: Prentice-Hall.

Bartolini, S. and Bonatti, L. (2004) "Social capital and its role in production: Does the depletion of social capital depress economic growth?" Working paper no. 421, Dipartimento di Economia Politica, Università degli Studi di Siena. www.econ-pol.unisi.it/quaderni/421.pdf

Bastelaer, T. van (2002) "Does social capital facilitate the poor's access to credit?" Annex 2 in C. Grootaert and T. van Bastalaer (Eds), *Understanding and measuring social capital: A multidisciplinary tool for practitioners* (pp. 237-264), Directions in Development, Washington, DC. The World Bank.

Becker, Gary S. (1993) *Human capital: A theoretical and empirical analysis, with special reference to education.* Chicago: The University of Chicago Press.

Besser, T. L., Recker, N. and Agnitsch, K. (2008) "The impact of economic shocks on quality of life and social capital in small towns" *Rural Sociology,* 73, 580–604.

Bhattacharyya, D., Jayal, N.G., Mohapatra, B.N., and Pai, S. (Eds) (2004), *Interrogating social capital – The Indian experience,* New Delhi: Sage

Bordieu, P. (1986). "The forms of capital" in J.G. Richardson, (Ed.), *Handbook of theory and research for sociology of education,* New York: Greenwood.

Bowles, S. (2004). *Microeconomics. Behaviour, institutions, and evolution.* New Delhi: Oxford University Press.

Brown, J. S., and Duguid, P. (2000). *The social life of information.* Cambridge, MA: Harvard Business School Press.

Bruni, L., and Sugden, R. (2000). Moral canals: Trust and social capital in the work of Hume, Smith and Genovesi. *Economics and Philosophy,* 16: 21–45.

Campbell, D. E. (2007). Social capital complications. *Journal of Public Administration Research and Theory,* 17: 532–534.

Carroll, T. F. (2001). *Social capital, local capacity building, and poverty reduction.* Social Development Papers no. 3. Manila: Asian Development Bank.

Chen, J., and Lu, C. (2007). Social capital in urban China: Attitudinal and behavioral effects on grassroots self-government. *Social Science Quarterly,* 88, 422–442.

Coase, R.H. (1990). *The firm, the market and the law.* Chicago: The University of Chicago Press.

Cohen, D., and Prusak, L. (2001). *In good company: How social capital makes organizations work.* Boston, MA: Harvard Business School Press.

Coleman, J. S. (1986a). Social theory, social research, and a theory of action. *American Journal of Sociology,* 91, 1309–1335.

Coleman, J. S. (1986b). *Individual interests and collective action.* Cambridge: Cambridge University Press.

Coleman, J. S. (1987). Norms as social capital. In Radnitzky and Bernholz (Eds.), *Economic imperialism: The economic approach applied outside the field of economics.* pp. 133–156. NY: Paragon.

Coleman, J. S. (1990). Social capital in the creation of human capital. In P. Dasgupta and I. Serageldin (Eds.), *Social capital: A multifaceted perspective* (pp. 13–39). Washington, DC: The World Bank.

Coleman, J. S., and Hoffer, T.B. (1987). *Public and private schools: The impact of communities.* New York: Basic.

Cornwell, E. Y., and Cornwell, B. (2008). Access to expertise as a form of social capital: An examination of race and class-based disparities in network ties to experts. *Sociological Perspectives*, 51, 853–876.

Dakhli, M., and De Clercq, D. (2003). Human capital, social capital and innovation: A multi-country study. Working Paper, Universitiet Gent, http://fetew.ugent.be/fac/research/WP/Papers/wp_03_211.pdf.

Dasgupta, P., and Serageldin, I. (2000). *Social capital: A multifaceted perspective*. Washington, DC: The World Bank.

Dasgupta, P. (2009). A matter of trust: Social capital and economic development. Paper prepared for and presented at the Annual Bank Conference on Development Economics (ABCDE), in Seoul (Korea). Washington, DC: The World Bank.

Durlauf, S. N., and Fafchamps, M. (2004). Social Capital. Working Paper no. 10485, Cambridge, MA: National Bureau of Economic Research, http://www.nber.og/papers/w10485.

Eichengreen, B. (1996). Financing infrastructure in developing countries: Lessons from the Railway Age. In A. Mody (Ed.) *Infrastructure delivery: Private initiative and the public good*. Washington, DC: Economic Development Institute, The World Bank.

Field, J. (2003). *Social capital*. New York: Routledge, Taylor & Francis.

Fukuyama, F. (1995). Trust: *The social virtues and the creation of prosperity*. New York: The Free Press.

Garip, F. (2008). Social capital and migration: How do similar resources lead to divergent outcomes? *Demography*, 45, 591–617.

Getz, C. (2008). Social capital, organic agriculture, and sustainable livelihood security: Rethinking agrarian change in Mexico. *Rural Sociology*, 73, 555–579.

Glaesar, E. (2000). The economic approach to social capital. Working Paper no. 7728, Cambridge, MA: National Bureau of Economic Research

Groot, W., Maassen van den Brink, H., and van Praag, B. (2006). *The compensating income variation of social capital*. DP No. 2529, IZA, Bonn: Institute for the Study of Labor.

Grootaert, C. (1997). Social capital: The missing link. In *Expanding the measure of wealth: Indicators of environmentally sustainable development*. Washington, DC: The World Bank.

Grootaert, C., and van Bastelaer, T. (2002). *Understanding and measuring social capital: A multidisciplinary tool for practitioners*. Directions in Development, Washington, DC: The World Bank.

Guiso, L., Sapienza, P., and Zingales, L. (2000). The role of social capital in financial development. Working Paper no. 7563, Cambridge, MA: National Bureau of Economic Research.

Harcourt, G. C. (1972). *Some Cambridge controversies in the theory of capital*. Cambridge: Cambridge University Press.

Harris, J., and de Renzio, P. (1997). Policy arena: "Missing link" or analytically missing? The concept of social capital. *Journal of International Development, 9*, 919–937.

Helliwell, J., and Putnam, R. D. (2000). Economic growth and social capital in Italy. In P. Dasgupta and I. Serageldin (Eds.), *Social capital: A multifaceted perspective* (pp. 253–268). Washington, DC: The World Bank.

Holliday, I., and Tam, W. (2001). Social capital in Hong Kong. *East Asia: An International Quarterly, 19*, 144–170.

Johnson, A. H., and Supple, B.E. (1967). *Boston capitalists and Western Railways.* Cambridge, MA: Harvard University Press.

Kikuchi, Yasushi (2004). *Development anthropology: Beyond economics.* Quezon City (Philippines): New Day Publishers.

Knight, J., and Yueh, L. (2002). The role of social capital in the labour market in China. Discussion Paper Series, Department of Economics, Oxford: Oxford University Press.

Krishna, A. (2000). Creating and harnessing social capital. In P. Dasgupta and I. Serageldin (Eds.), *Social capital: A multifaceted perspective* (pp. 71–93). Washington, DC: The World Bank.

Lucas, R. E. Jr. (2002). *Lectures on Economic Growth.* New Delhi: Oxford University Press.

Massetti, B. (2008). The social entrepreneurship matrix as a "tipping point" for economic change. *E:CO, 10*(3), 1–8.

Mauro, P. (1995). Corruption and growth. *Quarterly Journal of Economics, 110*, 681–712.

Miguel, E., Gertler, P., and Levine, D. (2004). Did industrialization destroy social capital in Indonesia? Working Paper CO3-131, Center for International and Development Economics Research, Berkley, CA: University of California, http://iber.berkeley.edu/wps/ciderwp.htm.

Min, S., Kim, S.K., and Chen, H. (2008). Developing social identity and social capital for supply chain management. *Journal of Business Logistics, 29*, 283–304.

Narayan, D. (1997). *Voices of the poor: Poverty and social capital in Tanzania.* Environmentally Sustainable Development Studies and Monographs Series, no. 20, Washington, DC: The World Bank.

Narayan, D., and Pritchett, L. (2000). Social capital: Evidence and implications. In P. Dasgupta and I. Serageldin (Eds.), *Social capital: A multifaceted perspective* (pp. 269–295). Washington, DC: The World Bank.

Navarro, V. (2008). Why "social capital" (like "disparities") is fashionable. *Anthropologica, 50*, 423–425.

North, D. C. (1990). *Institutions, institutional change and economic performance.* New York: Cambridge University Press.

North, D. (1994). Economic performance through time. *The American Economic Review. 84*, 359–368.

Ostram, E. (2000). Social capital: A fad or a fundamental concept? In P. Dasgupta and I. Serageldin (Eds.), *Social capital: A multifaceted perspective* (pp.172–214). Washington, DC: The World Bank.

Prakash, S., and Selle, P. (2004). *Investigating social capital. Comparative perspectives on civil society, participation and governance*. London: Sage.

Putnam, R. D. (1993). *Making democracy work: Civic traditions in modern Italy*. Princeton, NJ: Princeton University Press.

Putnam, R. (2000). *Bowling alone: The collapse and revival of American community*. New York: Simon and Schuster.

Reid, C., and Salmen, L. (2002). Qualitative analysis of social capital: The case of agricultural extension in Mali. In C. Grootaert and T. van Bastelaer (Eds.), *Understanding and measuring social capital: A multidisciplinary tool for practitioners* (pp. 85–107). Directions in Development, Washington, DC: The World Bank.

Renzio, P. de (2000). Bigmen and *Wantoks*: Social capital and group behaviour in Papua New Guinea. Working Paper no. 27, Queen Elizabeth House Working Paper Series (University of Oxford).

Rist, G. (2002). *The history of development: From western origin to global faith*. New York: Zed Books.

Sabatini, F. (2005). The empirics of social capital and economic development: A critical perspective. Department of Public Economics and SPES Development Studies Research Centre, University of Rome La Sapienza.

Schneider, J. A. (2006). *Social capital and welfare reform: Organizations, congregations, and communities*. New York: Columbia University Press.

Schneider, J. A. (2008). Social capital, civic engagement and trust. *Anthropologica, 50*, 425–428.

Sen, A. (2000). *Development as freedom*. New York: Anchor Books.

Serageldin, I. (1996). Sustainability as opportunity and the problem of social capital. *Brown Journal of World Affairs, 3*, 197–203.

Serageldin, I., and Grootaert, C. (2000). Defining social capital: An integrating view. In P. Dasgupta and I. Serageldin (Eds.), *Social capital: A multifaceted perspective* (pp. 40–58). Washington, DC: The World Bank.

Serra, R. (2004). "Putnam in India": Is social capital a meaningful and measurable concept at the Indian state level? In D. Bhattacharyya, N.G. Jayal, B.N. Mohapatra and S. Pai (Eds.), *Interrogating social capital: The Indian experience* (pp. 259–295). New Delhi: Sage.

Silberberg, E., and Suen, W. (2000). *The structure of economics. A mathematical analysis*. New York: Irwin-McGraw Hill.

Smart, A. (2008). Social capital. *Anthropologica, 50*, 409–416.

Smith, Adam (1910). *The Wealth of Nations*. London: Everyman's Library.

Sobel, J. (2002). Can we trust social capital? *Journal of Economic Literature*, 40, March, 139–154.

Solo, R. A. (2000). *Economic organizations and social systems*. Michigan: University of Michigan Press.

Solow, R. M. (2000). Notes on social capital and economic performance. In P. Dasgupta and I. Serageldin (Eds.), *Social capital: A multifaceted perspective* (pp. 6–10). Washington, DC: The World Bank.

Stiglitz, J. E. (2000). Formal and informal institutions. In P. Dasgupta and I. Serageldin (Eds.), *Social capital: A multifaceted perspective* (pp. 59–68). Washington, DC: The World Bank.

Streeter, D. R., *Seventh Letter. A journal of a Zen mountain dweller*. No date, no publisher.

Turner, J. H. (2000). The formation of social capital. In P. Dasgupta and I. Serageldin (Eds.), *Social capital: A multifaceted perspective* (pp. 94–146). Washington, DC: The World Bank.

Uphoff, N. (1996). *Learning from Gal Oya: Possibilities for participatory development and post-Newtonian social science*. London: Intermediate Technology Publications (first published by Cornell University Press, 1992).

Uphoff, N. (2000). Understanding social capital: Learning from the analysis and experience of participation. In P. Dasgupta and I. Serageldin (Eds.), *Social capital: A multifaceted perspective* (pp. 215–249). Washington, DC: The World Bank.

Van Buren III, H. J. (2008). Building relational wealth in the new economy: How can firms leverage the value of organizational social capital? *International Journal of Management*, 25, 684–691.

Weber, M. (1964). *The theory of social and economic organization*. New York: The Free Press.

Wong, S. (2007). *Exploring "unseen" social capital in community participation: Everyday lives of poor mainland Chinese migrants in Hong Kong*. Amsterdam: Amsterdam University Press.

Woodworth, W. P. (2008). Reciprocal dynamics: Social capital and microcredit. *ESR Review*, 10(2), 36–42.

Part I

Social Capital

Practice and Development

2

The Praxis of Social Capital

Wai-fong TING

I. Introduction

Few concepts in the social sciences can rival the power of social capital to arouse the interest of a wide spectrum of audience. Those who are interested, including academics, policy makers of governments around the world and international organisations, are keen not only to examine the concept itself, but also how to put it to use in everyday life, in interpersonal living and community building as well as public governance. The decade since 1999 has witnessed the exponential growth of studies related to social capital and most of them have contributed to our understanding of the nature of social capital, the forms of its existence, its benefits to individuals and society at large, as well as the trend of its development. Although it has been cautioned that despite the seemingly positive benefits, social capital is not a panacea, numerous scholars, practitioners, and governments still display keenness to find the right way to build social capital. These interests, however, are not always met with corresponding empirical study. Until now, little is known about the mechanism through which social capital can be built. In a simple sense, Putnam postulates that it is through participation in civil society that social capital can be built. However, this thesis has been severely contested by the Scandinavian social capital theorists, who argue that it is in the institutional model of the welfare state through which generalised trust can be developed. Despite their contribution in illuminating the respective roles of civil society and government, the debate has not been too helpful in addressing our concern for pursuing a model that can provide practical guidance on social capital development.

Against this backdrop, the present chapter aims to argue for a mixed model in which close collaboration between the state and an active civil society is necessary and sufficient for the formation of social capital. Based on the above, this chapter examines in detail the attributes of non-governmental organisations (NGOs) that are conducive to the creation of social capital. It is asserted that the profession of social work not only provides the practical know-how, but also safeguards the provision of a platform for participants of civil associations and NGOs to learn civic and democratic values, and thus contributes to the development of social capital.

In the following, we will first give a brief overview of what is already known about social capital. The subsequent section is a presentation of the current debate on whether the state or civil society is more effective as the source of social capital. The section that follows depicts the particularities of Hong Kong as the alternative model that is located outside the dichotomy captured in the current debate. A mixed model of government-NGO collaboration is then proposed as a promising way out of the dichotomous thinking. The final part of this chapter discusses our understanding of the capacity and propensity of social work as an active and effective agent in the creation of social capital.

II. The Basics of Social Capital

Definitions

It is commonly agreed that social capital is distinguished from other kinds of capital by its attribute of social relationships. Economic capital and human capital can be individually owned but social capital inheres in everyday interpersonal relationships, which cannot be separated from other actors and the structure of communities. Portes notes: "Whereas economic capital is in people's bank account and human capital is inside their heads; social capital inheres in the structure of their relationships" (Portes, 1998, p. 3).

Putnam identifies "several key features of social organisation, such as trust, norms and networks, that have the function of improving the efficiency of society by facilitating coordinated actions" (1993, 167). He further points out that social capital enables collectives of people to achieve more with their collective actions. In this light, the social capital could be defined as "networks of social relations that may provide individuals and groups with access to resources and supports" (Franke, 2005, p. 7).

Forms of Social Capital

Putnam suggests that social capital exists in different forms, namely bonding and bridging social capital. He described bonding social capital as "a kind of sociological superglue". He points out the bonding form of social capital is "by chance or necessity, inward looking and tend to reinforce exclusive". Bridging social capital, on the other hand, is like "a sociological WD-40" as these networks are "outward looking and encompass people across diverse social cleavages" (2000, p. 22).

Besides bonding and bridging social capital, other scholars (OECD, 2001a) add the category of linking social capital. This refers to relations between individuals and groups in different social strata in a hierarchy where power, social status and wealth are accessed by different groups. It is different from bridging social capital, which has been usually a horizontal category of interrelations, whereas linking social capital better captures an important vertical dimension of social capital.

Before Putnam, Granovetter (1973) acknowledged the significance of the strength of these comparatively "weak ties" (equivalent to bridging or linking type social capital) and proved these heterogeneous ties to be more valuable in combining resources from more diverse sources. Such networks are key to leveraging resources, ideas, and information from formal institutions beyond the community, which are particularly important for economic development (Woolcock, 2001).

Social capital may not be deliberately invested and may merely be a by-product of other activities (Coleman, 1990). Putnam (1993) considers it as "public good", that is, "not the private property of those who benefit from it" and its positive outcomes are deemed beneficial to the society (1993, p. 170).

Benefits of Social Capital

Social capital has been shown to correlate with a wide range of favourable policy outcomes. Empirical research shows that social capital can improve the individual as well as community level of economic performance by facilitating information flow and lowering transaction costs, notably through increasing trust (Fukuyama, 1995; OECD, 2001a). At the individual level, for instance, an unemployed person can be better off through ties formed by bridging social capital in a social network because a very large proportion of jobs are, in fact, filled by applicants who heard about them through word of mouth and personal contacts (Granovetter, 1973; Hannan, 1999; Montgomery, 1991; Six, 1997; Ting, 2006a; White, 1991). At the community level, the tragedy of double disadvantage, which was the phenomenon Wilson suggested in his work, *The Truly Disadvantaged*, that is, the rate of joblessness and poor people concentrates in the inner city and accumulates due to the lack of diversity of the neighbourhood, (Wilson, 1987), could be avoided by channelling new resources from more extensive and widespread bridging networks.

Social capital contributes to better governance too. Putnam (1993) has shown a positive correlation between trust and civic engagement and the quality of government. Subsequent research finds similar results in Germany (Cusack, 1999), Hungary (Schafft and Brown, 2000) and Russia (Petro, 2001). La Porta et al. (1997) show that high social trust was strongly associated with lower rates of government corruption at the national level, higher bureaucratic quality, higher tax compliance, infrastructure quality, and higher efficiency and integrity of the legal environment. Summarising all these findings, Halpern (2005, p. 194) concludes that "communities with high and egalitarian social capital foster more civic citizens who are easier to govern, a ready supply of co-operative political leaders, and a fertile soil in which effective government institutions can grow".

In a review of literature produced by the UK Office for National Statistics (2001), it is shown that previous research on social capital correlates high social capital with a multiplicity of desirable policy outcomes, which include psychological health and well being of citizens (Berkman and Glass, 2000; Brown and Harris, 1978); longer life expectancy (Kawachi, Kennedy, Lochner and Prothrow-Stith, 1997); lower crime rates (Halpern, 1999; Putnam, 2000); better educational achievement (Coleman, 1988); greater levels of income equality (Wilkinson, 1996; Kawachi et al., 1997); improved child welfare and lower rates of child abuse (Cote and Healy, 2001); and the cumulative effect that the well connected are more likely to be "housed, healthy, hired and happy" (Woolcock, 2001, p. 12).

The Dark Side of Social Capital

Social capital, on the other hand, has also its "dark side". A typical example often quoted in the literature is the association of mafia. They are groups with "clear associations with strong internal connections but generally do not lead to beneficial externalities for the wider community" (Coffe and Geys, 2007, p. 123). Another real life example can be found in Northern Ireland where the high level of trust and associational activity within the Protestant and Roman Catholic subcultures have generated high levels of intercommunity distrust and intolerance (Maloney, Smith and Stoker, 2000). Thus it could be seen that communities high in bonding social capital but low in bridging social capital can result in inter-group segregation or even conflict. Therefore, social capital theorists often favour bridging more than bonding social capital as it is argued to be more likely to generate positive externalities than bonding social capital (Coffe and Geys, 2007).

Trend

Putnam (1995) presented extensive empirical evidence of an alarming decline of civic and associational life in American over recent decades. The average membership rate in 32 National Chapter-based associations in the USA has fallen over recent decades. On average, membership rates slightly less than halved between the peak in the early 1960s and 1997 (Putnam, 2000, p. 55). Apart from formal associational life, the informal social connections of American people declined as well. The average number of times of entertaining friends at home fell from 14–15 times a year to only 8 times a year in 1990 (Putnam, 2000, p. 98). Even informal interpersonal or group activities like going on picnics, going out to bars, night-clubs, discos and taverns showed a similar fall (Halpern, 2005, p. 206). Political participation in the US was also in steep decline. For instance, the participation rate in American presidential elections fell by 29% over a 40-year period (Halpern, 2005, p. 203); giving as a proportion of GNP fell by 29% over a period of 35 years, and blood donations dropped by 20–25% in the same period (Halpern, 2005, p. 207). Refusals to participate in surveys and voluntary returns of public census forms recorded similar falls. To sum up, as stated by Halpern (2005), social capital has shown an overall decline across a wide range of domains in the USA from 1960 to 2000.

Putnam's classic works on explicating the trend of declining social capital, although focused on a region of Italy and on the United States nationally, influenced other researchers in exploring this phenomenon over the globe. For other countries, according to Aldridge and Halpern (2002) and OECD (2001a), Australia is declining in social capital, France is stable or declining from a relatively low base, while the UK has the same situation but the fall starts from a high base.

The declining trend of social capital found in many countries, notably the US, therefore, is by no means universal, as Sweden and the Netherlands are experiencing an increase from an already high base. Recently, social capital theorists and researchers in the Scandinavian countries have come up with a whole range of empirical evidence suggesting that, due to different institutional arrangements, particularly that of welfare, the Scandinavian countries are among the "odd man out" amidst the declining trend of social capital in many Western democratic countries (Hooghe and Stolle, 2003; Maloney and RoBteutscher, 2007; Wollebaek, 2008). Despite the differences in the trends found in different countries, the importance of social interaction and voluntary associations are underscored. This is probably a result of the loyal affiliation to the Tocquevillian tradition that associational participation is the most important mechanism for the formation of social networks and the generation of norms of trust and reciprocity.

III. The Formation of Social Capital: Civil Society or the State?

The above studies reveal that social capital is falling in many western societies and this alarming trend has attracted much attention from academics in many social sciences disciplines (sociology, political sciences, economic, social work etc.), policy makers of governments (USA, UK, Australia, Canada, Hong Kong SAR, etc.) around the world and international organisations (World Bank, UNDP, OECD etc.). Together or alone in their own field, they make numerous attempts to explain the tendency of this fall, with a view to developing strategy that could halt this downward trend. However, before one can explain the reasons social capital is being eroded, perhaps one needs to go back to the theories and empirical evidences of the who, how and by what social capital is formed in the first place. This section presents and discusses two dominant views regarding the formation of social capital, as well as criticisms of them.

The Role of Civil Society and the Mechanism of Social Capital Formation

More than a century and a half ago, Alexis de Tocqueville started on an interesting journey in linking the relationship between associational life and democracy. To him, association has the ability to unite people's individualistic thinking and direct them towards a collective goal. It could thus be envisaged that people could learn civic virtues by attending the Tocqueville school of democracy. Following the Tocqueville tradition, Putnam (1993, 2000) asserts that citizens' participation in voluntary organisations is positively linked to the social capital manifest both at the micro/individual and macro/aggregate level. To him, voluntary associations are indispensable in the building and accumulation of bonding and bridging social capital. These assertions are indeed based on a ground-breaking study that Putnam undertook in Italy more than a century after Tocqueville's project.

In his classical study of the regional differences in Italy, Putnam concluded that vibrant community life, referring to the existence of dense social networks that provides channels for citizens to affiliate, was closely associated with the effectiveness of the government. Putnam further distinguishes two types of networks, namely the vertical and the horizontal. Vertical social networks sponsor social interactions that are characterised by dependence, whereas social interactions in horizontal networks are typically more egalitarian and that norm of trust and a shared sense of responsibility are fostered. In making this distinction, Putnam unambiguously expresses his preference for civic or voluntary associations, the informal social ties or horizontal social networks, over vertical social networks. He also dismisses the role of formal networks composed of various kinds of professionals in the creation of social capital.

To Putnam, voluntary associations contribute to the formation of social capital in several ways. First, voluntary organisations offer opportunities for members to learn the virtues of trust, the habits of cooperation, solidarity, and public spiritedness which, according to Putnam, are at the core of social capital. This has come to be known as the "internal effect" of voluntary associations, or the effect that occurs at the individual level (Putnam, 1993, 2000). Second, Putnam postulates that participation in voluntary associations brings about "external effects". To him, participation increases social connections among participants, which in turn help to end social isolation and stimulate the development of democratic competencies and inculcates civic and moral virtues in members (Wollebaek, 2008,). Other theorists of social capital also support the view that trust and the norm of reciprocity that people generate in associations could also spread to the whole community, encompassing citizens who are not equally active in associational life. In other words, interaction in voluntary associations has positive externalities on the entire community, or the rainmaker effect (Van der Meer, 2003). To

Putnam and those who agree with him, the mechanism of associational participation is like a school of democracy where participants or members of the associations learn the values and behaviour appropriate to become a citizen of the democratic society. This indeed is a school of thinking that advocates the important role played by civil society in the formation of social capital. This thesis, despite its overwhelming popularity and having gained the support of many scholars and governments around the world, faces many challenges and criticisms.

Critique of the Civil Society School

The first and foremost challenge comes from Stolle who questions the assumptions that the "civil society school" makes have not yet been empirically proven. To her, it seems that there are a lot of "unknowns" that need to be answered before Putnam's thesis can stand. For instance, do voluntary associations actually act in the ways that Putnam and others have described (Stolle, 2003)? What aspects of the "face-to-face" interaction are really necessary and sufficient for the formation of the norms of trust and reciprocity? Are all associations alike, and capable of the kinds of social capital effects that Putnam and others have anticipated? Without such empirical evidence, Stolle could only accept the claims that the relationship between "membership in voluntary associations" and virtuous "attitudes of trust, reciprocity and cooperation" are hypotheses still to be proven (Stolle, 2003, p. 23). This lack of empirical evidence is due to the fact that most of the data generated from the national surveys, namely the General Social Surveys, the National Election Studies, and the World Values Survey, do not combine the indicators of social capital with measures of structure of individual associations, or the content of interaction and the degree of social contact, etc. Nor do these studies examine in detail the respondents' participation in different types of associations and the kinds of associational life that are conducive to the formation of social capital. Without such data, it would be difficult to ascertain the group-level characteristics as sources of social capital (Stolle, 2003).

The second powerful challenge points to the plausible explanation of "socialisation" as the mechanism through which participants of associations learn the values of trust, reciprocity and collective action. According to Hooghe (2003), the logic of socialisation used to explain the creation of social capital among members of associations rests on the understanding that, through sustained and face-to-face interaction with others, members are not only socialised into more democratic and pro-social values, but also, based on these values of trust and reciprocity, they will develop a generalised trust in other citizens or institutions of society. Quoting the work of social psychology on group interaction, Hooghe explains that the phenomenon of value congruence that occurs can indeed influence individual group members to adopt the prevalent and dominant values in the group (Hooghe, 2003). However, he cautions that the interaction only enforces already existing values but does not introduce qualitatively new values. Arising from this observation, the social capital outcomes for group interaction depend on whether the norms of trust and reciprocity are pre-existing among at least some members of the group. Alternatively, for interactions to be able to produce social capital outcomes, these groups have to purposefully adopt and reinforce the norms of trust and reciprocity in the group. This suggestion points to the importance of the mission and objectives of the association that sponsors the group, the nature of groups, the contents of group interaction as well as the human factor, such as the character of the group leader/facilitator and their knowledge and "skills" through which these norms are cultivated.

The process of socialisation has been further contested, for instance, by Uslaner (2000), who casts doubt on whether particularised trust can be transformed into generalised trust, as he thinks that people do not develop trust in total strangers just on the basis of the people whom they know and trust. Even if this could happen, to Uslaner, voluntary associations are not exclusive in bringing about this effect; the family, school and neighbourhood also should be able to do so. Moreover, the assumption that prolonged interaction will lead to higher levels of trust within the group seems to be again just a hypothesis and empirical evidence is needed to make this claim firm.

Finally, the thesis of self-selection poses further challenges to the logic of socialisation by postulating that the attitudinal difference between the joiners and non-joiners can be explained not by the behaviour of "joining" and the subsequent face-to-face interaction with other joiners in the association, but by the very fact that those who join are by their predisposition more trusting, more inclined to volunteer and to join with others in collective good actions (Hooghe, 2003). All in all, the core belief of the civil society school has been challenged and while their respective responses have yet to emerge, the limitations pointed out by the critics are clear.

The Role of Government
in the Creation of Social Capital

In the early stage of social capital studies, the role of government or state was rarely put on the agenda, most probably due to the overwhelming success and influence of Putnam's work. This model suggests that social capital is basically a product of civil society and has little to do with the state. Along this line of thinking, a more elaborate view holds that, indeed, one benefit of social capital is its impact on effective governance both at local, regional and national levels. Specifically, it is held that communities with a high level of social capital are able to foster more civic citizens and produce a steady supply of co-operative political leaders which are the essential ingredients of effective government (Halpern, 2003). This claim was later coined the "bottom-up" model and it allegedly adopts a linear thinking in which state/government performance is seen as a function of the social capital that exists.

While not disagreeing with the above view, some authors have begun to evaluate this claim and suggest that "the state plays a fundamental role in shaping civil society" and thus, social capital (Tarrow, 2006, p. 395). Mettler (2000), while criticising Putnam's model as losing sight of the political and institutional factors, advocates "bring[ing] the state back in to the study of civic life" (2000, p. 363). This view was echoed and elaborated by the authors of the "institutional school of social capital" mostly come from the Scandinavian countries. It is generally agreed among this camp of social capital theorists that the phenomenal growth of the third sector can be largely attributed to state intervention (Skocpol, Ganz and Munson, 2000). However, they are also quick to qualify this position with the caveat that only some forms of government and certain kinds of government intervention or institutional arrangements are conducive to the formation of social capital.

According to the "institutional school of social capital", there are many aspects of a government that matter for the development of social capital. First and foremost, a democratic government is conducive to the development of egalitarian relationships in both the vertical and horizontal dimensions. A negative example is given in which a repressive or authoritarian government is destructive to social capital as it discourages spontaneous group activities and the development of trust (Booth and Richard, 1998). Worse still, these governments build their power on the foundation of mistrust among their citizens. This was evidently the case in the Cultural Revolution in China in the 1960s. It was an era in which the young Red Guards of Chairman Mao were encouraged to report on the misdeeds of their parents, relatives, friends, teachers, co-workers, and so forth. As Sztompka has observed, this "culture of mistrust", which has persisted in the post-communist era among the Eastern European countries, could probably explain why they consistently rank lower than western democratic countries in comparable international surveys on interpersonal trust and social capital (Sztompka, 1995; Halpern, 2005). Stolle (2003) suggests that some theorists of social capital tend to overgeneralise these negative examples and hence judge any form of government intervention as detrimental to social capital. To vigorously illuminate this argument, Stolle and other Scandinavian scholars have joined together since the late 1990s to make a case for state intervention in the creation of social capital.

In trying to solve the "Scandinavian puzzle" of why the Scandinavian countries, unlike many of their western counterparts, do not follow the downward trend in social capital, the Scandinavian social capital theorists, as represented by Rothstein and Stolle (Rothstein, 2002, 2004; Rothstein and Stolle, 2003a, 2003b; Stolle, 2003) have proposed and tested several hypotheses that are developed based on the relationships between differential government measures or institutional arrangements of welfare provision and the level of social capital. The results of these studies lend support to their argument that it is the institutional arrangement of welfare provision, rather than just civic associations, that accounts for the high social capital in the Scandinavian countries. In short, it is suggested that the welfare state has the potential either to make or break social capital, depending not on the size, but the actual design of the welfare state (Kumlin and Rothstein, 2005). The reasoning behind this argument is multifaceted.

First, it is common that people living in a welfare state come into contact with many different types of public agencies and services. It is suggested that people's attitude of trust is partly shaped by the contacts they make with public welfare state institutions and the concept of "procedural justice" is used to help explain this working. According to Dworkin (1977) and Rothstein (1998), people are not only concerned with the outcome of their contact with officials of public organisations, but also with the "fairness" in the process leading to the outcome. If an individual citizen is being treated with "equal concern and respect" by government institutions and their representatives, he or she would feel satisfied that procedural justice has been met. Kumlin and Rothstein (2005) suggest that it is the "design" of the welfare state that determines whether procedural justice will occur. There are in general two major designs of welfare state. In the "needs testing" design, citizens' eligibility to receive services is based on "needs" that are assessed by public organisation employees. This places great demands on the officials to make decisions on who is eligible for the service of which they are the gate keepers. In this process, it is inevitable for them to develop an "interpretive" or discretionary practice which is often informal and less explicit in nature and could easily be suspected of being prejudicial and stereotypical (Kumlin and Rothstein, 2005). In response, the citizens in this needs-testing model of welfare state would use their creativity and intelligence trying to outwit the officials, or the system, in order to get the services they need, for instance, by withholding information. This, according to Hermansson (2003), could easily turn the official-client relationship into a vicious spiral of "distrust-control-further distrust". The link between procedural justice and interpersonal trust can be exemplified by the people drawing inferences about others' trustworthiness from their experiences of the public service officials. Thus if mistrust prevails, then the prospect of interpersonal trust of this particular society would be gloomy.

The other design is the universal model of welfare state, in which programmes and services are often universal and do not require the interpretation of officials. People will naturally feel that they are treated equally and fairly. Moreover, the content of the universally provided welfare programmes could also impact on the social capital outcomes. Again, Stolle (2003) argues that the way the welfare state tackles "inequality" will have an effect on the generalised trust in the society. He uses examples of measures taken by the Scandinavian countries in addressing issues of income and gender inequality to illustrate the relationship between government intervention and social capital outcome. For instance, it is noted that in these countries, progressive income tax is used extensively to tackle income inequality, and public policies that facilitate women's associational and social participation are adopted which make it easier for women to reconcile paid work and unpaid family obligations. Subsequently, a sense of generalised trust in the society will certainly be generated among the benefactors of these policies.

Finally, it is further argued that if the government has the capacity "to monitor free-riding, to punish defection and to direct a relatively impartial and fair bureaucracy" (Stolle 2003, p. 34), the social capital outcome of that society would optimistically be positive.

Critique of the Institutional Model

The welfare state, as one model of social arrangements in which the state resumes primary responsibility for the welfare of its citizens, emerged in the European countries from the late nineteen century. Its emergence is said to be the harbinger of state provision of care "from cradle to grave". While the welfare state is applauded by many as an exemplar of humanitarian and altruistic collective action, it also attracts a great deal of criticism. The familiar critics no doubt come from the liberals, who accuse the welfare state of infringing upon individual freedom. Moreover, it is accused of being highly inefficient, compared with the market, in the distribution and redistribution of resources in the society. However, in the context of social capital building, we will focus on the following arguments that the welfare state actually kills social capital.

Wolfe (1989) is an often quoted critic of the welfare state. According to him, the welfare state has a devastating moral effect of squeezing out civil society. In a traditional society or non-welfare state, ordinary citizens will or are normatively expected to take up the responsibility of caring for their young, sick, frail, and disabled. Once the welfare state comes of age, the same ordinary citizens will just refer or bring the needy family members to the state-run welfare bureaucracy and leave them in the "care of strangers" (Weick, 2006). Moreover, as the scope of services provision in the welfare state is so immense, a lot of its citizens become one kind or another caring/helping professional employed by the state. Instead of caring for our own folks, the welfare state turns us into workers attending to the "needs of strangers" (Ife, 2002). Consequently, when social obligations become public, the intimate ties of the society will be weakened and the norm of reciprocity will be "crowded out" (Zijderveld, 1998).

Another problem of the welfare state is its "moral corruption" of citizens. By providing a wide range of services to citizens but not requiring them to contribute to the national good, the urge and compulsion among the citizens to contribute will be reduced (van Oorschot, 2003). This "will to contribute" is a common virtue among Protestants and the welfare state's measures erode the individuals capacity to enact this virtue (van Oorschot, 2003). Finally, as the government assumes a major share of the financial burden through taxation in the provision of care, citizens in the welfare state may find it unnecessary to contribute, other than paying taxes, and this results in the further erosion of philanthropy in the society. The care for our needy family members and relatives, the will to contribute and the urge to do philanthropy are all normative behaviours that substantiate a vibrant civil society. The existence of the welfare state indeed could, according to its critics, crowd out the civil society (van Oorschot, 2003; Kumlin and Rothstein, 2005).

The above discussion on the role of civil society and the state seems to present a scenario in which the two sides are rivals for the status of champion for social capital creation. Like any competition, a "winner-loser" position seems inevitable, but is this inevitable? Could a middle-of-the-road position be possible and be taken? The above review of the two positions does not just disclose each camp's dissatisfaction with the other, but the criticisms launched by one camp on the other in fact reveal hints for the emergence of a third model. Rather than answering these criticisms one by one, we would like to tackle them by thinking and looking outside the frameworks proposed by the two camps, i.e., to locate the possible existence of a third model which blends in essence the two models. The circumstances of Hong Kong will be highlighted as an example of how such a third model is possible in addressing the issues of concerns as discussed above. Before that, we recapitulate the various issues raised by the two camps.

The first issue concerns the agents of social capital formation. Must it be the civic associations, as Putnam suggests, or the institutional welfare model as the Scandinavians suggest? What about the role of charitable non-government organisations? The second issue highlights the mechanism and process through which social capital can be created. According to Putnam, the frequent face-to-face interaction of association members is sufficient for social capital development. This reveals a severe lack of details exemplifying the working of the mechanism and the content of interaction, as well as the role of the leader/facilitator in these organisations or interactions. Third, as the role of the leader/facilitator and the content of the activities are crucial ingredients in social capital development, the "who" and "what" questions need to be addressed. Fourth, as suggested by the Scandinavian scholars, it is not the size of the welfare state, but the design, i.e., the universal mode of provision which can safeguard "procedural justice". An interesting question might emerge here: Are these models of welfare provision so pure that there is either the "universal" or the "needs-tested" model? In fact, a mixed mode is often the case and it would be of interest to find out the attributes, role and contribution of such a mode in safeguarding procedural justice and thus the creation of social capital.

As we wish to depict Hong Kong as a possible third model in the creation of social capital, we therefore should discuss its unique circumstances in: the model of welfare provision; the relationship between the government and civil society, or the NGO sector, in providing for the citizens; the composition and operation of the NGOs; the landscape of participants in the NGOs, and the mechanism for participation. The following will succinctly explain our thesis that a blending or mixed model with a large NGO sector is indeed crucial in helping to create social capital.

IV. Hong Kong:
The Blending of Civil Society
and the State in the Creation of Social Capital

At the centre of the debate on whether the role of state or civil society is more important in the creation of social capital is the issue of how much the state intervenes in or provides for the livelihood of its people. In particular, it has been argued that the kind of model in welfare provision that a government adopts has a significant impact on social capital formation. Thus we will begin the exploration by identifying the model of welfare provision in Hong Kong. A comparison with both Sweden and the USA in terms of the magnitude of state provision will then be made in order to locate Hong Kong's position along the institutional-residual continuum of the model of welfare provision. Following on from this, a description of the scope and horizon of Hong Kong's civil society will be given, with particular reference to its relationship with government in the provision of welfare. Given its unique role in the delivery of welfare programmes, we would like to review whether civil society, or the third sector that is composed of several hundred non-governmental organisations (NGOs), still has the vision and capacity to build social capital or is just joining hands with the government in the destruction of social capital, as the Scandinavian scholars have professed. If these organisations do have an important role to play, then an examination into the "what" and "who" they are and "how" the task of building social capital is done becomes crucial if we need to answer the various questions raised on the mechanism of social capital creation.

Welfare Provision in Hong Kong

Hong Kong has long been described as adopting a residual model of welfare in which the government only provides for those who cannot help themselves. Thus if one is unemployed or sick in Hong Kong, what one can expect from the government is a safety net in which only the minimum protection is provided. This might sound mean, yet Hong Kong's spending plan in the year 2008–09 is US$6.1 billion, equivalent to 19.2% of its GDP (Budget Speech 2008 Hong Kong Special Administrative Region (HKSAR)), reflecting an increase of 30% over the past ten years (annual compound growth rate of 2.7%). Out of this budget, close to 60% is intended to cover social services including housing, education, health and social welfare for the citizens. The budget allocated to social welfare has increased by over 80.3% over the past ten years (annual compound growth rate of 6%), though most of the increase goes to Comprehensive Social Security Assistance (CSSA) (Budget Speech 2008, HKSAR). This increase may be impressive; but it seems insignificant when compared with Sweden, where close to 30% (OECD, 2001b) of GDP is spent on welfare alone. However, when the US figure of 14.8% (OECD, 2001b) comes into the picture, Hong Kong does not seem to do too badly, especially when considering that Hong Kong's per capita GDP (US$29,149) is much lower than that of both Sweden (US$47,069) and the US (US$43,594) (Wikipedia, country profiles of USA, Sweden and Hong Kong, 2008).

The second issue we would like to address here is the "mode of provision" of social services in Hong Kong. As discussed in Kumlin and Rothstein's paper (2005), the mode of provision of welfare in the Scandinavian countries is basically universal. In this system, all citizens are entitled to welfare benefits without being tested for eligibility. In this regard, Hong Kong seems to adopt a mixed mode, somewhere in between the universal and the selective mode of provision. For example, Hong Kong has an elaborate public housing programme under which 30% of the population lives in government subsidised rental housing flats and another 18% in government subsidised home ownership flats (Government of Hong Kong SAR, 2006). This programme is not universal, however, and those who benefit from this programme have to be means-tested. However, the health service, which resembles the National Health Service in the UK, is universal and the government pledges to "ensure no one in Hong Kong is deprived of medical care because of lack of means" (Hong Kong Year Book, 2006, p. 164). Education-wise, the government provides nine years of free and compulsory education for all. Together with the recently introduced vouchers for families to send their children to kindergartens and the heavily-subsidised senior secondary school and university education, Hong Kong can claim to have a mixed mode or partial universal provision of education services to all. Instead of going into details about these services, we consider it more productive to focus only on examining the details in the welfare service arena as it bears directly on the creation of social capital in Hong Kong.

> The Government is committed to maintaining a caring and just society. To engender a social environment that promotes harmony, it continues to place emphasis on family solidarity, fosters mutual care in the community and promotes partnership among different segments of the community. While ensuring a safety net of last resort for those in need, it also encourages them to be self-reliant and actively participate in economic and social life. (Hong Kong Year Book, 2006, p. 194).

The above pledge by the government summarises well the mixed mode of welfare service provision in Hong Kong. To fulfil this commitment, the government provides a range of social welfare services either through financial support or direct services. The financial support, called social security assistance in Hong Kong, is provided through a series of social security assistance schemes including the Comprehensive Social Security Assistance (CSSA) Scheme and the Social Security Allowance (SSA) Scheme, and is primarily means-tested, with the exception of the Higher Old Age Allowance and the Accident Compensation Schemes. Of the total social welfare spending, social security payments occupy more than two-thirds of the budget (71.7% in 2006) while the services in kind provided for families, the elderly, disabled persons, the community, etc., account for only 19.9% of the welfare expenditure. All these services, whether provided directly by the government (through the Social Welfare Department) or by non-government organisations (NGOs) with government funding, are primarily non-means-tested. In these services, the government and the NGOs collaborate closely to fine tune the development and delivery of these welfare programmes. Taking families and children facing problems of domestic violence as an example, a three-pronged approach to service planning and implementation is adopted to meet the needs of families. The primary level of intervention aims to provide prevention and education to the family/community prior to the emergence of problems. At the secondary level, a range of supportive services including support groups and intensive counselling services are provided for at-risk families. At the tertiary level, specialised services and crisis intervention are provided so as to contain or curb further damage to individuals and families (Hong Kong Year Book, 2006). For young people, there is also a comprehensive range of services provided at schools and in communities. These include the school social work service providing counselling and development services for all students studying in the 492 secondary schools in Hong Kong. Moreover, there are 133 Integrated Children and Youth Services Centres (ICYSCs) providing children and youth centre services, outreach social work services and family life education service for all young people and their families in their communities. All these services are provided free of charge to all those in need by professionals (clinical psychologists and social workers) employed either by the Social Welfare Department or NGOs. After reviewing the above, it might now be justifiable to say that Hong Kong is by no means a welfare state that is based entirely on the institutional model. Yet with the comprehensive coverage and diversified range of services provided to all in the community, we also cannot dismiss the government role in financing and organising social welfare in Hong Kong with a view to bring about a more "just and harmonious society". If this is the case, then what relevance does it have to the ongoing debate on the relative role played by the state and civil society in the formation of social capital? To us, it is becoming obvious that a third model does exist in which there is close collaboration between the government and the NGOs sector in the production of social capital in Hong Kong.

The Contribution of Welfare Sector NGOs in Building Social Capital

The discussion above has clearly pointed out that the Hong Kong government will not be able to accomplish its welfare mission without the contribution of the vibrant third sector that is made up of a large group of non-profit organisations, now commonly known as non-governmental organisations (NGOs), in Hong Kong. We argue here that it is the NGO sector, which is made up of nearly 400 organisations of varying sizes, that takes up a major role in the development of social capital in Hong Kong over the past four to five decades, through its provision of social services to the community. Before we go on to examine this phenomenon, a brief sketch of the demographic data of the NGO sector might be necessary.

Having their genesis more than half a century ago, NGOs today provide more than 90% of education and welfare services in Hong Kong. With regular or contractual funding from the government, the welfare sector NGOs engage a large number of community members to serve on the organisational boards and employ more than 40,000 full-time staff to serve an annual turnover of 57 million service users. Among the employees, over 8,000 are registered social workers. These social workers are employed by the NGOS which in turn are funded mostly by the government, however, like their counterparts in the UK and the US, their professional activities are subject to the scrutiny of their professional body and its code of conduct. So, even though the pay cheques come from the government, the bureaucratic rules and regulations are not their only practice guidelines. They also need to follow closely the professional practice protocol. As the central thesis of this paper is to explicate the role NGOs and social workers play in the development of social capital, the following sections will be devoted to elaborate on this argument.

NGOs provide fertile ground for the development of social capital in a number of ways. First, every NGO has an advisory or directory board that recruits members of the community to serve as board members. The appointments are honorary and members serve on the board as volunteers. These board members are mostly successful professionals or entrepreneurs or even celebrities, whose socio-economic backgrounds are very different from the employees and service users of the NGOs. This system provides a bridging function between these parties and thus lays the ground for the development of bridging and even linking social capital.

Second, among the 400 NGOs, many of them are also founded by faith-based groups, mostly Christian (Protestant and Roman Catholic). For those NGOs that are not faith-based, their founders include Native or Clansman groups, Chambers of Commerce; alumni groups (of universities or a prestigious secondary school); district-based resident groups; groups that concern a particular functional community (e.g. the elderly, children and young people, single parents, chronic illness etc.), and so on (Chan, 2005). Despite the differences in their religious, cultural and social backgrounds, these organisations are often united in their mission in advocating love, care and concern for the society and its citizens (not just their own members). Their mission statements are unambiguously civic oriented. This further qualifies the attributes of the organisations (or associations) mentioned in the "civil society" school (and neglected by the "institutional" school) of social capital. In other words, it is not just any (civic) associations, like sports clubs, or (government) organisations like the Social Welfare Department, but organisations that are governed by a clear civic mission, like the welfare sector NGOs in Hong Kong.

Furthermore, as the NGOs are all government partners in the provision of welfare services, they thus serve as a bridge to link the service users with the government, albeit indirectly over issues that concern the livelihood of the public in general and the service recipients in particular. It should be noted that not all kinds of efforts to link citizens and government officials/departments are effective nor that the linking relations built up can be sustained over time (Ting, 2006b). However, when the employees or key staff of NGOs are professional social workers who, on the one hand, have the skills and techniques in interpersonal and intersystem communication and are not necessarily subject to the bureaucratic command but by their professional code of ethics, on the other hand, the outcome of the linking efforts will be akin to that of linking social capital. In the following, we will illuminate this argument by examining the ways in which social work as a profession contributes to the creation of social capital in Hong Kong.

The Contribution of Social Workers in the Formation of Social Capital

The large number of welfare sector NGOs in Hong Kong employ extensively registered social workers to implement the vast variety of services in the various social welfare programmes. To what extent these social workers are equipped to achieve the welfare objectives in general and to contribute in the building of social capital in particular is the central question to be examined here.

The social work code of ethics

The code of practice of any profession not only reflects the belief it upholds, but also stipulates the standard of behaviour considered appropriate for its members. From a glimpse into the social work code of ethics, we could easily identify the basic values and beliefs of social workers as conducive to the development of norms of trust, reciprocity, respect, mutual help, mutual support and the strengthening of interpersonal relationships for the betterment of individuals, families, communities and society at large (Social Workers Registration Board, 2008). Moreover, there are very minute details stipulating that the social workers should aspire to treating the clients, colleagues, agencies, professionals and society with dignity and to be responsible not just as a professional social worker, but as a civilised and good citizen. Bearing this code in mind, the social workers in the NGOs are instrumental in translating this set of values and beliefs in their daily contact with the service users. It would not be difficult to imagine the civic outcomes of the contacts made between the social workers and the large number of service users. This code of ethics is by no means the only element in the profession that is imperative to the building of social capital. Indeed, social work training programmes internationally are deemed necessary and sufficient in inculcating a set of values as well as knowledge and skills that are once again effective in helping individuals/society to address social problems in general and conducive to the building of social capital in particular.

More than case work – A rich body of knowledge and skills

To a lot of people, social workers are problem solvers, thanks to the prominent work *Social casework: A problem-solving process* (Perlman, 1963), published by a pioneer social worker. However, many observers of social work are not aware that social casework is just one strand of practice in the profession of social work. At the dawn of the profession in the early twentieth century in the USA, social work was already practised in a community context, via the famous Settlement Movement. Social workers then worked in the community of poor and disadvantaged people and casework was not the popular method. Instead a lot of work that was done focused on fostering mutual help and support among the community residents. Although this strand of practice did not vanish, its significance and popularity was overtaken by the more individualised or casework approach to address the predicaments of the disadvantaged people. Some disappointed social work scholars alarmingly alleged this turn as meaning that social workers have fallen to become "unfaithful angels" who have forgotten about the "social" side of practice (Specht and Courtney, 1994). While this overall leaning towards clinical practice continues, nonetheless the "dual focus" persists in the profession until today. We do not want to join in the debate, as both strands of practice are imperative in the profession for those in need. However, what we want to highlight is that the two strands of practice have different implications for the creation of social capital.

The more individually oriented caseworkers adopt mostly psychological theories to inform their practice. This orientation necessarily sees the problems that the "client" encounters as arising from the inner psyche and the solution is also inevitably to be located within the client's psychic strength. In addressing these problems, to socialise the client into a responsible civic person is not the social worker's priority concern. Moreover, the one-to-one context of practice also does not facilitate the "client" learning from people other than the social workers, thus limiting the formation of a wider social or supportive network. Without doubt, effective casework practice might help address or even solve the problems that the "clients" are facing, but it would seldom impact on or change the persons' value or behaviour towards the civic direction. As mentioned earlier, right from the genesis, social work has a dual focus in its mission and adopts a wide spectrum of social science disciplines to underpin its theory and practice. So besides being informed by the psychological theories, social workers also rely on psychosocial, sociological and even political theories to inform their practice with groups and communities. For brevity, the following will describe the non-clinical strand of social work practice, i.e., social work with groups and community, with a focus on its knowledge.

Social work with groups

Depending on the purposes, the types of groups sponsored by social workers include friendship groups, uniform groups, service or volunteer groups, interest groups, committees or task groups, consciousness-raising groups, educational groups, growth groups, remedial groups, socialisation groups, self-help or mutual aid groups and social action groups. Also depending on the value orientation and the theoretical underpinnings, social work groups can be based on one of the three theoretical models; namely the Social Goals, the Reciprocal and the Remedial Models. The Remedial model, with the purposes of intervention in eliminating the psycho-social and or behavioural problems of group members, is often practised in clinical settings such as mental health hospitals or prisons by clinical social workers, psychologists or psychiatrists. Like social casework, this model of practice addresses individual problems more than cultivating civic values and fostering altruistic behaviour among the group members.

However, the Reciprocal and the Social Goals Models are often associated with practices that aim to socialise the group participants into civic-oriented citizens. For instance, the primary concern of the Social Goals Model is with social order, civic value, communal belongingness and social integration, and the ultimate goal is to cultivate a class of community-oriented and integrated citizens. The purposes of this practice, therefore are, first, to develop and enhance the members' social consciousness and potentials, as well as their sense of responsibility towards others in the society. Moreover, social workers would also facilitate the development of members" social competence, self-esteem and social power. The third purpose is to cultivate in group members a broader knowledge base and skills in civic participation. The outcomes of this model of intervention are the development of local leaders who have the awareness and ability to effect social change for the benefit of the society (Ho and Tse, 1996). The Reciprocal Model aims to achieve mutual aid and openness among members, between the groups and the related social system. The focus of practice is on fostering the relationship between the individuals and the environment with a view to enhancing the functioning of both. Social workers practising this model believe that the group is a mutual aid system which has the capacity for mutual support and problem solving. As Gitterman and Shulman have rightly pointed out, the mutual aid system, as informed by the ideas of Dewey (1916) and Mead (1934), believes that there exists a kind of reciprocity between individuals and their social surroundings (Gitterman and Shulman, 2005, p. 21). The two authors further suggest that the dynamics of mutual aid are expressed as "sharing data", "a dialogical process", "feeling of being in the same boat", "mutual support", "mutual demand" and so on (Gitterman and Shulman, 2005, pp. 21–24).

Social work with communities

Parallel to the practice with groups, social work also has a strong record in practices with communities. Again, the practice with communities can be distinguished by three particular models of practice; namely, social planning, locality development and social action. Among the three models of practice, the locality development model is the most relevant to the building and development of social capital. According to Rothman (1987), this approach to community practice presupposes that changes in the community (problems or concerns) would only come about through broad participation of the community residents. Therefore, the aim of locality development is to promote self-help among residents to enable them to find solutions to their problems and, in the process, people are helped to develop a strong sense of responsibility for the conditions within the community and to learn the skills and knowledge for collaborative practice. In achieving these aims, the social workers need to plan and carry out tasks that would stimulate and increase the residents' awareness of their life situations, problems, needs and the immediate social environment that maintain this environment. Moreover, social workers will also provide opportunities to develop among residents good interpersonal relationships, a sense of neighbourliness and mutual help and to encourage their active participation in community affairs. Last but not least, they will also develop in the residents leadership skills such as public speaking, chairing meetings, negotiation and lobbying with government officials and other sectors of the society. To summarise, we can say that community organisation, one brand of community practice, is a process in which the social workers, together with the community residents, identify the needs of the community, set objectives and then take action in relation to these needs and objectives. In this process, the participants also extend and develop co-operative and collaborative attitudes and behaviour in the community (Ross, 1967).

Finally, the description of the work of social workers could not be complete without mentioning very briefly the kind of programmes and activities that social workers plan and implement for groups and communities of residents. As a common practice, social workers entering the community will conduct a community study through which the needs and problems as well as assets and resources will be identified, through interviewing and talking to individuals and groups of residents, including both ordinary residents and leaders of organisations. Having made an initial assessment, the social worker would then conduct community gatherings in which the residents could meet and exchange views of the community in relation to its past, present and future. It is also through these contacts that social and neighbourhood networks are built and originally isolated or strangers in the community are connected and have a platform to meet others in the community. Eventually, plans to address problems and meet needs would be discussed democratically and only plans that are formulated with consensual support would be adopted and implemented. While plans are implemented, ongoing monitoring and evaluation processes will also commence until the objectives are achieved.

Sometimes, goals and objectives need to be revised and strategies amended when the constraints of reality become insurmountable. While the outcome might be uncertain, the process nonetheless is democratic, participative, educational and informative, and also through this process, participants learn the values and skills of participation in contemporary participative democracy. It is common for the social workers to provide even more intensive training to more active and willing individuals in the community. In these instances, groups based on the social goals and reciprocal models mentioned above will be organised. These groups resemble very much the school of democracy that Putnam and Tocqueville advocate. It is from these contexts that residents, who are now members of the organisation implementing the community develop -ment project, form social networks and learn the norms of trust and reciprocity. Through ongoing participation in the activities, they will have the opportunity to put these values into practice with their fellow residents and people in the wider community and society.

The thesis of how social capital is built and by whom had indeed been neglected in the literature on social capital. The above description depicts social workers as professionals who are well prepared and equipped to contribute to the development of social capital in their daily practice. To move the discussion forward, the next section will elaborate on actual practice in building up social capital in the local context. We intend the description of the praxis of social capital to enrich our understanding on the how social capital is built by a well prepared and equipped group of practitioners. Hopefully this will fill the theory-practice gap left open by all the theoretical discussion of social capital in the past two decades.

V. The Praxis of Social Capital – Two Practice Examples

Social workers who have reviewed the major literature on social capital would feel perplexed by an interesting but sarcastic phenomenon, and the author of this paper is one example. Often, the themes of discussion, like those presented at the beginning of this chapter, are fascinating as they all point to a new and exciting direction which matches so well with the values and mission of the social work profession. When reading on, two responses are often noted. First, we would say, "Yes, this (the creation of social capital in terms of building trust and reciprocity and social networks among participants or users of our services) is what we have been doing all along". Second, we would wonder why social workers and our work are not particularly mentioned or recognised in the literature as contributing to the building of social capital. While we do not intend to speculate on the reasons behind this phenomenon, we wish to present the following two practice examples as illustration and evidences of social workers' contribution in social capital formation in Hong Kong.

Social Work Groups with Secondary School Students – The Building of Social Capital Among Secondary School Students in Hong Kong

As mentioned above, there have been very few works, especially of the empirical type, analysing mechanisms through which social capital can be built. This thus leaves a big gap in spelling out clearly the mechanisms and means through which social capital can be augmented (Stolle, 2003). One of the best known theses about social capital is that membership in association activities is positively linked to the level of trust. Thus the author of this paper has launched an empirical practice research in Hong Kong , in 2005 in which groups of secondary school students were recruited to participate in two common types of social work groups based on the Reciprocal and Social Goals Model. The purpose of the practice-research was to address the following concerns:

a. Does participation in associations, which is more amenable to social work intervention, enhance social capital, which is crucial to many social interactions and cooperation that go beyond the boundaries of kinship and friendship, and even the boundaries of acquaintance?

b. If the answer to the above is affirmative, then how and why does it happen? What are the mechanisms and processes that operate? and

   c. Could the mechanisms and processes be augmented or promoted through purposely designed social work group intervention programmes.

Two groups were planned and implemented for students of two secondary schools, with one group aiming at integrating the students with a group of mentally-challenged residents in the community in planning and implementing community programmes; and the second group focused mainly on the students' learning the skills of volunteering in carrying out various kinds of community services. In the half year's participation, students of both groups planned and participated in activities such as "flag selling" to raise funds for community organisations; activities such as a Christmas party for children, mentally challenged, and elderly people, and singing Christmas carols with mentally challenged people on the street; making handicrafts for elderly people, house cleaning services for elderly people; helping a youth centre to distribute programme promotion leaflets, etc.

Pre- and post-participation measurements showed that the group members experienced more positive changes in norms of generalised trust and reciprocity than the control group. For instance, students in the experimental groups (participants of the two groups) showed a sharp decrease in "distrust" of people coming from a different background (an item designed to test generalise trust) whereas the control group show a moderate increase (Ting and Sze, 2007). This seems to suggest that, after participating in the groups, students think that people who come from a different background are not difficult to get along with, and they develop higher confidence and readiness to make contact with people they are not familiar with. This demonstrates that the group programme does have a positive effect on cultivating generalised trust level among the students. Moreover, the students who participated in the groups also showed a rather large increase in the amount of time (from less than 5 hours per month to 10 hours per month) they were willing to volunteer after they participated in the groups, whereas the control group students showed a slight decrease (remaining less than 5 hours per month) (Ting and Sze, 2007). This again demonstrates that the group programme has a positive effect in cultivating the spirit of volunteerism among the group members.

Community-based Social Capital Intervention Programmes – The Sham Shui Po Child-Friendly Network

In the 2001 Policy Address, the then Chief Executive of Hong Kong Special Administrative Region, Mr C. H. Tung, announced the setting up of a $300 million Community Investment and Inclusion Fund (CIIF) [1] that aims to provide seed money to support collaborative efforts of community organisations and the private sector in building social capital among the communities in Hong Kong. Since its inauguration in 2002, the fund has supported more than 170 projects all over Hong Kong. The following is one example in which the author of this paper was involved. The aims and objectives of the project are to:

a. enhance the community well-being of Shum Shui Po through creating a sustainable network that builds primarily on a child-friendly community network initiative;
b. mobilise resources within the community to solve its own problems and develop itself into a child-friendly community.

The project began by recruiting from the Sham Shui Po community residents who are parents of young children from low-income families; volunteers; schools, kindergartens and nurseries; small business vendors as well as other community organisations. Through a series of "family-" and "community-focused" programmes, the various sectors of the community were drawn together to contribute for the well-being of the disadvantaged groups, in this case, children and parents of low-income and newly arrived families. Subsequently, through participating in the family focused programmes, the parents learnt the skills of not just taking care of themselves, but also developing trust first in other parents (bonding social capital) and then to the general population in the community, including other parents, teachers of schools other than the one their children go, paediatricians, shop owners/keepers as well as government officials/organisational representatives in the

---

1 Community Investment and Inclusive Fund (CIIF), Hong Kong SAR, http://www.ciif.gov.hk.

community (bridging social capital). Finally, the parent participants who benefited from the project again demonstrated their their post-participation changes lie not just in the norms of trust and reciprocity, but in actual behaviour.

A two-year longitudinal study which documents the programme content and measures attitudinal and behavioural changes of project participants was designed and instituted right from the beginning of the project (Chan and Ting, forthcoming). As mentioned already, the study recorded obvious development of bonding and bridging social capital among the project participants. Most importantly, the study also documented that project workers who are registered social workers consistently employed social work knowledge and skills in facilitating the building of social capital. This undoubtedly lent evidence to our claim that social workers are indeed the most well-prepared and ready group of professionals whose knowledge and skills' repertoire are useful and effective in the building of social capital.

We also wish to highlight that these two practices operate under the auspices of two typical NGOs, as described in section IV. These organisations are long standing NGOs (one faith-based and one non-faith-based) and are prominent welfare service providers in Hong Kong. They also extensively engage professional social workers who in turn pledge allegiance to the profession's code of ethics. Moreover, their practices are delivered within the organisation's framework (in particular its civic oriented mission) and underpinned by the profession's knowledge and skills. Under these circumstances, it is almost certain that their practices are geared towards the building up of mutual trust and mutual help among the programme participants and the bridging between them and the wider community and other sectors in the society, that is, the development of bridging and linking social capital. The examples here supplement the picture depicted by the institutional school (in which the government plays a major role in laying the infrastructure and the mechanism for social capital formation) by instituting the role played by NGOs and professional social workers in the development of social capital.

We are also satisfied that the two practice examples, with the empirical data generated, are able to fill the theoretical as well as practice gap raised by the institutional school and omitted by the civil society school of social capital mentioned earlier. In these two practice examples, we are able to make transparent what it is in Putnam's civic associations that help to cultivate the norms of trust and reciprocity, core elements in the concept of social capital. When further examining the mechanism of social capital formation, several essential components become apparent. First, the nature of the organisation that sponsors the programmes does matter. Although the civil society school of social capital seems to contend that any voluntary organisations will do in providing a platform for citizens' interaction, yet, it mentions little about the attributes (e.g. mission, organisational make-up, etc.), the personnel orchestrating the interactions, as well as the content and format of interaction. The two practice examples which vividly describe the "who", professional social workers; "what" rather well structured and facilitated group and community programmes; and "how" carefully designed, implemented and evaluated programmes etc., could provide initial substance to fill these gaps.

VI. Conclusions

This chapter began with our concern about the lack of discussion on the praxis of social capital and the detailed delineation of the agents and mechanisms of social capital formation. The discussion above has hopefully shed light on the possible "third" model in which neither the civil society nor the state alone should be held responsible for the creation of social capital. Instead, the participation of civil society, with its large government-funded NGO sector and its close collaboration with the government, is a viable third model. Moreover, the charitable nature of the NGOs and their faith-based characteristics ensure that the pro-social and civic values are upheld and transmitted together with the welfare services they provide. Furthermore, these NGOs are often staffed by teams of non-clinically orientated social workers, whose compliance to the profession code of conduct ensures the democratic values are being respected and transmitted; and their practice competence in using the social work groups and community development approaches have been demonstrated as effective in the development of social capital. Finally, the two practice examples in the creation of social capital provide empirical evidence that supports the further development of the praxis of social capital. The author of this chapter hopes that this discussion may serve as an overture that could stimulate future work in this area.

References

Aldridge, S. and Halpern, D. (2002) *Social capital: A discussion paper*. London: Performance and Innovation Unit.

Berkman, L. F., and Glass, T. (2000). Social integration, social networks, social support and health. In L.F. Berkman and I. Kawachi (Eds.), *Social epidemiology* (pp.174–190). Oxford: Oxford University Press.

Booth, J., and Bayer, R. P. (1998). Civil society and political context in central America. *American Behavioral Scientist, 42*, 33–46.

Brown, G., and Harris, T. (1978). *Social origins of depression*. London: Tavistock.

Chan, C. (2005). *Study on the third sector landscape in Hong Kong*. Central Policy Unit, Hong Kong Special Administrative Region.

Chan, W. K., and Ting, W. F. (forthcoming). A study of the mechanism of social capital development: The case of Sham Shui Po Child-friendly Network. MPhil thesis, Department of Applied Social Sciences, Hong Kong Polytechnic University.

Coffe, H., and Geys, B. (2007). Toward empirical characterization of bridging and bonding social capital. *Nonprofit and Voluntary Sector Quarterly, 36*, 121–139.

Coleman, J. S. (1988). Social capital in the creation of human capital. *American Journal of Sociology, 94*, Supplement: S95–S120.

Coleman, J. S. (1990). *Foundations of Social Theory*. Cambridge, MA: Harvard University Press.

Cusack, T. R. (1999). Social capital, institutional structures and democratic performance: A comparative study of German local governments. *European Journal of Political Research, 35*(1), 1–34.

Dewey, J. (1916). *Democracy and education*. New York: Macmillan.

Dworkin, R. (1977). *Taking rights seriously*. London: Duckworth.

Franke, S., (2005). *Measurement of Social Capital: Reference Document for Public Policy Research, Development, and Evaluation*. Ottawa: Policy Research Initiative.

Fukuyama, F. (1995). *Trust: The social virtues and the creation of prosperity.* London: Hamish Hamilton.

Gitterman, A., and L. Shulman (Eds.) (2005). *Mutual aid groups, vulnerable and resilient populations, and the life cycle.* New York: Columbia University Press.

Granovetter, M. (1973). The strengths of weak ties. *American Journal of Sociology, 78,* 1360–80.

Gidron, B., Kramer, R., and Salamon, L.M. (1992). Government and the third sector in comparative perspective: Allies or adversaries? In B. Gidron, R. Kramer and L.M. Salamon (Eds.), *Government and the Third Sector: Emerging relationships in Welfare States* (pp. 1–30). San Francisco: Jossey-Bass.

Government of Hong Kong SAR (2006). *Hong Kong year book 2006.* Hong Kong: Information Services Department, Government of Hong Kong SAR.

Halpern, D. (1999). Social capital: The new golden goose. London: Institute for Public Policy.

Halpern, D. (2005). *Social Capital.* Cambridge (UK) and Malden, MA: Polity.

Ho, K. W. and Tse, M. H. (1996). *Working with groups.* Hong Kong: Hong Kong Polytechnic University.

Hannan, C. (1999). *Beyond networks: "Social cohesion" and unemployment exit rates.* Institute for Labour Research, Discussion paper 99/28. Colchester: University of Essex.

Harrison, L., and Huntington S. (Eds.) (2000) *Culture matters: How values shape human progress.* New York: Basic Books.

Hermansson, J. (2003). *Politik pa upplysningens grund. Om den demokratiska reformismens mojligheter och problem.* Malma: Liber.

Hooghe, M., and Stolle, D. (Eds.) (2003). *Generating social capital: Civil society and institutions in comparative perspective.* New York: Palgrave Macmillan.

Hooghe, M. (2003). Voluntary associations and democratic attitudes: Value congruence as a causal mechanism. In H. Hooghe and D. Stolle (Eds.), *Generating social capital: Civil society and institutions in comparative perspective* (pp.89–111). New York: Palgrave Macmillan.

Ife, J. (2002). *Community development. Community-based alternatives in an age of globalization.* Frenchs Forest, NSW: Pearson Education Australia.

Knack, S. (2003). Groups, growth and trust: Cross-country evidence on the Olson and Putnam hypotheses. *Public Choice, 117,* 341–355.

Kawachi, I., Kennedy, B.P., Lochner, K., and Prothrow-Stith, D. (1997). Social capital, income inequality and mortality. *American Journal of Public Health, 89*(9), 1491–1498.Kumlin, S. and Rothstein, B. (2005). Making and breaking social capital: The impact of welfare-state institutions. *Comparative political studies*, 38(4), 339–365.

La Porta, R., Lopez-de-Silanes, F., Shleifer, A., and Vishny, R.W. (1997). Trust in large organizations. *American Economic Review*, 87, 333–338.

Maloney, W., and Robteutscher, S. (Eds.) (2007). *Social capital and associations in European democracies: A comparative analysis*. London: Routledge.

Maloney, W., and Robteutscher, S. (2007). The associational universe in Europe: Size and participation. In W. Maloney and S. Robteutscher (Eds.) *Social capital and associations in European democracies: A comparative analysis* (pp. 39–51). London: Routledge.

Milofsky, C. (Ed.) (1988). *Community organizations Studies in resource mobilization and exchange*. New York: Oxford.

Mead, F. H. (1934). *Mind, self and society*. Chicago: University of Chicago Press.

Mettler, S. (2002). Bringing the state back in to civic engagement: Policy feedback effects of the GI Bill for World War II veterans. *American Political Science Review*, 96, 351–365.

Montgomery, J.D. (1991). Social networks and labour-market outcomes: Toward an economic analysis. *American Economic Review*, 81, 1408–1418.

OECD (2001a). *The well-being of nations. The role of human and social capital*. Paris: Organisation for Economic Co-operation and Development.

OECD (2001b). *Welfare expenditure report* (Microsoft Excel Workbook), Paris: Organisation for Economic Co-operation and Development.

Perlman, H. H. (1963). *Social casework: A problem-solving process* (2nd ed.). University of Chicago Press.

Petro, N. (2001). Creating social capital in Russia: the Novgorod model. *World Development*, 29(2), 229–244.

Portes, A. (1998). Social capital: Its origins and applications in modern sociology. *Annual Review of Sociology*, 24, 1–24.

Putnam, R. D. (1993). *Making democracy work: Civic traditions in modern Italy*. Princeton, NJ: Princeton University Press.

Putnam, R. D. (1995). Turning in, turning out: The strange disappearance of social capital in America. *Political Science and Politics*, 28, 1–20.

Putnam, R. D. (2000). *Bowling alone: The collapse and revival of American community*. New York: Simon and Schuster.

Reimer, B. (2004, June 8). *Measuring social capital at the community level*. Retrieved December, 2008, from http://www.pri-prp.gc.ca/doclib/Reimer_0604_2004.pdf.

Roberts, W., and Northen, H. (1976). *Theories of social work with groups*. New York: Columbia University Press.

The Praxis of Social Capital

Ross, M. G. (1967). *Community organization: Theory, principles and practice.* New York: Harper & Row.

Rothman, J. (1987). Models of community organization and macro practice perspectives: Their mixing and phasing. In F.M. Cox (Ed.), *Strategies of community organization: Macro practice* (pp. 3–26). Itasca, Ill.: F.E. Peacock Publishers.

Rothstein, B. (1998). *Just institutions matter: The moral and political logic of the universal welfare state.* Cambridge: Cambridge University Press.

Rothstein, B. (2002). Sweden:Social capital in the social democratic state. In R. Putnam (Ed.), *Democracies in flux: The evolution of social capital in contemporary society* (pp. 289–332). Oxford: Oxford University Press.

Schafft, K. A., and Brown, D. L. (2000). Social capital and grassroots development: The case of Roma self-governance in Hungary. *Social Problems, 47*(2), 201–219.

Six, P. (1997). *Escaping poverty: From safety nets to networks of opportunity.* London: Demos.

Skocpol, T., Ganz, M., and Munson, Z. (2000). A nation of organizers: The institutional origins of civic voluntarism in the United States. *American Political Science Review, 94*(3), 527–546.

Stolle, D. (2003). The sources of social capital. In M. Hooghe and D. Stolle (Eds.), *Generating social capital: Civil society and institutions in comparative perspective* (pp. 19–42). New York: Palgrave Macmillan.

Sztompka, P. (1995). Vertrauen: Die fehlende Ressource in der Postkommunistischen Gesellschaft. In B. Nedelmann (Ed.), *Politische Institutionen im Wandel* (pp. 254–278). Opladen: Westdeutscher Verlag.

Tarrow, S. (1996). Making social science work across space and time: A critical reflection on Robert Putnam"s *Making Democracy Work. American Political Science Review, 90,* 389–397.

Ting, W. F. (2006a). *A study of the social situations of ethnic minority women in Hong Kong.* Hong Kong: Hong Kong Christian Service, Project SASA (South Asian Support Alliance) and Department of Applied Social Sciences, Hong Kong Polytechnic University.

Ting, W. F. (2006b). *Final report for evaluating the outcomes and impact of the Community Investment and Inclusion Fund (CIIF).* Hong Kong: Department of Applied Social Sciences, Hong Kong Polytechnic University.

Ting, W. F., and Sze, Y. H. (2007). *A study of the effectiveness of social capital intervention programs in local secondary schools.* Unpublished research report. Department of Applied Social Sciences, Hong Kong Polytechnic University.

Uslander, E. M. (2002). *The moral value of trust.* Cambridge: Cambridge University Press.

Van der Meer, J. (2003). Rain or fog? An empirical examination of social capital's rainmaker effects. In M. Hooghe and D. Stolle (Eds.), *Generating social capital: Civil society and institutions in comparative perspective* (pp. 133–151). New York: Palgrave Macmillan.

van Oorschot, W. (2003, November). *Different welfare states, different social commitments*. Paper presented at the First Annual Conference of the European Social Policy Network, Copenhagen, Denmark.

Weick, A. (2006). In the care of strangers. In A. Lightburn and P. Sessions (Eds.), *Handbook of community-based clinical practice* (pp. 39–45). Oxford: Oxford University Press.

Wilkinson, R. (1996). *Unhealthy societies: The afflications of inequality.* London: Routledge.

White, M. (1991). *Against unemployment.* London: Policy Studies Institute.

Wilson, W. J. (1987). *The truly disadvantaged: The inner city, the underclass, and public policy.* Chicago: University of Chicago Press.

Wolfe, A. (1989) *Whose keeper? Social science and moral obligations.* Berkely: University of California Press.

Wollebaek, D. (2008). Voluntary associations, trust, and civic engagement: A multilevel approach. *Nonprofit and Voluntary Sector Quarterly, 37*(2), 249–263.

Woolcock, M. (2001). The place of social capital in understanding social and economic outcomes. *Canadian Journal of Policy Research, 2*, 11–17.

Zijderveld, A. (1998). The vertical division of the European welfare state. *Society 35*, 62–71.

3

Bridging Social Capital – Theories and Practice

Alice Ming Lin Chong

and Grace Fung-Mo Ng

I. Introduction

Communities today, developed or otherwise, are facing rapid and sometimes radical changes that disrupt social institutions and disconnect social relationships on a scale that is unprecedented. The dynamic changes in the social and economic environment demand different types of adaptability, resilience and entrepreneurship from individuals and communities to succeed. In communities with relative material abundance, such as Hong Kong, it is no longer abject poverty that threatens the sense of social security and harmony. It is more often the fear, uncertainty and doubt associated with the negative experience of change that accentuate the risks of social marginalisation, disconnection and possible exclusion from mainstream society. Policy makers, academics and researchers alike have been searching for ways to reduce the negative impacts of change and to foster a sense of social harmony. Social capital, with its impacts on social trust, participation and connectivity (Putnam, 1993, 2000 and 2002) has been advocated as an effective way to enhance social networks and to build stronger communities.

Social capital has been variously defined. Some see it as a feature of communities, such as the extent of interpersonal trust between citizens, norms of reciprocity and density of civic associations (Kawachi, Kennedy and Glass, 1999). Robert Putnam (1993, 2000, and 2002), who popularised the notion of social capital, sees it mostly in terms of social trust, participation and connectivity. Others point out that it is just a re-packaging of what sociologists have long referred to as "social networks" (Johnson, Headey and Jensen, 2003). Social capital is also sometimes used interchangeably with social cohesion, social support, civic engagement and other similar concepts. For example, in a World Health Organisation document on the social determinants of health, Wilkinson and Marmot (2003) assert that social cohesion – defined as the quality of social relationships and the existence of trust, mutual obligations and respect in communities – helps to protect people and their health.

For *academics*, social capital includes too many facets, is imprecise and too vexing a concept for vigorous empirical testing. Yet precisely because of its multi-faceted and inter-disciplinary nature, the concept of social capital holds much fascination for *practitioners,* such as social workers, community development workers, and promoters of corporate social responsibilities who find many principles of social capital building to be consistent with those of their own professional training.

Social capital is multidimensional, consisting of at least three dimensions: *bonding, bridging* (Putnam, 2000) and *linking* (Woolcock, 2001). Of all these dimensions, this paper examines the theories and practices of *one specific aspect* of social capital – *bridging social capital.* The reasons to single out bridging social capital are twofold. First, while all three dimensions of social capital facilitate some kind of networking, it is essential to go beyond bonding social capital to bridging different groups and social entities for real capacity building. Second, human service professions such as social work and community work have acquired a rich array of practical experience in bonding people of similar needs and characteristics together, with the aim of enhancing their mutual help, reciprocity and intra-group solidarity. Yet there is insufficient emphasis and literature on bridging external and diverse groups and entities to secure new resources and opportunities. In the following, we will analyse the dynamics and reasons leading to positive impacts and effects of bridging social capital through the application of the "intergroup contact theory" from social psychology (Pettigrew, 1998). Relevant examples from social capital development projects funded by the Community Investment and Inclusion Fund (CIIF) of the Hong Kong Special Administration Region (HKSAR) Government will be cited to illustrate the different strategies and good practices that facilitate bridging. Implications for human services professionals and social development advisors will be highlighted. Such practices will be of particular relevance to Chinese, Asian and other societies that are facing the challenge of rapid social change with the risks of social alienation and relative or intergenerational poverty.

II. Building Social Capital – The Hong Kong Experience

In his 2001 Policy Address, the then Chief Executive of the HKSAR Government announced the establishment of the CIIF[1] as a new policy initiative. The CIIF is a seed fund with an initial injection of HK$300 million to encourage mutual help and concern through support for community initiatives that build capacity, increase connectedness across social groups, promote tripartite partnerships and develop social capital. It aims to create conditions and new opportunities for increasing community participation.

In our view, the CIIF attempts a breakthrough in linking concepts and policy with practice. The CIIF has since operationalised a social capital development framework that integrates various interpretations of social capital into a simple and coherent framework, as presented in Figure 1. The framework serves as a process to promote paradigm shift, especially amongst the community, local stakeholders and business partners in how new social problems and realities are to be analysed, re-interpreted and addressed.

---

1   A background brief on the CIIF is in the annex.

Figure 1: CIIF Social Capital Framework

Social capital – components, strategies & outcomes

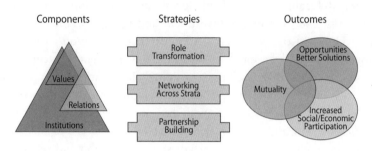

The "components" of social capital in this CIIF framework are based on key definitions drawn from academics involved in the World Bank and other sociologists: *social norms* (individual attitudes and social values), *networks*, and *institutions*. The "Strategies" deployed in social capital development included: "*Cognitive*", "*Relational*" and "*Structural*" dimensions, incorporating psychological and sociological concepts of "*role transformation*", "*social trust*", within in-group "*bonding*" and horizontal "*bridging*" across heterogeneous groups and collaboration in vertical "*linking*" partnerships across institutions, sectors and power hierarchies. This CIIF framework encompasses practically all aspects of social capital in concepts as well in application even though this paper examines primarily the bridging social capital elements in detail.

III. The CIIF – Promoting Bridging Across Generations and Social Backgrounds

Putnam (2000) argued that while bonding social capital, defined as the strength of relationships glued amongst in-group members, is helpful for "getting by", bridging social capital, defined as the network of relationships between people from different social categories, is crucial for "getting ahead". Putnam's emphasis on bridging social capital is reflected in the social capital strategies promoted by the CIIF. Since its formal launch in August 2002, the

CIIF has taken on an active role in promoting social capital development through its application guide[2], the funding criteria it applies, funding agreements over outcome indicators, interaction with the project teams throughout the project development, review and monitoring processes, the independent evaluations it commissions and the annual sharing forum it hosts. The assessment criteria applied by the CIIF include: alignment with achieving social capital outcomes, the robustness of the proposal strategies, track record, strength of networks of the applicants, level of collaboration and shared ownership from stakeholders and sustainability of the social capital outcomes to be achieved. The CIIF provides a unique case study in bridging social capital strategies being promoted ahead of bonding ones. The CIIF has been encouraging the adoption of social capital strategies that aim to bridge across social strata, ages, cultures and ethnicities to be systematically applied in the 176 projects that the CIIF has supported to date[3], with good practice models being generated and substantiated with independent evaluative data accumulated over a five-year period. New data and knowledge is continuously being generated.

In addition to the quarterly performance data collected by the CIIF on "social capital outcomes" achieved by each of its funded projects, the effectiveness and meso-level impacts of these social capital initiatives were independently evaluated from multiple perspectives by the CIIF Evaluation Consortium[4] formed by seven research teams from five universities in Hong Kong in 2004. The research findings of these seven Consortium studies, covering 56 social capital initiatives, were largely affirmative of the efficacy of

---

2 The CIIF Application Guide and Forms are accessible at the CIIF website: http://www.ciif.gov.hk.

3 As of October 2009, the CIIF has provided funding support for 200 social capital initiatives distributed in all 18 districts in Hong Kong, mobilising over 4,700 tripartite partners in implementation, involving over 530,000 participants, with over 20,000 ex-service users taking on the role of core volunteers, establishing over 440 mutual help networks that form a protective "safety" net for over 14,000 families.

4 The first CIIF Evaluation Consortium co-ordinated seven separate research studies undertaken between December 2004 and March 2006, covering 56 social capital initiatives funded by the CIIF at that time.

specific social capital strategies being promoted by the CIIF to enhance the health, well-being and hence social inclusion of the community. [5] These projects have shown enhanced social engagement and participation, with positive impact on the well-being of people, families and communities that are often considered vulnerable or marginalised. Project participants include older people, at-risk youth, new arrivals, middle-aged unemployed, ethnic groups, ex-mental health patients. Families include those supported by sole parents, working parents, families on Comprehensive Social Security Assistance (CSSA) or families on low income; and communities include rapidly growing new towns or redeveloped housing estates, where residents are socially disconnected from their relatives, friends and neighbours, resulting in a high level of social alienation; or old communities that are losing population and energy. The variety of the over 3000 collaborators is extensive, including schools, businesses, corporate volunteer groups, retiree associations, professionals, housing estate management and hospitals etc., offering a rich array of bridging social capital potentials.

IV. What is Bridging Social Capital?

Social capital harbours at least three dimensions: *bonding, bridging* (Putnam, 2000) and *linking* (Woolcock, 2001). The first one is "bonding" which refers to intra-group, internal or inclusive "bonding" (Putnam, 2000) among homogeneous relationships within a family, group (e.g. new arrivals) or community (including geographic community, such as new town; or functional

---

5   The 2006 research findings were largely affirmative of the social capital strategies being promoted but could not be considered conclusive on the *sustainability* of the outcomes achieved because most of the 56 initiatives were only in the first two years of implementation. Most of the CIIF projects are being funded for up to three years to enable some of the medium-term impacts to be achieved. The social capital initiatives supported by the CIIF are generating a rich source of data for a second-phase action research to be undertaken with more refined research questions including reexamining the crucial question of sustainability.

community, such as particular ethnic minority group). Bonding social capital is good for promoting reciprocity, and for mobilising solidarity. It usually provides a sense of belonging which fulfils the immediate needs for belonging, love, emotional support and solidarity (Terrion, 2006).

The second is inter-group or external "bridging" and refers to the connections with diverse social groups or heterogeneous relationships between different families, groups and communities. Bridging social capital would be useful in mobilising external resources and information diffusion (Putnam, 2000). Bridging networks are better for linkages to external assets and information diffusion.

The third is "linking" social capital (Woolcock, 2001). Woolcock sees bridging as horizontal connections made outside of the immediate network but with those who are similar in terms of demographic characteristics, including socioeconomic status, beliefs and values, life experiences, and existing social capital. Woolcock (2001) thus adds a third dimension, i.e., the linking social capital which refers to a vertical relation that helps individuals gain access to resources from formal institutions for social and economic development (Woolcock, 1999). In linking social capital, individuals or groups forge "alliances with sympathetic individuals in position of power . . . in order to leverage resources, ideas, and information from formal institutions beyond the community" (Woolcock, 2001: 13). This thus opens up access to jobs, opportunities, advice, and other resources (Terrion, 2006).

The concepts of bridging and bonding are found in different fields and settings. For instance, they are applied in companies and organisations to help with information access and retrieval (e.g. Edelman, Bresnen, Newell, Scarbrough and Swan, 2004; Newell, Tansley and Huang, 2004). Bridging and bonding social capital are also applied in intervention programmes to promote resilience among vulnerable children (e.g. Garcia-Reid, 2007; Kao and Rutherford, 2007) and among impoverished and immigrant families (e.g. Terrion, 2006). They are shown to be positively associated with youth well-being (Beaudoin, 2007), health (Folland, 2007), and mental health (Almedom, 2005).

In particular, bridging social capital has benefits beyond what bonding social capital can offer, as bridging enables impoverished groups to secure resources that are not available among their homogenous members, but can be mobilised through interactions and ties with members across heterogeneous groups. Kim and Schneider (2005) found that bridging social capital helps adolescents' transition to post-secondary education after high school graduation, resulting in more educational resources and better future occupations. Bridging, operationalised as parent participation in school programmes about post-secondary opportunities and financial aid, predicted greater odds of their children's enrolment in post-secondary institution in the year after high school graduation. Parental participation in school programmes builds bridging social capital with other parties which possess the information and resources that are not possessed by the parents themselves or within their families.

V. From Bonding to Bridging Social Capital

Both bonding and bridging social capital have their different contributions in enhancing cohesion, relatedness, reciprocity and trust among the participants, and in building a harmonious society. However, a comparison of the nature and impacts (intended and unintended) of bonding and bridging social capital reveals that bonding social capital alone is not sufficient for real capacity building, nor for reducing social segregation and alienation. It is essential to go beyond bonding social capital to bridging different groups and social entities. In the following paragraphs, we compare bonding and bridging social capital in terms of three main areas: the networking approach, the resources in transaction, and the outcomes.

1. *Network approach*: Bonding social capital is more inward looking, focusing on strengthening communication and interaction among members of a specific family, group or community. Bridging, on the other hand, refers to the outward-looking networks and encompasses people across diverse social cleavages who are heterogeneous in their age, socio-economic status, experiences, or needs.

2. *Resources in transaction*: In bonding social capital, the resources of internal members of an individual family, group or community would be mobilised to promote the sense of solidarity and identity, to work or cooperate on some common tasks or to achieve common goals. Being members of a homogeneous group, the resources that could be mobilised are relatively similar in nature. By contrast, in bridging social capital, diverse resources (including information, knowledge, expertise, physical and material resources) are tapped from stakeholders of different backgrounds, age, social strata and geographic regions in order to achieve some common goals.

   Although soliciting resources from similar others (such as people of the same community, backgrounds or people facing similar risks or challenges), as in the case of bonding social capital, can enhance individual capacity to some extent, it is not conducive to soliciting those outside resources. Assets and opportunities that are otherwise sufficiently diversified supplement individuals and groups in areas where they are lacking, resulting in complementarity of strengths and weaknesses. The latter benefits require bridging social capital.

3. *Outcome:* Bonding social capital enhances intra-group solidarity, sense of belonging, mutual trust and reciprocity among members of the same group, family or community. It fosters the spirit of self-help and mutual aid that is much emphasised in many human services such as social work and community work. On the other hand, in the building of social capital process, bonding social capital may unintentionally segregate members from those of other groups and social entities, thus aggravating stereotypes, misunderstanding and distrust between groups. Putnam (2000) refers to this unintended but undesirable consequence of bonding social capital as "negative" social capital.

   Bridging, on the other hand, may broaden perspectives, extend the basis for social identity and foster individualised trust towards people who are very different from themselves but with whom they have formed close networking and collaboration relationships. Very often, individualised trust can even be generalised to members of the other groups with whom there is no direct contact (Pettigrew, 1998). Bridging can also bring about positive role change among participants, from being the recipients of help to achieving self-efficacy and self-reliance, and then moving on another step to helping others who are different from themselves.

Putman (2000) has eloquently differentiated the strengths and differences of bridging and bonding: bridging social capital can generate broader identities and reciprocity among heterogeneous groups; whereas bonding social capital bolsters our narrower selves, and, by creating strong in-group loyalty, may also create strong out-group antagonism. Bonding people with similar others often reinforces social stratification along racial, gender and class lines (Putnam, 2000). Putnam views bonding social capital as a kind of sociological superglue, whereas bridging social capital provides a sociological WD-40.[6]

In a nutshell, the policy objectives of many modern economies such as Hong Kong have been to help people to help themselves, and to foster mutual help. Bonding social capital may be a way to actualise these. However, if we want to achieve the paradigm shift from relying on welfare to self-reliance and then to contributing to society, and if we want to enhance social solidarity and social harmony, bridging social capital has a lot to offer. In a sense, bonding social capital can provide the foundation for bridging, for individual, family, group or community to venture outside itself and its boundary, and to network with people with different characteristics or backgrounds.

---

6   WD-40 stands for "Water Displacement, 40th formula" and is the trademark of a widely used penetrating oil (cleaner, lubricant and anti-corrosive solution) spray. It was developed in 1953 by Norm Larsen (then working for the Rocket Chemical Company) to eliminate water and prevent corrosion. The product is currently sold for many household uses.

VI. Mechanisms of Bridging

The literature has abundant examples of various efforts and projects building social capital in different parts of the world (including both developing and developed societies), covering target groups of different ages, gender, backgrounds and needs. However, there is a dearth of theories to explain why such positive outcomes and impacts should result.

Research suggests that the intergroup contact theory may shed light on the mechanism behind bridging social capital. This theory was originally proposed by Allport, a social psychologist, in 1954, and further expanded by Pettigrew (1998). Allport's theory conceptualises the conditions and processes through which the intergroup contacts and cooperation can lead to the reduction of prejudices and discrimination, which is also a major outcome of bridging social capital. "In-group" is a social group towards which an individual feels loyalty and respect, usually due to membership in the group. In-group members enjoy privileges over "out-group" members. The contact and cooperation between in-group and out-group echo the connection between heterogeneous social groups as defined in bridging social capital. The conditions and processes that are identified by the intergroup contact theory (Pettigrew, 1998) may help to explain the mechanism whereby bridging social capital can reduce social prejudice and social segregation, and enhance social solidarity.

The intergroup contact theory (Pettigrew, 1998) identifies four key conditions for intergroup contact to produce positive outcomes. First, in the intergroup cooperation task, members of the in-group and the out-group should accept each other as equal partners. Second, they should have common goals. The importance of common goals was also explicated by Sherif and Sherif's (1953) conceptualisation of the pursuit of "superordinate goals", which are goals desired by both groups that can only be realised by joint efforts. Third, the joint efforts should be based on role relationships that are interdependent rather than competitive. Fourth, authority, law, or custom provide social sanctions and support for intergroup contact and cooperation.

Pettigrew (1998) further posits four processes for the occurrence of change. Prejudice reduction and associated positive effects would result when: (i) in-group members learn new knowledge about the out-group, dislodging the latter's previous negative images; (ii) temporary and initial acceptance of the out-group during cooperation serves as a precursor for future attitude change; (iii) in-group and out-group members build affective ties and friendship during the cooperation; and finally (iv) in-group members gain insights that their own norms and customs turn out to be not the only ways of viewing the social world.

In the process of change, the operation of the four development processes as identified in intergroup contact theory would lead to the reduction of excessive in-group pride, learning of new ways from the out-group, disconfirmation of previous stereotypes, and access to resources outside the in-group. These dynamics bring about the reduction of prejudices, mobilise additional resources and promote the building of relationships.

Empirical studies are needed to operationalise the principles and processes identified in intergroup contact theory and to verify their applicability in bridging social capital. For the time being, these principles and processes seem to provide some plausible ways to identify the factors that are required to reduce stereotypes as well as to build intergroup solidarity; and to explain the positive process of change that is involved. Intergroup contact theory, as a general explanation of the positive effects of human interaction among groups of diversity, can shed light on the dynamics of bridging social capital.

VII. Strategies
to Foster Bridging Social Capital

Relevant case studies from social capital development projects funded by the CIIF will be cited below to illustrate the different strategies and good practices that would bring about bridging social capital. They also serve to illustrate principles and process of the intergroup contact theory where appropriate.

Bridging Elders with the Community

The rate of suicide among older people in Hong Kong is among the highest in the region, even though Hong Kong tops its neighbours in terms of GDP and per capita income. The loss of purpose, value, respect, and meaningful roles in the family or a place in the community are probably contributing factors.

One initiative by the CIIF is the "Elder Shop". Older people who used to be passive participants in a social centre for older people are now the part-owners and part-operators of a shop supported by the CIIF. This "Elder Shop" has changed the roles of the older participants completely and has extended the bonding relationships amongst the older people to one of bridging across other social groups with elements of linking in respect of partnerships with other organisations. The elders now operate this Elder Shop as a traditional corner store, giving neighbours a drop-in place, where the much valued Chinese traditional soup is served and where the elders, along with women and youth volunteers, operate voluntary or fee-paying community services teams for their community. These groups of elders have earned almost HK$2 million in three years to support their operation post-CIIF funding. More importantly, they are further advancing their roles as "adopted grannies" to children and parents from families in need, in a partnership project involving schools. Ranging in age from the 60s to the 80s, the elders are busily engaged in their community, they report much improved health and feel younger and happier. This illustrates the efficacies of the *role transformation* strategies to achieve positive, active and healthy ageing. Moreover, the project provides numerous and regular opportunities for older people *to interact and work with "others"* (Pettigrew, 1998), i.e., people of different backgrounds such as housewives, youth volunteers, and customers of their shop, thus reducing possible negative stereotyping about older people and enhancing mutual understanding and good will.

Bridging Across Generations

Social disengagement or dropping out from society is often a precursor to poor health, drug abuse and low motivation among youth. Bridging social capital strategies in the form of cross-generation and cross-strata mentoring that link up volunteer mentors and young people are being used in a number of CIIF projects, such as the Red Apprentices project. Over 250 at-risk youths were matched with volunteer mentors from the professions, the arts (such as modern dance) and the corporate sector (such as property management). These partnerships demonstrated bridging and linking social capital in operation. Apart from teaching job-related skills, the mentors helped build confidence, life values, and sense of direction to the young people through the special mentoring relationships that had been established. Over a two-year period, a success rate of more than 80% was achieved (as measured by changes in lifestyle, return to study or gainful employment) for these 250 youngsters. Many of them have even become self-employed. The project also serves to illustrate the four processes of change (Pettigrew, 1998) that bring about affective ties and friendship between the mentors and the young people. Both mentors and the at-risk youth learned more about each other through the projects, previous stereotypes were dislodged, mentors became aware of and began to appreciate the uniqueness, vigour and strengths of the formerly-at-risk youths, while the latter discovered that they could indeed learn a lot from their mentors, despite their difference in age, lifestyle and socio-economic background.

Bridging and Mutuality

Neighbours used to be considered central in the Chinese social support networks, with the notion that help from close neighbours is sometimes more timely than those from distant relatives. But in Hong Kong, as a result of dwindling family size and dislocation in community relationships, support from families and neighbours is dissipating. The majority of Hong Kong families now live in housing estates with apartment buildings over 30 storeys high, and where neighbours no longer know each other despite their physical proximity. Weaving new safety nets in the "vertical" communities, fostering trust and re-creating connections among neighbours, has been a key focus for the CIIF. Special models such as a system of floor mentors and estate leaders are being evolved to co-ordinate semi-formal networks of support amongst neighbours. Modern day co-operatives are being formed to provide after-school care, healthy meals, escort to medical consultations, home repair services etc., by connecting people to a network of neighbours with ready access to timely practical assistance, emotional and social support. This has resulted in new work opportunities being created, increased social and economic participation, a sense of community well-being and reduced child/elder neglect. These community networks are facilitating civic engagement at the neighbourhood level and form the basis of a more resilient, caring and safer communities which represent a "superordinate goal" shared by all in the community.

Bridging between New Arrivals and Locals

Hong Kong has a sizeable and growing population of new arrivals from the mainland. Whilst the majority of new arrivals (Leung, Chan, Cheung and Ng, 2007) have settled successfully, a small percentage have faced difficulties. The host community tended to respond in two extreme ways: either exaggerating every failure as evidence of abuse of services by the new arrivals, or favouring the provision of special customised services, such as interpretation services, training, or socialisation programmes exclusively for new arrivals. Despite their good intentions, the efficacy of the latter services is often questionable. They often serve to reinforce the marginal status of new arrivals and create additional hurdles for their social integration. However, a simple role-switching strategy being applied in a number of CIIF initiatives involving new arrivals has achieved quite impressive outcomes. Instead of putting the new arrivals into conventional roles as trainees, they are being encouraged to be the tutors (in areas of their competence, such as speaking Putonghua) for locals in a community-learning centre. Within six months, most participants had made friends with the locals; within 18 months, over 120 new arrivals and 80 local families had joined the network, and by the end of the second year, they formed a self-managed and self-funded local mutual care cooperative enabling some parents to seek open employment, creating part-time work for others as tutors and providing opportunities for volunteering for others. The role switching provided the platform for both locals and new arrivals to perceive each other as equal, it gave the new arrivals a sense of confidence and respect, and helped to bridge them with the locals and enriching the neighbourhood support networks for all.

Bridging Across Social Strata

Collaboration across the home, school and community is a common theme of several bridging social capital initiatives supported by the CIIF. Weaving *community safety nets* in support of families is one of the key social capital strategies preferred by the CIIF and schools. Parent-teachers associations especially have the potential to play a critical bridging role between the homes and the community. Most of the initiatives involve engaging parents with community volunteers and mentors from different socio-economic backgrounds such as university students, retirees from the public sector or professional bodies and corporate volunteers in programmes such as after-school care and developmental extension activities for young children, mentorship for youth or capacity building for parents. At a simple level, immediate needs of society for care are met. At another level, fragile nuclear families are connected to other families through some of the fellow participants or community volunteer helpers, who are often their neighbours. Such connections form a protective shield around the children and their families, thus strengthening their resilience. For the volunteer helpers, their relational networks are expanded, as they often become the adopted "grannies" of the families they mentor. At a third level, the status of the participants evolves as they progress from being helped to becoming helpers, and eventually becoming the participant leaders of the projects. Their self-esteem is often significantly elevated when their involvement in these projects is brought to the same discussion table as project partners with school principals, senior business people as corporate volunteers, doctors, local stakeholders such as city councillors, committee members who are prominent persons and government officials, whom they normally do not get to meet, much less influence. Such CIIF initiatives have paved the way for people who may otherwise be at the margin of the community to become more active and effective in civic engagement.

VIII. Conclusions
and Practice Implications

The strengthening of social relationships alone has been instrumental in bringing about personal, economic and social benefits for individuals and communities. Social capital has been shown to increase personal competence, cushion the impact of adversities and facilitate social inclusion for individuals and groups segregated from mainstream society. The four basic tenets of the CIIF projects, viz. the community building orientation, empowerment approach, fostering self reliance and inter-sector collaboration, have become working assumptions or theories of change in building social capital.

The potential values of developing bridging and linking social capital is easier to embrace than to practice as they require professions, social groups and institutions to operate out of their comfort zones. The social capital development strategies outlined above have presented new challenges and opportunities for human service professionals such as the social workers and community workers as well as for promoters of corporate social responsibilities in terms of meaningful business-community engagement. The outcomes achieved with elders, youth and the community at large have precipitated considerable shifts in paradigms and practice orientation amongst the project staff (mostly social workers), the participants and collaborators in order to achieve bridging social capital.

a. The first practice change is for community builders, social change agents and project workers to take on *different roles*. Staff must have sufficient trust in and work systematically to build the capacity of the participants to assume more active roles, facilitate them to take increasing responsibility and then even take control. Much also depends on the engagement, development and reinforcement mechanism being put in place to enable the participants to gain confidence, as well as feel respected and rewarded in order to sustain their motivation to take on further responsibilities.

b. The second practice change is a shift from one of providing help to the vulnerable to one of identifying, developing and maximising their strengths as the main problem solving strategy.

c. The third shift in approach is on extending the horizon of traditional service recipients by bridging them with people from different backgrounds or with complementary strengths so that they can develop social trust to these people, forge more lasting mutual help relationships and access to new resources.

d. The fourth requires professionals to move out of operating centre-based programmes to working with people in their communities.

Overall, bridging social capital strategies require a shift from professional-led service provision to *community initiation, engagement, cooperation, empowerment, self-management* and *shared ownership*, which hopefully will result in stronger social networks, social connectivity, improved individual and community health and community-business engagement.

References

Almedom, A. M. (2005). Social capital and mental health: An interdisciplinary review of primary evidence. *Social Science & Medicine, 61*, 943–964.

Beaudoin, C. F. (2007). The impact of news use and social capital on youth well-being: An aggregate-level analysis. *Journal of Community Psychology, 35*, 947–965.

Community Investment and Inclusion Fund (CIIF) Evaluation Consortium Reports, 2006, to the Legislative Council Welfare Services Panel, HKSARG, available from CIIF website, http://www.ciif.gov.hk.

Folland, S. (2007). Does "community social capital" contribute to population health? *Social Science & Medicine, 64*, 2342–2354.

Frank, John W. (1995). The determinants of health: A new synthesis. (Working Paper no. 54). Toronto, Ontario: The Canadian Institute for Advanced Research.

Garcia-Reid, P. (2007). Examining social capital as a mechanism for improving school engagement among low income Hispanic girls. *Youth & Society, 39*, 164–181.

Hawe, P., and Shiell, A. (2000). Social capital and health promotion: A review. *Social Science and Medicine* 51: 871–885.

Johnson, D., Headey, B., and Jensen, B. (2003). *Communities, social capital and public policy: Literature review.* Melbourne Institute Working Paper no. 26/03, Melbourne Institute of Applied Economic and Social Research, University of Melbourne, Australia.

Kao, G., and Rutherford, L. (2007). Does social capital still matter? Immigrant minority disadvantage in school-specific social capital and its effects on academic achievement. *Sociological Perspectives, 50,* 27–52.

Kawachi, I., Kennedy, B. P., and Glass, R. (1999). Social capital and self-rated health: A contextual analysis. *American Journal of Public Health*, 89(8), 1187–1193.

Kim, D. K., and Schneider, B. (2005). Social capital in action: Alignment of parental support in adolescents' transition to postsecondary education. *Social Forces, 84,* 1181–1206.

Knorringa, P., and Staveren, I. (2006). *Social capital for industrial development: Operationalizing the concept.* Vienna: United Nations Industrial Development Organisation.

Leung, K. K., Chan, W. C., Cheung, C. K., and Ng, S. H. (2007). *How recent migrants from the Chinese Mainland acculturate in Hong Kong: Success factors and policy implications*, paper presented to the AASP Conference organised by the Asian Association of Applied Psychology, Kota Kinabalu, Sabah, Malaysia, 25–28 July 2007.

Macinko, J. and Starfield, B. (2001). The utility of social capital in research on health determinants. *The Milbank Quarterly*, 79(3), 387–421.

Mitchell, R., Bartley, M., and Shaw, M. (2004). Combining the social and the spatial: Improving the geography of health inequalities. In Paul Boyle et al. (Eds.), *The geography of health inequalities in the developed world: Views from Britain and North America.* Aldershot, UK: Ashgate.

Newell, S., Tansley, C., and Huang, J. (2004). Social Capital and Knowledge Integration in an ERP Project Team: The Importance of Bridging AND Bonding. *British Journal of Management, 15,* S43–S47.

Pettigrew, T. F. (1998). Intergroup contact theory. *Annual Review of Psychology, 49,* 65–85.

Putnam, R. D. (1993). *Making Democracy Work.* Princeton, NJ: Princeton University Press.

Putnam, R. D. (1995). Bowling alone: America's declining social capital. *The Journal of Democracy, 6,* 65–78.

Putnam, R. D. (2000). *Bowling alone: The collapse and revival of American community.* New York: Touchstone Books/Simon & Schuster.

Putnam, R. D. (2002) *Democracies in flux: The evolution of social capital in contemporary society.* New York: Oxford University Press.

Raphael, D., and Curry-Stevens, A. (2004). Conclusion: Addressing and surmounting the political and social barriers to health. In Dennis Raphael (Ed.) *Social determinants of health: Canadian perspective.* Toronto, Ontario: Canadian Scholars' Press Inc.

Sherif, M., & Sherif, C. W. (1953). *Groups in harmony and tension: An integration of studies in intergroup behavior.* New York: Harper & Row.

Terrion, J.L. (2006). Building social capital in vulnerable families: Success markers of a school-based intervention program. *Youth and Society, 38,* 155–176.

Veenstra, G. (2000). Social capital, SES and health: An individual-level analysis. *Social Science and Medicine, 50,* 619–629.

Veenstra, G. (2004). Location, location, location: Contextual and compositional health effects of social capital in British Columbia, Canada. *Social Science and Medicine, 60,* 2059–2071.

Wilkinson, R. and Marmot, M. (Eds.) (2003). *Social determinants of health: The solid facts.* 2nd edition, Copenhagen, Denmark: World Health Organisation.

Woolcock, M. (1998). Social capital and economic development: Towards a theoretical synthesis and policy framework. *Theory and Society, 27*(2), 5–208.

Woolcock, M. (2001). The place of social capital in understanding social and economic outcomes. *Isuma, 2*(1), 11–17.

Ziersch, A. M., Baum, F.E., MacDougall, C., and Putland, C. (2004). Neighbourhood life and social capital: The implications for health. *Social Science and Medicine 60,* 71–86.

Annex

Brief on the CIIF

(with further information available from the CIIF website
<http://www.ciif.gov.hk>)

In his 2001 Policy Address, the former Chief Executive of the HKSARG announced the setting up of the HK$300 million CIIF to promote the development of social capital through encouraging mutual support in the neighbourhood, community participation and cross-sectoral partnerships. The rationale for this policy initiative is that "social capital" fosters social harmony and is considered by the World Bank to be the essential social glue that strengthens the resilience of a community during times of major social and economic changes.

Expected impact of social capital strategies

The CIIF was set up to develop social capital comprehensively rather than for addressing poverty per se. At a conceptual level, development agencies such as the World Bank and the European Union consider social capital to have an impact on poverty reduction as it provides the essential fourth capital, other than human, financial and infra-structural capitals, to achieve enhanced social and economic outcomes by changing mindsets, building relationships and creating new opportunities through institutional collaboration. At a practice level, projects funded by the CIIF do promote self-reliance and enhance employability through capacity building, transforming vulnerability into strength, connecting the disadvantaged to job opportunities through extended networks, and creating new employment opportunities through new tripartite partnerships, and businesses exploring new ways to exercise their corporate social responsibilities. Within this context, *the CIIF promotes bridging and linking aspects of social capital ahead of bonding social capital* and makes contributions to reducing the risks of inter-generational poverty through promoting social capital development.

Funding consideration

Supporting community-initiated projects is one of the strategies adopted by the CIIF to promote this relatively new concept of social capital development in Hong Kong. The CIIF invites project proposals twice a year. It generally supports projects with funding for up to three years. Project teams are encouraged to trial and apply social investment- and tripartite partnership-type of strategies in their projects to achieve clearly specified social capital outcomes. Project teams are required to indicate their plan for sustainability from the start, to ensure that social capital outcomes such as positive changes to participants' attitudes, mutual help networks, shared ownership by collaborators and work opportunities etc. once created can be sustained beyond the project funding period. Experience tells that many successful projects do not require continued funding from the government because of the support networks established, partnerships formed and changes entrenched.

Updated progress

As of March 2008:

(a) a critical mass of projects has been achieved; a total of 12 batches of applications have been processed, with funding of over \$160 million allocated in support of 176 proposals;

(b) the geographical coverage is wide – the projects span all 18 districts and in communities at different stages of development, including older communities such as Southern District and Sham Shui Po, new towns such as Tung Chung, Tseung Kwan O and Tin Shui Wai, and redeveloped communities such as Shek Pei Wan;

(c) the project scope and target groups are broadening – the projects involve over 320,000 participants from different age groups, social strata and cultural/ethnic backgrounds in a variety of capacity building, networks and community building initiatives; and

(d) the culture of cross-sectoral collaboration is gradually gaining roots – over 3,000 project partners, including non-governmental organisations, schools, businesses, professional groups, resident associations, hospitals, district councils and government departments, are jointly implementing these projects.

Evaluation and research evidence

The CIIF attaches great importance to evaluating the effectiveness of its operation, the strategies that it promotes and the impact of projects that it funds. It has been collecting feedback from various sources, including quarterly reports/assessments by the project teams, site visits and review meetings with the project teams, participants and partners, as well as independent evaluation studies. The first set of seven independent evaluation studies were undertaken by a CIIF Evaluation Consortium composed of research teams involving 16 academics from five universities in Hong Kong. These 15-month studies took place between December 2004 and March 2006. Findings from these studies were reported to the Welfare Services Panel of the Legislative Council of Hong Kong in May 2006 and the full reports of these studies are publicly available through the CIIF website http://www.ciif.gov.hk

Overall, both academic evaluation and participants' reports have affirmed the effectiveness of the social capital building strategies promoted by the CIIF, particularly with regard to:

(a) undoing negative labelling effects and focusing instead on capacity building – this is found to be effective in empowering disadvantaged groups and there is strong evidence of positive social and economic results;

(b) bridging people from different ages, social backgrounds, or ethnicities – in terms of broadening peoples' perspectives and motivating them to change, this is more effective than reinforcing the bond within homogenous groups; and

(c) emphasising sustainability – initiatives such as mentoring which build in-depth relationships are more instrumental than one-off programmes in fostering trust and reciprocity at times of need.

There is also substantive evidence that CIIF projects have created differences in individuals and their hosting communities. Examples include:

(a) transformed roles and enhanced capacity – over 20 000 participants who may otherwise have remained as service recipients have been transformed into volunteers and project organisers, serving others in need, actively contributing to the development of their respective communities and increasing their own employability;

(b) closer mutual-help relationships and stronger neighbourhood support networks – over 340 mutual help networks have been established. They are managed by the participants themselves and support over 10 000 families in need;

(c) social and economic inclusion involving cross-generation and cross-strata mentorships – over 1000 volunteer mentors from a variety of occupational backgrounds and corporate volunteers have become "life navigators" for families in need and re-connected over 3000 marginalised young people to mainstream society. These reduce the risks of inter-generational poverty;

(d) enhanced partnership across institutions and sectors – many projects have successfully built multi-sectoral partnerships such as home / school / community partnerships and health / welfare / community partnerships;

(e) indigenous models in social capital building are emerging, such as –

- flexible neighbourhood-based after-school care;
- designated "floor mentors" in residential buildings as core members of neighbourhood support networks;
- modern apprenticeship/mentorship schemes made possible through tripartite partnership; and
- "elder shops" and "adopt a granny" initiatives that promote cross-generational collaboration and positive ageing;
- increased social and economic participation – over 3500 full-time or part-time, paid or volunteer jobs have been created through cross-sector partnerships ; and

(f) over 20 self-sustaining co-operatives of different scales have been established. One example is the Lok Kwan Home Repair Cooperative Project, launched in 2003 with CIIF funding support with the aim of changing the mindset of a group of unemployed artisans and home workers to re-engage with the community and explore alternative work opportunities through volunteering, mutual help and partnerships. When this group of workers reached the stage of forming a work co-operative, business managers from substantive partnering corporations served as volunteer mentors of the project team and shared with the workers their professional knowledge on contracting, risk and financial management, as well as branding and promotion. Such assistance has helped the co-operative scale up the business part of the operation. The workers have, in turn, contributed to the community by sharing their expertise through mentoring other community volunteers, and providing guidance to secondary students on taking up their trades. The co-operative now has over 200 members, and is being self-managed by a team of members, earning in excess of $7 million in business even after CIIF funding expired.

4

Social Capital
in Hong Kong Since 1997

Adelaide Pui Ki HUNG
Kwan Kwok LEUNG
and Sik Hung NG

The first of July 1997 marked Hong Kong's transition from a British colony to a Special Administrative Region (SAR) of China. Since then, Hong Kong has been making a conscious effort under the "one country, two systems" blueprint of development to reposition itself as a political part of China while retaining its pre-1997 legal system and capitalistic form of economy. On its way, it was put under severe test by the Asian financial crises in the second half of 1997, the collapse of the overheated property market soon after, and the outbreak of the frightening SARS epidemic and bird flu in 2003. Those tumultuous first years, and the diving fortunes of the middle class, contrasted sharply with the optimistic buoyancy of an unprecedented level of affluence that the populace had enjoyed just prior to the transition. In the political arena, the incomplete success of the Chief Executive and his Executives to command the civil service, and of the Hong Kong SAR Government to govern effectively in a decisive way, also compared poorly with the apparent authoritativeness and effectiveness of the former colonial Governor and government. All these seemed to make the post-1997 developments look like a turn for the worse. Paradoxically, though, they served to remind Hong Kong people of the gravity of the historical mission they were destined to bear as Hong Kong SAR's first generation in the making of a new Hong Kong. The massive protest in 2003, when half a million people took to the street in the summer's simmering heat, had a similarly positive after-shock effect of making people sit up and reflect on the kind of society they would wish to have for themselves and for their children.

Hong Kong the British colony and Hong Kong the SAR of China therefore offer a rather unique case to look at social capital and its potential for the development of a modern complex city that has been, and will continue to be, at the confluence of Chinese and Western cultures. This chapter first reviews studies of social capital in Hong Kong published over the last ten years or so to see how the concept of social capital has been applied to the local context, its measurement issues, and broad changes in the stock of social capital over time. In this part of the chapter, the focus will be on academic studies. The second part will focus on governmental attempts to understand and apply the concept of social capital to a range of projects aimed at social inclusion and the redesigning of social services for the new era. In the third and final part of the chapter, a summary will be made of recent studies that attempt to evaluate the outcomes of a major governmental initiative on building social capital among individuals and groups who have been marginalised or underprivileged.

I. Social Capital in Hong Kong: Academic Studies

In academic discourse published in journals and monographs, the concept of social capital seems frustratingly diverse and hopelessly complicated. Our starting point is a layperson's conception of social capital that makes good intuitive sense and, despite its Western origin and antiquity, is surprisingly Chinese and modern.

> The individual is helpless socially, if left to himself . . . If he comes into contact with his neighbor, and they with other neighbors, there will be an accumulation of social capital, which may immediately satisfy his social needs and which may bear a social potentiality sufficient to the substantial improvement of living conditions in the whole community. The community as

> a whole will benefit by the cooperation of all its parts,
> while the individual will find in his association the
> advantages of the help, the sympathy and the fellowship
> of his neighbors. (L. J. Hanifan, an American reformer
> in the progressive era, cited by Putnam, 2000, p. 19).

The stock of social capital envisioned by Hanifan in the quotation above anticipated several of the most fundamental features of social capital now found in the modern literature. The fact that it is confined to neighbours within neighbourhoods would suggest that it is primarily a form of bonding social capital, and not a bridging or linking social capital (these apply respectively to social capital between neighbourhoods and between the neighbourhood as a sector of society and a different sector such as the local government). Its structure of face-to-face associations, aptly described as a form of "fellowship", would refer to an element of structural social capital, whereas its evolving norm of cooperation among neighbours would point to another element of social capital that is more cognitive in nature than structural. It is interesting that Hanifan distinguished between two categories of the benefits of social capital, one relating to individuals' personal socio-psychological needs such as help and sympathy, and the other relating to living conditions for the neighbourhood as a whole. Hanifan can be said to have anticipated the multi-dimensional nature of social capital outcomes and the corresponding need for multi-disciplinary study. At a deeper level still, Hanifan realised clearly the social nature of social capital and how this would make the term relatively distinct from other similar terms such as human capital or financial capital. In a nutshell, social capital is social because its formation depends on interpersonal associations and relationships connecting two or more individuals, rather than on their respective human or financial capital per se. It cannot be owned individually, unlike human or financial capital, but only collectively through its use. As Hanifan has put it so aptly, "The individual is helpless socially, if left to himself . . . (but if) he comes into contact with his neighbor, and they with other neighbors, there will be an accumulation of social capital . . ." (cited in Putnam, 2000, p. 19).

Recent decades have seen an explosion of studies on the conceptualisation (Bourdieu, 1977) and measurement (Grootaert and van Bastelaer, 2002; van Deth, 2003) of social capital, its applications to sociological theories (Coleman, 1988) and implications for a range of issues such as democracy (Putnam, Leonardi and Nanetti, 1993), community involvement (Putnam, 2000), poverty (Collier, 2002), crime (Graycar, 1999), and policy (Halpern, 2005). The World Bank (2007) has also initiated a number of studies especially on social development in underdeveloped countries.

In Hong Kong, relevant studies in social capital are few in number but interesting because they address issues arising from Hong Kong's specific situation post-1997, rather than merely echoing overseas studies. A·number of such issues can be gleaned from this body of local scholarship, including democratisation and political engagement, sense of community and belonging to the new Hong Kong and to China, public trust in the "de-colonialised" government now run by Hong Kong Chinese, and the evaluation of a government-led initiative on building social capital in disadvantaged groups and communities.

Largely following Hall's (1999) British study of social capital, Holliday and Tam (2001) measured social capital in Hong Kong on the bases of membership of voluntary associations, voluntary work, charitable donations, informal sociability and social trust. They interpreted data culled from archives over the past three decades to mean that "Hong Kong seems to be rather lacking in the reserves of social capital found in some other parts of the developed world . . . In fact, Hong Kong looks a little like those parts of Italy or Russia where social capital has never really developed" (Holliday and Tam, 2001, 166). The authors were cautious in their speculations from this finding, and were in fact reluctant to predict that democratisation and political engagement would be doomed in post-1997 Hong Kong despite Putnam's general prediction of a strong correlation between (lack of) social capital and (ineffectual) democratisation. Instead they pointed to Hong Kong's wealth, its international links and widespread support for the Democratic Party in the late 1990s as causes for optimism about Hong Kong's further democratisation. This piece of scholarship exemplifies the development of indigenous social capital research and reminds researchers and policy makers of the need to ground the interpretation of data in the local context, instead of routinely echoing overseas findings.

As already noted, the return of sovereignty over Hong Kong to China was a protracted process, marked by hard-hitting negotiations between China and Britain, and marred by a number of grave events such as the 1989 Tianmen Square incident and the outbreak of the Asian financial crises in 1997 (see also Ng, 2007). Hong Kong people's sense of community and belonging to the territory, already weak according to researchers (e.g., Lau, 1985), was put to severe test, and the mass emigration of relatively well-off residents triggered by the Tianmen Square incident served notice for the post-1997 government to strengthen the citizens' sense of belonging and inculcate patriotism toward the Chinese mainland. This local concern set the scene for a social capital research agenda that was quite different from that in "mainstream" social capital research. La Grange and Yip (2001) articulated the difference succinctly in their discussion of social belonging and social capital:

> Thus the debate about social belonging has a major political/territorial component in Hong Kong . . . . Consequently academic research has focused on why residents choose to emigrate, while policy has focused on what can be done to persuade people to stay or return. This compares quite starkly with much of the social capital literature's focus on lower-income ethnic minorities and efforts to integrate them into mainstream society; in Hong Kong the debate is framed in terms of people's attitude to reunification with China, and the distribution of residents' loyalties between Hong Kong and the Mainland (p. 305).

One policy tool in Hong Kong was to use home ownership to anchor people's sense of social belonging, but the effect of home ownership turned out to be spurious as soon as other variables were controlled (La Grange and Yip, 2001). However, although the hope for building a strong sense of social belonging through home ownership has been misplaced, according to these authors, home ownership (and housing policy more generally) can still play an important role in other aspects of social capital such as neighbourhood stability. The opposite side of the same coin – how urban renewal may disrupt existing neighbourhoods – was picked up in a study by Ng, Kam, and Pong (2004). Hong Kong is a highly urbanised city and has accumulated a huge stock of residential buildings erected in the 1960s to cater for the population explosion, most of which are now in a dilapidated condition and in need of renewal. Their demolition and the subsequent relocation of residents on a massive scale is bound to disrupt the existing neighbourhoods, pose problems of adjustment for residents to integrate in their new neighbourhoods, but also offer the government and community groups opportunities for building new neighbourhoods (Ng et al., 2004).

A third topic in local studies of social capital is public trust in the government, which is becoming increasingly important and politicised in the aftermath of Hong Kong's transition from a British colony to a Special Administration Region of China. Citing works published before 1997, Brewer and Hayllar (2005) made the observation that although the former colonial government lacked legitimacy it was able to shore up public trust in its governance through "market-oriented economic development and to meet basic needs in housing, education and health" in the early days, and later, through "administrative reforms to improve the quality of the public services" (p. 478). Paradoxically, the Hong Kong SAR Government now run by Hong Kong Chinese has had a much tougher ride. The massive protest against the Government on 1 July 2003 amounted to a vote of no confidence, but it was conducted peacefully and was effective in triggering a change of the Government's Chief Executive. Thus post-1997 changes in the level and nature of public trust in the government are an important area of social capital research. The two case studies conducted by Brewer and Hayllar (2005) represent a major step forward in this direction, showing, in one case, how trust that had taken decades to build up through government/civic society partnership in the provision of school-based education could be ruined quickly within a few years; and in the second case, the severe handicap posed by a low-trust environment to the government's attempt to initiate cross-sector collaboration to build a large-scale arts hub in the city for the wider region in Southeast Asia.

A fourth topic in local social capital research is the evaluation by academics of the outcomes of a government-initiated project on building social capital in disadvantaged groups and communities. The Community Investment and Inclusion Fund (CIIF), a Hong Kong SAR Government policy initiative established in 2002 to promote and develop social capital in Hong Kong (see Part 2 below), instigated an evaluation research consortium formed by seven multi-disciplinary research teams from five local universities in Hong Kong. The objectives of the consortium of researchers were to assess the effectiveness of social capital development strategies promoted by the CIIF, review insights and good practices from the CIIF project implementation, identify critical success factors and make recommendations for the future development of social capital (CIIF, 2008). Key findings from the evaluation of the CIIF projects include: bonding and bridging social capitals were being built up steadily but the linking social capital was still relatively weak; the building of trust and reciprocity was effective; structural, cognitive and collective social capitals had been established at individual and organisational levels; the intergenerational project was implemented effectively; and personalised trust had increased though the situation was less certain with respect to generalised trust (CIIF, 2008). Stimulated by the government's initiative on the CIIF project, the collaborative research made jointly by the consortium of university researchers has formally raised the profile of social capital development and research in the community (see Section II and Table 1 below).[1] It is expected that this trend will continue in the future.

---

1 A new course on Social Capital and Sustainable Development was introduced in an undergraduate programme in a tertiary institution in Hong Kong, and an international conference on "Social capital and volunteering in modern ageing cities: Building intergenerational inclusion" was organised in December 2008 in Hong Kong.

II. Social Capital in Hong Kong: Government Initiatives

An impetus for social capital development in 2001 arose from intensified social and political concerns, some of which were to promote social solidarity, social inclusion, community participation, and mutual assistance in the new Hong Kong as a SAR of Mainland China. Others were to foster or reinforce positive values through investing in capacity building of individual capabilities, bringing about paradigm shifts from top-down delivery of welfare to bottom-up and more sustainable forms of self-reliance such as active capacity building, building networks within a specific group and between groups, and enhancing cooperation among different social strata. In recognition of the role of social capital in sustainable social development, the Chief Executive of the Hong Kong SAR Government in his 2001 Policy Address emphasised the importance of promoting joint efforts between government, corporate bodies, and the third sector promoting and building social capital for Hong Kong (Tung, 2001). Based on the Chief Executive's initiatives, the Government announced the setting up of a HK$300 million CIIF to provide seed money to support the collaborative efforts of community organisations and the private sector. From 2001 to 2009, the number of citations of the CIIF (社區投資共享基金) in the Hong Kong Chinese printed media has increased from 55 to 83 (156 at the zenith in 2008) per annum (Table 1). Over the same period of time, citations of social capital (社會資本) have increased from 63 to 304 per annum in Hong Kong and from 622 to 3,568 per annum in the Chinese mainland. These figures clearly show that the concept of social capital and what it represents has diffused into public discourse.

In 2004, the Home Affairs Bureau (HAB) of the Hong Kong SAR Government devised a framework for a Creativity Index (CI), which had social capital as one of its key components (Home Affairs Bureau, 2004). To measure social capital, the HAB used 21 indicators, namely, three indicators for the development of social capital, twelve for norms and values, and six for social participation, some of which were from the World Value Survey. The resulting Social Capital Index (SCI) was used to compare levels of social capital over time. Overall, the levels of social capital in Hong Kong from 1999 to 2004 were found to have increased from 72.45 to 100 (using 100 as a nominal reference for 2004).

Table 1:
Media Coverage on Social Capital in Hong Kong and the Chinese Mainland by WiseSearch as of 14 July 2010 (by citations)

Search Date	Social Capital		CIIF	
	Hong Kong	Chinese Mainland	Hong Kong	Chinese Mainland
2009	304	3,568	83	1
2008	202	2,842	156	1
2007	246	2,073	120	0
2006	204	1,863	115	0
2005	194	2,019	115	4
2004	183	2,260	108	0
2003	143	1,919	59	0
2002	141	936	68	1
2001	63	622	55	0
2000	42	301	0	0
1999	45	12	0	0
1998	10	0	0	0
Total (01/1998–12/2009)	1,777	18,415	879	7

More recently the concept of social capital has been promoted in Hong Kong for developing better social well-being and building a more compassionate and cohesive community. The Secretary for Labour and Welfare, Matthew Cheung Kin-chung, at the Fifth Annual Forum of the Community Investment and Inclusion Fund (CIIF) held in 2007, highlighted that

. . . social capital was a new thinking in welfare policy . . . The cost-effectiveness of social capital far exceeds that of direct financial aid. The problem of poverty gap and cross-generation poverty cannot be solved by money alone, not to mention that care and concern are invaluable. As public resources are limited, we have to help people to help themselves and foster mutual aid and co-operation to achieve an all-win situation (Labour and Welfare Bureau, 2007).

From the perspective of public policy, social capital is capable of building up the capacity of individuals, bringing about changes in people's mentality from welfare dependency to self-reliance, establishing networks within a specific group and between groups, and enhancing cooperation among different social strata. Social capital is perceived to be the essential component in enhancing social solidarity and social inclusion, which in turn builds a strong and harmonious society. It is clear that social capital plays a crucial role in paving the way for Hong Kong's future welfare policies. Just as significant, cross-sector partnership is seen as an effective way to further promote social capital in Hong Kong. As Professor Lau Siu-kai, Head of the Central Policy Unit of the Hong Kong SAR Government, has commented recently in his Opening Remarks at a social capital symposium, "The Government of the HKSAR has been taking a keen policy interest in social capital . . . one important strategy to achieve this [the development of strategies to enhance social capital] was to develop the tri-partite partnership between government, the business community and the third or not-for-profit sector" (Lau, 2007).

The government has provided a vehicle to enable the participation of individuals in social organisations through territory-wide social service organisations. The strategies of investing in capacity building through civic engagement provide opportunities for individuals to interact, acquire skills, and change their mindsets. Further, the strategy of promoting partnership among CIIF-funded projects, the government, community groups, schools, and business operators, and so forth, enables the building of collaborative platforms for different individuals and groups, which otherwise would rarely meet to share experience or transfer knowledge. The enhanced network and the continued interaction therein foster ties, trust, and cohesion among participants that could lead to collective actions yielding individual and social benefits.

III. Social Capital in Hong Kong: Evaluation Studies of Government Initiatives

In Hong Kong, researchers and policy makers obtain an overview of a wide range of social concerns by using various social indicators.

Within the generic framework of social indicators, the development of indicators for the specific measurement of social capital is only beginning. Since 1997, Hong Kong has undergone considerable restructuring in both the social and economic arenas. In this section an attempt will be made to conceptualise and measure social capital with a view to supporting an integrated approach to the development of social capital research in Hong Kong.

As part of the evaluation research consortium referred to earlier, Leung, Chan, Chan, and Ng (2006) have studied the effectiveness of the CIIF-funded projects in developing social capital in Hong Kong. Both qualitative and quantitative instruments were adopted in the study to measure social capital, including documentary and literature review, in-depth interviews, and a self-administered questionnaire. Based on the research literature (especially Grootaert, 2002) and in the light of the Social Capital Assessment Tool (SOCAT) developed by the World Bank for assessing social capital, Leung et al. (2006) used three sets of indicators to measure the three dimensions of social capital in the Hong Kong context. As shown in Figure 1, structural social capital was assessed on the bases of the density and diversity of membership, as well as the extent of participation in the decision-making process whereas cognitive social capital was measured by solidarity, trust, cooperation, and conflict resolution. To measure collective action, the frequency of collective action, the type of activities undertaken collectively, and the extent of willingness to participate in collective action were used.

Questions relating to structural social capital included the frequency of participation in community and social activities, perceived degree of participation, diversity of memberships, and the participation in the decision making process of organisations and/or committees. The resulting 13-item scale had a Cronbach's alpha reliability of 0.74. Results showed that the mean score was 25.78, which was slightly below the scalar mid-point.

Cognitive social capital was measured by 31 items covering perceived mutual trust and care in the community, cooperation, solidarity, inclusion, self and mutual help, self-confidence, and so forth. The scale had a Cronbach's alpha reliability of 0.94. Results showed that the level of cognitive social capital was 89.22, which was well above the scalar midpoint and relatively higher than the level of structural social capital.

Figure 1:
Structural Social Capital, Cognitive Social Capital and Collective Action

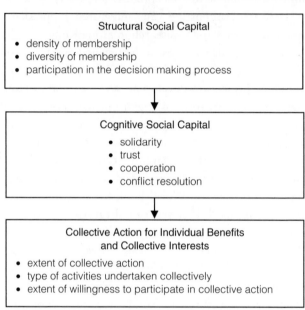

Collective action was measured by nine items that covered changes in voting in elections, participation in protests or demonstrations, contact with influential or community leaders, and volunteering for charitable organisations. The reliability of the scale was 0.89. The mean level of collective action was 16.67, which was slightly above the scalar mid-point, relatively higher than structural but lower than cognitive social capital.

Correlational analysis revealed positive correlations between structural and cognitive capital, and importantly, between these two forms of social capital and collective action (see Table 2). Although the positive correlations between structural and cognitive social capitals, on the one hand, and collective action on the other do not mean that collective action results from structural and cognitive social capitals in the causal sense, they lend support to the theoretical argument that posits the flow of impact from structural and cognitive social capitals to collective action. Of the two kinds of social capital, cognitive capital in particular was highly correlated with collective action, suggesting its primary importance.

Table 2:
Pearson's Correlation Coefficients
among Dimensions of Social Capital (N=184)

	Cognitive social capital	Collective action
Structural social capital	0.33**	0.18*
Cognitive social capital		0.56**

* $p < 0.05$, ** $p < 0.01$ (2-tailed)

In a more recent study, Leung, Chan, Cheung and Ng (2007) have adopted a social capital approach to the identification of factors that contributed to the successful acculturation made by recent arrivals (migrants) from the Chinese mainland when they settled in Hong Kong. Successful acculturation was measured by scales relating to psychological adjustment, social integration and achievement at school or in the workplace. Consistent with the ideas of Lareau and Horvat (1999) and Tang (2002), results from a survey of 2,846 new arrivals (1,390 students, 1,091 younger adults and 365 older adults) showed that a cyclic model of possession/access, activation, and reproduction/accumulation of capital fitted the acculturation data. Possession of capital refers to social capital that had existed prior to or on arrival in Hong Kong. Activation of capital is the process that makes use of existing social capital to create or reproduce social capital, whereas accumulation of capital is the process of concentrating and centralising social capital through the possession and activation of capitals in order to produce success in psychological adjustment, social integration and achievement (see Figure 2).

The results showed that the migrants' access to social capital at the time of arrival was an important basis for producing further capital after their arrival. Social capital accessed by migrants after arrival in Hong Kong had a greater impact than the same capital that had already existed prior to their arrival. Importantly social capital was not automatically activated, but must be either activated by the migrants themselves, or by a third party such as an NGO or the government. Furthermore, the activation also depended on the skills of and efforts made by migrants to compete with local people. As illustrated by Lareau and Hovat's (1999) analogy of card playing, cards are capital held by the players who must have the skill and experience to interact with other players so that they can play the game and win. New arrivals were already at a disadvantage because they had little social capital to begin with. Even for those with greater access to social capital, they often lacked the skills and knowledge to activate the capital in the new environment.

Figure 2: A Process Model of Social Capital

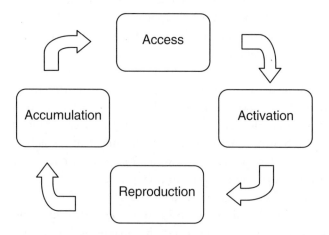

The findings above and others from the survey suggest that in order for migrants to succeed in Hong Kong, it is vital for local governments in the Chinese mainland to enhance applicants' social capital before their migration, and for the Hong Kong SAR Government to integrate them as early as possible once they arrive in Hong Kong, and to provide them with skills and knowledge to activate their capital. As social capital exists in the form of relationships among people in society, in principle it can be shared by all and with a communal effort it can become self-generating through continuous inputs from activators in a continuous cycle.

IV. Conclusions

Social capital is essential to the sustainable development of a community. The present chapter has focused on Hong Kong to provide a case study of social capital research and practice. It is clear from the review of relevant research that the study of social capital in and about Hong Kong is only beginning. Though limited in number, they have contributed to the development of indigenous scholarship of using the concept and method of social capital for understanding post-1997 Hong Kong and its development. At the same time, the practice of social capital has burgeoned with government- and NGO-assisted projects playing pioneering roles. Social capital projects associated with the government's CIIF alone have succeeded in mobilising over 300,000 participants from different sectors in social capital building since 2002 (see Chong and Ng's chapter in this volume). A notable feature of this on-going indigenous initiative has been the forging of links between practice and research by the successful engagement of academic researchers in five universities to undertake a multi-faceted evaluation study of the projects from multi-disciplinary perspectives. Future opportunities exist for further collaboration of this kind as CIIF-funded projects increase in number, variety and maturity. A critical development would be the diffusion of social capital theory and practice in the design of new and self-sustaining forms of social services and social enterprises.

As Hong Kong positions itself in its development toward a modern cosmopolitan multi-cultural city with Chinese characteristics, it continues to enhance its stock of human capital through immigration and the recruitment of expatriate professionals. The connection between human capital and social capital represents a fruitful area of social capital research in Hong Kong (and elsewhere). For example, the empirical study of how new arrivals in Hong Kong from the Chinese mainland may succeed in the new land of their choice can be approached from a social capital perspective. As shown in this chapter, the conceptual model of social capital process arising from the study of new arrivals would be useful for assessing changes and trends in different forms of social capital, and for shedding light on the dynamical process of accessing, activating and accumulating social capital for the betterment individuals' life conditions.

Acknowledgements

The authors acknowledge funding support from the City University of Hong Kong (projects #7002398 and #9610056) and the Community Investment and Inclusion Fund for studies that have contributed to the present chapter.

References

Berman, S. (1997). Civil society and political institutionalization. *The American Behavioral Scientist*, 40 (5), 562–574.

Bourdieu, P. (1977). *Outline of a theory and practice* (translated by R. Nice). Cambridge: Cambridge University Press.

Bourdieu, P. (1985). The form of capital. In J.G. Richardson (Ed.), *The handbook of theory and research for the sociology of education*. New York: Greenwood.

Brewer, B., and Hayllar, M.R. (2005). CAPAM Symposium on networked government: Building public trust through public-private partnerships. *International Review of Administrative Sciences*, 71, 475–492.

Bryant, C., and Norris, D. (2002). Measurement of social capital: The Canadian experience. Paper prepared for the OECD-UK ONS International Conference on Social Capital Measurement in London, 25–27 September 2002. Retrieved 2 December 2009 from, http://www.oecd.org/dataoecd/21/48/2381103.pdf.

Chan, A., and Lin, P. (2006). *An evaluation study on the impacts of CIIF intergenerational programmes on the development of social capital in Hong Kong*. Hong Kong: Asia Pacific Institute of Ageing Studies, Lingnan University.

Chan, K. T. (2006). *Social investment and social network: Analysis of the collaboration between third sector and private sector in CIIF-funded projects*. Hong Kong: Department of Applied Social Sciences, Polytechnic University of Hong Kong.

Chan, K. H., Chong, A., and Ng, S.H. (2006). *Social trust and its antecedent conditions in the development of social capital*. Hong Kong: Department of Applied Social Studies, City University of Hong Kong.

CIIF (2008). Community Investment and Inclusion Fund. Evaluation consortium. Retrieved 25 August 2008 from http://www.ciif.gov.hk.

Coleman, J. (1988). Social capital in the creation of human capital. *American Journal of Sociology*, 94 (Supplement), S95–S120.

Colletta, N. J., and Cullen, M. L. (2002). Social capital and social cohesion: Case studies from Cambodia and Rwanda. In C. Grootaert and T. van Bastelaer (Eds.), *The role of social capital in development: An empirical assessment*. Cambridge: Cambridge University Press.

Collier, P. (2002). Social capital and poverty: A microeconomic perspective. In C. Grootaert and T. van Bastelaer (Eds.), *The role of social capital in development: An empirical assessment*. Cambridge: Cambridge University Press.

Grange, A. L., and Yip, N. M. (2001). Social belonging, social capital and the promotion of home ownership: A case study of Hong Kong. *Housing Studies, 16*(3), 291–310.

Graycar, A. (1999). Crime and social capital. Paper presented at the 19th Biennial International Conference on Preventing Crime, Melbourne, Australia.

Grootaert, C. (1999). *Social capital, household welfare, and poverty in Indonesia*. Local Level Institutions Working Paper no. 6. Washington, DC: The World Bank.

Grootaert, C. (2002). Quantitative analysis of social capital data. In C. Grootaert and T. van Bastelaer (Eds.), *Understanding and measuring social capital: A multidisciplinary tool for practitioners*. Washington, DC: The World Bank.

Grootaert, C., and van Bastelaer, T. (2002). Social capital: From definition to measurement. In C. Grootaert and T. van Bastelaer (Eds.), *Understanding and measuring social capital: A multidisciplinary tool for practitioners*. Washington, DC: The World Bank.

Hall, P. A. (1999). Social capital in Britain. *British Journal of Political Science, 29*, 417–461.

Halpern, D. (2005). *Social capital*. Cambridge, UK: Polity Press.

Herreros, F. (2004). *The problem of forming social capital: Why trust?* New York: Palgrave Macmillan.

Holliday, I., and Tam, W. (2001). Social capital in Hong Kong. *East Asia, 19*, 144–170.

Home Affairs Bureau (2004). Home Affairs Bureau of the Hong Kong Special Administrative Region Government. *A study on creativity index*. Retrieved 9 May 2008 from http://www.hab.gov.hk/file_manager/en/documents/policy_responsibilities/arts_culture_recreation_and_sport/HKCI-InteriReport-printed.pdf.

Knack, S., and Keefer, P. (1997). Does social capital have an economic payoff? A cross-country investigation. *The Quarterly Journal of Economics, 112*(4), 1251–1288.

Krishna, A. (2002). *Active social capital: Tracing the roots of development and democracy*. New York: Columbia University Press.

Krishna, A., and Uphoff, N. (2002). Mapping and measuring social capital through assessment of collective action to conserve and develop watersheds in Rajasthan, India. In C. Grootaert and T. van Bastelaer (Eds.), *The role of social capital in development: An empirical assessment* (pp.85–124). Cambridge: Cambridge University Press.

Labour and Welfare Bureau. (2007). Social capital concept embodies spirit of welfare policy. Retrieved 11 December 2007 from, http://www.lwb .gov.hk/eng/press/15112007a.htm.

Lareau, A., and Horvat, M. (1999). Moments of social inclusion and exclusion: Race, class and cultural capital in family-school relationships. *Sociology of Education, 72*, 37–53.

Lau, S. K. (1985). *Society and politics in Hong Kong*. Hong Kong: The Chinese University Press.

Lau, S. K. (2007). Opening remarks of Professor Lau Siu-kai, Head of the Central Policy Unit of the Hong Kong SAR Government, at the Symposium on "Social Capital in Modern Cities" at the City University of Hong Kong, held on 19 November 2007. Retrieved 2 December 2009 from http://www.cpu.gov.hk/english/documents/conference/20071119%20 Opening%20Remark.pdf.

Leung, K. K., Chan, K. H., Chan, W. T., and Ng, S. H. (2006). *Report on an evaluation study on the effectiveness of implementation of community investment and inclusion fund (CIIF)*. Hong Kong: Quality Evaluation Centre, City University of Hong Kong.

Leung K. K., Chan, W. C., Cheung, C. K., and Ng, S. H. (2007). How recent migrants from the Chinese mainland acculturate in Hong Kong: Success factors and policy implications. Presented at the Seventh Conference of Asian Association of Social Psychology (AASP), Kota Kinabalu, Malaysia, 25–28 July 2007.

Mok, B. H., Ngai, S., and Cheung, C. K. (2006). *A study of professional contribution to the sustainability of self-help groups and their social capital created in CIIF Projects*. Hong Kong: Department of Social Work, Chinese University of Hong Kong.

Narayan, D., and Pritchett, L. (1999). Cents and sociability: Household income and social capital in rural Tanzania. *Economic Development and Cultural Change, 47* (4), 871–897.

Ng, S. H. (2007). Biculturalism in multicultural Hong Kong. *Journal of Psychology in Chinese Societies, 8*, 121–140.

Ng, S. H., Kam, P. K., and Pong, R. W. M. (2005). People living in ageing buildings: Their quality of life and sense of belonging. *Journal of Environmental Psychology, 25*, 347–360.

Nielsen, K. (2003). Social capital and systematic competitiveness. In C. Dannreuther and W. Dolfsma (Eds.), *Globalisation, social capital and inequality: Contested concepts, contested experiences* (pp. 33–52). Cheltenham (UK): Edward Elgar.

Onyx, J., and Bullen, P. (2001). The different faces of social capital in NSW Australia. In P. Dekker and E.M. Uslaner (Eds.), *Social capital and participation in everyday life* (pp. 45–58). London: Routledge.

Ostrom, E., and Ahn, T. K. (2003). *Foundations of social capital.* Cheltenham (UK): Edward Elgar.

Portney, K. E., and Berry, J. M. (1997). Mobilizing minority communities: Social capital and participation in urban neighborhoods. *The American Behavioral Scientist, 40* (5), 632–644.

Putnam, R. D. (2000). *Bowling alone: The collapse and revival of American community.* New York: Simon & Schuster.

Putnam, R. D., Leonardi, R., and Nanetti, R. Y. (1993). *Making democracy work: Civic traditions in modern Italy.* Princeton, NJ: Princeton University Press.

Reid, C., and Salmen, R. (2000). *Understanding social capital – Agricultural extension in Mali: Trust and social cohesion.* Washington, DC: The World Bank.

Tang, H. H. (2002). *New arrival students in Hong Kong: Adaptation and school performance.* Hong Kong: University of Hong Kong.

Tung, C. W. (2001). Policy Address 2001: Building on our strengths, investing in our future. Retrieved 15 December 2007 from http://www.policyaddress .gov.hk/pa01/high_e.htm.

van Deth, J. W. (2003). Measuring social capital: Orthodoxies and continuing controversies. *International Journal of Social Research Methodology, 6*(1), 79–92.

Warren, M. R., Thompson, J. P., and Saegert, S. (2001). The role of social capital in combating poverty. In M.R. Warren, J.P. Thompson and S. Saegert (Eds.), *Social capital and poor communities.* New York: Russell Sage Foundation.

Westlund, H. (2006). *Social capital in the knowledge economy: Theory and empirics.* New York: Springer.

Wong, D., Leung, J., Law, C. K., and Chui, E. (2006). *Building social capital: A formative programme review of CIIF projects Hong Kong.* Department of Social Work and Social Administration, University of Hong Kong.

Wong, S. (2008). Building social capital in Hong Kong by institutionalising participation: Potential and limitations. *Urban Studies, 45,* 1413–1437.

Woolcock, M., and Narayan, D. (2000). Social capital: Implications for development theory, research, and policy. *The World Bank Research Observer, 15* (2), 225–249.

World Bank (2007). Social capital. Retrieved 15 December 2007 from http://web.worldbank.org/WBSITE/EXTERNAL/TOPICS/EXTSOCIAL DEVELOPMENT/EXTTSOCIALCAPITAL/0,,contentMDK:20194767~me nuPK:418848~pagePK:148956~piPK:216618~theSitePK:401015,00.html.

Part II

Social Capital Connectivities

5

Social Capital and Community:
A Review of International
and Hong Kong Development

Joe Cho Bun LEUNG

I. Introduction

Recent tragedies and accidents in the home due to child neglect, child abuse, and the lack of child care services, as well as the plight of deprived communities, have instigated public debates on the functions of neighbourhood support and community provision. What is happening to our neighbourhoods? Is there evidence of widespread mistrust among people in the same neighbourhood but from different backgrounds? Is there hostility and discrimination towards new arrivals, ethnic minorities, social assistance recipients and other vulnerable groups? Indeed, increased mobility, privacy-oriented architectural design, new modes of communication and increased social diversity are factors contributing to the breaking down and fragmenting of our communities. The need to build stronger trusting community relationships or social capital at the community level has received increased attention around the world.

The Chief Executive of the Hong Kong Special Administrative Region Government has advocated the "people-first" policy and the need for public engagement. In essence, community has emerged as a strategic place to engage people and promote active citizenship. In his 2006–07 Policy Address, the Chief Executive said (Tsang, 2006, p. 49):

Mutual concern and mutual aid among neighbours is a strong support for families. We encourage community building and friendly neighbourhoods. There are individual new towns where inadequacies occurred in the course of past development, resulting in imbalances in certain aspects of community development. These imbalances meant that we are unable to provide a suitably favourable environment for the development of healthy families . . . In the future, the government will allocate resources according to the different conditions in the districts, and strengthen district planning and coordination.

The Chief Executive has highlighted the importance of community building to provide the necessary support to families, and the need to redress the imbalances in community development through government intervention. In the UK, people have ever higher and diverse expectations of public services. The UK Local Government White Paper published in 2006, *Strong and Prosperous Communities* (Department for Communities and Local Government, 2006, p. 20), explained:

People no longer accept the "one size fits all" service models of old. They want choice over the services they receive, influence over those who provide them, and higher service standards. We want this to be the case everywhere – for people to be given more control over their lives; consulted and involved in running services; informed about the quality of services in their area; and enabled to call local agencies to account if services fail to meet their needs.

This vision of responsive local government echoes the "people-centred" or "community-based" approach to good government. We believe that the active involvement of citizens in social and public affairs is critical to improve their quality of life and achieve the objectives of public policies. People want to be informed, consulted and involved about the policies affecting their lives. Public and social services have to be devolved and empower people to manage their own lives. Overall there is a renewed interest in bringing "community" back to the policy agenda, particularly in tackling poverty and social exclusion. Geographical community is increasingly recognised as an important focus for policy implementation and for civil renewal. As the UK Secretary of State for Communities and Local Government claimed in the recent *Action Plan for Community Empowerment* (2007), it is a "duty of the government to involve local people". In reinventing the governance of Britain, community empowerment "marks a new relationship between government and citizens". He claimed that: "There isn't a single service or development in Britain which hasn't been improved by actively involving local people".

Overall, community building promises to rebuild the relationships between people themselves and between the government and the people at the community level. Central to the notion of community building is the concept of social capital. It has been described as a "glue" that holds people together in a social collectivity and a "lubricant" that enables different community groups to work together collaboratively and smoothly. In short, social capital facilitates the analysis and policy formulation to strengthen community capacity. This chapter reviews the relationship between community building and social capital, and the policy development of community building efforts in both selected countries and Hong Kong.

II. The Concept of Community Revisited

Facing an increasingly individualised, polarised, divided and heterogeneous society, there is a worldwide resurgence of interests in those related buzz words or contested concepts, notably community building, social capital and partnerships. Primarily, these concepts are regarded as pivotal in policy formulation, promoting responsive policy, maintaining social stability, and reducing social exclusion. Community building involves the attempt to empower local people to make decisions and choices in their own lives and improve their life chances. A key challenge for governments is to identify and harness the strength of community ties and resources contributing towards a just and harmonious society. Building partnerships that cut across different sectors, namely the public, the private (market) and civil society (non-governmental organisations and community organisations) has emerged as an integral part of the community building process.

"Community" is a vague and over-used concept with no agreed meanings. In a general sense, it refers to a group of people with shared characteristics, such as place, belief, values, functions and interests. Modern community is no longer based on locale, but it is a product of our interactions. In fact, new communities can be formed whenever communication links can be made (Bruhn, 2007, p. 233). Modern community is based on social networks with common interests and values where face-to-face interactions may not be necessary. Sociologists have been concerned with the impact of urbanisation and individualised life style on community as a place. The notion of the "loss of community" marks the phenomenon of declining community participation, mutual trust and cohesiveness. From the perspective of social capital, Putnam has vividly described the changing community situation in the United States, with declining informal relationships, participation in voluntary association and civic activities (Putnam, 2000, 2002). In general, he recognises the worrying trend of declining "community engagement", "community spirit" and "sense of community". In many countries, levels of social interactions, informal and formal social networks, membership of community organisations and voluntary groups, political participation, volunteering and charity donations are found to be on the decline. The situation seems to be more serious among socially excluded groups.

Community has been studied by a variety of disciplines, including sociology (socialisation, culture, and social capital), psychology (sense of community), economics (community economy, employment), philosophy (communitarianism), public administration (local government and governance) and social work (community development, community building). More recently the focus on community has shifted towards the study of "social capital" – the sense of connectedness and formation of social networks (Putnam, 2000).

In this chapter, without getting into the rhetoric of definitional debates, community is narrowly confined to mean geographical locality, or "place". Community is not concerned with the abstract debate on rebuilding social solidarity and cohesion, but the practical approach to resolving local issues and engaging people. "Community" is focused on its importance as a strategic platform for promoting community engagement and civil renewal, policy formulation and implementation, as well as social care networks.

1. Community Engagement and Civil Renewal: Civic participation is at the very heart of democracy and is its lifeblood. Local community has been regarded as one of the cornerstones of democracy where residents can exercise their rights and responsibilities and participate actively in the public realm, particularly through maintaining dialogue between residents and locally elected representatives. It promotes effective local democracy, with strong and accountable political leadership (Home Office, 2003; Blunkett, 2003; Jochum, et al., 2005).

According to the Department for Communities and Local Government of the UK government, civil renewal is (Home Office, 2003):

> about people and government, working together to make life better. It involves more people taking responsibility for tackling local problems, rather than expecting others to. The idea is that government can't solve everything by itself, and nor can the community: It's better when we work together.

There are three key ingredients to civil renewal: (a) active citizens: people with motivation, skills and confidence to speak up for their communities and organisations; (b) strengthened communities: community groups with the capacity and resources to bring people together, and (c) partnership with public bodies: public bodies willing and able to work as partners with local people.

Community engagement includes the mobilisation of interests and support in social movements, policy consultation, volunteering, corporate social responsibility, the cultivation of local representative leadership, and the mitigation of local conflicts. Communities are places where the third sector, including non-governmental organisations, faith groups, charities, social enterprises, cooperatives and community organisations, has been most active. These community organisations are important channels for public engagement and involvement in community affairs. Evidence on the benefits of community engagement has been documented in a report in the UK (Rogers and Robinson, 2004). They include the reduction of crime and anti-social behaviours, the improvement of health and education, the promotion of employment and economic growth, and the robust implementation of urban regeneration projects.

2. *Policy Formulation and Implementation*: Decentralised and community-based service delivery can enhance policy responsiveness, "joined-up" action and partnerships tackling cross-cutting social issues. Community-based intervention allows flexibility to tailor-make solutions to address local social issues (Daly and Davis, 2002; Wang, 2003; Kjaer, 2003; Department of Health, 1998).

3. *Social Care Network*: Strong social networks are pivotal to support social programmes targeting impoverished and deprived communities. Community activities can include action to build social capital (enhancing mutual trust, volunteering, and collective actions), provide informal care services, and influence government decisions on public services (Richardson, 2008; Means, et al., 2008). It can reduce community problems relating to crime, employment, anti-social behaviour, domestic violence, social exclusion and hard-to-reach vulnerable groups. Mutual trust, or social capital more generally, is regarded as the glue that holds different community groups together, and is the essential ingredient for building community. As an important social asset and resource, community building contributes to the promotion of social stability, social cohesion and collaborations.

In sum, community building can be referred to as the building of social capital at the neighbourhood level. Social capital is essential for civic renewal, policy implementation and the promotion of social care network. Through norms and networks of civic engagement and collaborations for collective benefits, the quality of life at individual level as well as collectively, can be enhanced (Hooghe and Stolle, 2003).

There has been an upsurge of interest in the study of social capital, especially after the work carried out by Putnam. The focus has been on definitions, measurements (structural-cognitive, formal and informal, thick and thin, inward-looking and outward-looking, and bridging and bonding) and impacts (negative and positive). There are again numerous definitions of social capital. Social capital is related to the quality (pattern and intensity) of social relationships and networks, implying shared values, mutual trust and collaboration (OECD, 2001). Social capital is found to have contributed to economic development, poverty alleviation, crime prevention, and achievements in health, education, and employment (Field, 2005; Hardin, et al., 2003; Dekker and Uslaner, 2001; Montgomery and Inkeles, 2000; Baron, et al., 2000; Lin, et al., 2001; Performance and Innovation Unit, 2002; The National Economic and Social Forum, 2003). More importantly, social capital is referred to as the resource or capacity of the community to take collective actions for the common good.

Traditionally, the concern of community building was on the building of "bonding social capital", the cohesiveness among members of the same organisation, network or group. Bonding social capital can provide people, particularly vulnerable groups, with key supporting resources for job seeking and emotional support. On the other hand, there are also reservations that bonding social capital can be inward-looking and exclusive. Other types of social capital, namely, "bridging social capital" and "linking social capital", which describe the connectedness between groups with different backgrounds and power, have received more attention. Bridging social capital implies the building of partnerships across groups within the same sector (e.g., NGOs in the welfare sector), whereas linking social capital goes beyond a particular sector and refers to cross-sector partnerships (e.g., between welfare and business sectors).

Overall, the missing link in research on social capital has been on how social capital can be created, particularly through government intervention and policy. Various studies have indicated that the local community can be a vital platform for service delivery providing support to the older people, the disabled, children and the socially excluded. Strengthening the social capital of the unemployed is vital to promote their effective integration back into the labour market (Holzer, 1996; Dickens, 1999; Auspos, 2006).

From the bottom-up perspective, community engagement can be considered as a form of grassroots-based social movement. As a form of collective behaviour or collective action for achieving common objectives, social movements have functioned as an important vehicle for articulating and advocating a collectivity's interests and claims (Snow, et al., 2004). Social movements are marked by the use of non-institutionalised means of action, such as petitioning, campaigning, advocacy, protests and possibly, civil disobedience. Daily news coverage of social movements covers a wide variety of both international and local contested issues, including democratisation, animal rights, civil rights, welfare rights, human rights, immigration, religious freedom, anti-free trade, nuclear weapons, world poverty etc. Those relating to community issues would include conservation, housing, homelessness, social service provisions, transportation, and urban planning. Citing World Values Survey Data, Norris showed that an increasing number of people have reported participation in demonstrations (Norris, 2002). To be sure, social movements have somewhat become a "routinised avenue for expressing publicly collective grievances". As a field of study, it has received growing interest from academics (Snow, et al., 2004). Social movements, with the emphasis on the use of confrontational approaches to redress grievances, can enhance bonding social capital within a particular group or bridging social capital among groups within a sector, but not necessarily the linking social capital between the deprived and the mainstream social sectors.

Overall, the notion of community does not simply try to recapture the lost form of social solidarity, but it is now a popular area-based approach to address social, political and economic issues. With the upsurge of governments' interest in decentralising administration so as to enhance the responsiveness of policy and programmes and promote community engagement, community building is perceived as vital to the maintenance of social stability and the promotion of a cohesive society.

However, there may be a large gap between different societal sectors and the government in their understanding and expectations of community building. Some people believe that community building can create greater understanding and confidence, inform policy making, enhance policy support, and ensure responsive and accountable services. Others see community building as creating unrealistic expectations and tensions, as well as additional administrative costs. However, it is our firm belief that community building is not simply a utopian ideal, but a core commitment of good governance.

Finally, community is an important platform for the residents, community organisations and government departments to work together. It is also a place where people can be given a much bigger say in the services they receive and in the quality of communities in which they live. The vision of civil renewal is strong, active, and empowered communities, capable of taking responsibility to define the problems they face and tackle them together. Facing declining community relations and social capital, a key challenge is to identify and harness the strength of community ties and resources contributing towards a just and harmonious society. More importantly, it involves the building of positive relationships across different groups, cultures, parties, departments and organisations as envisioned in the concepts of bridging and linking social capitals.

III. Community Building and Community Capacity Building

Community building has been referred to as a locally-focused approach to collective problem-solving of public problems and to promote socially valuable forms of connectedness, sustained stakeholder engagement, a sense of common purpose, and greater institutional capacity (Briggs, 2002; Chaskin, et al., 2001; Gittell and Vital, 1998). The approach focuses on creating relationships among local interested stakeholders, taking collective problem-solving actions. More importantly, society should build bridges that link or integrate people of different income, occupation and culture together.

Community capacity is:

> the interaction of human capital, organisational resources, and social capital existing within a given community that can be leveraged to solve collective

problems and improve or maintain the well-being of that community. It may operate through informal social processes and/or organised efforts of individuals, organisations, and social networks that exist among them and between them and the larger systems of which the community is a part (Chaskin, et al., 2001).

Community capacity building is:

activities, resources and support that strengthen the skills and confidence of people and community groups to take effective action and leading roles in the development of their communities (Home Office, 2004).

Four outcomes of community capacity building have been identified (Home Office, 2004):

a. Social capital and cohesion – enabling communities to develop a common vision and sense of belonging where people from different backgrounds feel valued for the part they can play in making their community a better place to live, as well as having the ability to network beyond their neighbourhoods.

b. Community self-help – building the capacity of community-led service providers to plan and deliver activities and programmes to meet local needs.

c. Participatory governance – enabling citizens, individually and collectively, to have a greater say in decisions that affect their communities' well-being.

d. Sustainable involvement – increasing the confidence and capacity of individuals and groups to participate actively in their communities in ways and through structures that are supported and maintained within those communities.

Overall, communities should be empowered and facilitated to develop the capacity to participate actively in local public life, including elections, community organisations, holding local representatives and officials accountable, and articulating their views on policies and services affecting the local quality of life.

Promoting community engagement requires a change in community governance – a more open government which can demonstrate greater accountability, transparency and responsiveness (OECD, 2003). A modernised government requires public officials to be accountable for their actions, provide accessible information to the public and listen and consult key community stakeholders. Open government is increasingly recognised as an essential ingredient for democratic governance, social stability and economic development (OECD, 2005).

IV. Experiences of Selected Countries

Singapore

In Singapore, the semi-governmental organisation, the "People's Association" (PA) is responsible "to connect the people and the government for consultation and feed back". It seeks to "leverage on these relationships to strengthen racial harmony and social cohesion, to ensure a united and resilient Singapore". The mission is:

- To promote active citizenry and multi-racial harmony.
- To provide affordable access to life-skills and lifestyle activities.
- To connect the citizens for community bonding and volunteer work.
- To bring the people closer to one another and to the government.

Apart from being funded by the government, the chairperson of PA is the Prime Minister, and members are key government ministers. At the community level, Citizens' Consultative Committees were formed in 1955 to spearhead community building efforts within the constituencies. Together with the Community Development Councils, they provide services to help needy people with self-reliance financial assistance and work assistance schemes. It has a network of 1800 grassroots organisations, including community centres (100), Residents' Committees (550) and Neighbourhood Committees (100). They organise a wide range of social, cultural, educational and sporting activities and programmes to create opportunities for residents to interact, thereby strengthening social cohesion. They include services for the elderly and young people, as well as community leadership development. In particular, PA organises dialogues and seminars to allow its grassroots organisations and people of all walks of life to provide feedback on national policies and initiatives. Including the Mayor, all council members of community development councils are appointed by the PA, with financial allocation from the government ($1 for each resident, and a matching grant from the government of $3 for every $1 donated).

In addition, PA reaches out to achieve dialogue with grassroots organisations, including ethnic-based organisations, trade associations, professional groups, youth and women's organisations (People's Association website; Community Development Council website). Programmes include assisting the needy (social assistance and employment assistance), bonding people (arts and culture, youth, elderly, health lifestyle programme), and connecting the community (corporate partner scheme, district meeting, community partnership). The Singaporean model rests on the leadership of an over-arching semi-governmental organisation to assume a mixed responsibility of policy and political communication, connecting the public, and service delivery.

Mainland China

In the urban district, the street office, which is an extension of the district people's government, administers a population of around 50,000 people. Under its supervision are "self-governing" community residents' committees formed by popular elections. Each residents' committee covers a population of around 3000–5000 residents. In recent years, they have been renamed community residents' committees. Other types of residents' organisations within a street office include residents' congresses, community consultative committees and community owners' committees. Community Party organisations including a party branch, Community Youth League, women's federation organisation, and unions.

With the decline of the work units in "connecting" the people, the Chinese government has tried to re-invigorate the "community" to replace some of the social, political and economic functions of the traditional work units. Facing a more mobile and heterogeneous community, neighbourhood governments and community organisations have to assume the political functions of maintaining political communication with different community groups, particularly those without local household registration. Maintaining political stability through the mitigation of community conflicts has been a key role for the community-based government. At the same time, the community has emerged as the key platform for the delivery of public and social services. Local residents' committees are delegated to manage and deliver local services. A variety of social services are provided. They include health clinics, social assistance and charity supermarkets for the poor, nurseries for children, home-care and residential care services for the older people, welfare factories for the disabled, and probation services for young people with behavioural problems. Public services include the management of environment, market, family planning, household registration and crime control. Categories of community services include (Leung, 2000; Ministry of Civil Affairs, 2009):

a. Social security – services for the older people, retirees, homes for the aged, social assistance and employment services for the unemployed.
b. Medical care – community clinics.
c. Culture and education – recreational, cultural, sports, interests activities.
d. Community security – registration and monitoring of residents without household registration, security and fire patrols, emergency and crisis management.
e. Convenience service – shopping centres, parking spaces, nurseries, public toilets, and household repair and maintenance.
f. Environment and sanitation – tree planting, garbage collection, sewage system maintenance, market and hawker management.

g. Administrative affairs – information on the work of the residents' committees and street offices, hotlines, and collection of public opinion.

h. Legal services – legal education and advice, mediation services, legal aid for the disadvantaged, and probation services for ex-prisoners.

Overall, community participation has been heavily government-sponsored, government-financed and government-led. Until now, completely independent NGOs or community organisations have been rare. Community organisations have been delegated to implement a heavy load of management responsibilities, and have been heavily dependent on government for funding support. If community organisations desire to develop quality service provisions, they have to rely on commercial businesses to support their operations. Under the policy of "socialisation" of public services, the government has to rely more on community organisations to deliver public and social services, particularly through the purchase of services. Development of community building and community services has been very uneven, and significant variations are found between cities and provinces, and even among districts in the same city. In terms of social capital building, community building in China focuses on the building of trust and communication vertically between the people and the government.

The United Kingdom

The New Labour government which came to power in 1997 pledged itself to promote active citizenship and community engagement at all levels and in all policy areas. Civil renewal forms the centrepiece of the government's reform agenda (Blunkett, 2003). The New Deal for Communities, launched in 1998, concentrated on nurturing social capital. After the disturbances in several cities, such as Bradford and Oldham in England in 2001, associated with populations from different cultural and racial backgrounds, building community cohesion and civil renewal has received top government priority (Blunkett, 2003). According to the review report, these communities are deeply divided and separated on racial, generational and religious lines, manifested in education, community bodies, employment, worship, language, and social and cultural networks (Home Office, 2001a). Some communities had responded to this challenge with vigour and determination, while other communities had shown less commitment and determination to confront the issues. Unfortunately, the review team has the following observations (Home Office, 2001b):

> The programmes devised to tackle the needs of many disadvantaged and disaffected groups, whilst being well intentioned and sometimes inspirational, often seemed to institutionalise the problems. The plethora of initiatives and programmes, with their baffling array of outcomes, boundaries, timescales and other conditions, seemed to ensure divisiveness and a perception of unfairness in virtually every section of the communities we visited.

In addition, the costs of such community engagements included "burn-out" of key local community players, intra-community tensions, and the demands placed on the time and resources of workers and organisations (Office of Deputy Prime Minister, 2003). The Labour government's 2005 manifesto promised enhanced powers for neighbourhood governance, including community funds for neighbourhood to spend on local priorities, the ability to own community assets and powers to trigger action in response to antisocial behavior (Lund, 2007).

Under the Cabinet Office, the Office of the Third Sector has been responsible for formulating policies in relation to community participation, social enterprises, and voluntary and community sector development. It is mainly responsible for the promotion of volunteer development and building relationships with community organisations. The Department for Communities and Local Government is responsible for the promotion of community cohesion and civil renewal. Community cohesion is described as the ability of communities to function and grow in harmony together rather than in conflict. Community cohesion implies common values and a civic culture of tolerance, respect for differences, inter-group cooperation, social participation and civic engagement, support for political institutions, equal access to services, acknowledging social obligation and willingness to assist others (Community Cohesion Unit, 2003; Home Office, 2003; Local Government Association, 2002, 2003, 2004;). The Local Government Association defined a cohesive community as one where (Local Government Association, 2002):

- there is a common vision and a sense of belonging for all communities;
- the diversity of people's backgrounds and circumstances is appreciated and positively valued;
- those from different backgrounds have similar life opportunities; and
- strong and positive relationships are being developed between people from different backgrounds and circumstances in the workplace, in schools and in neighbourhoods.

The Egan Review (Department for Communities and Local Government, sustainable communities website) also indicates the need to build sustainable and balanced communities:

> Sustainable communities meet the diverse needs of existing and future residents, their children and other users, contribute to a high quality of life and provide opportunity and choice. They achieve this in ways that make effective use of natural resources, enhance the environment, promote social cohesion and inclusion and strengthen economic prosperity.

According to the Office of the Deputy Prime Minister, sustainable communities are (Office of Deputy Prime Minister, 2003):

> places where people want to live and work, now and in the future. They meet the diverse needs of existing and future residents, are sensitive to their environment, and contribute to a high quality of life. They are safe and inclusive, well planned, built and run, and offer equality of opportunity and good services for all.

For communities to be sustainable, they must offer; decent homes at prices people can afford, good public transport, schools, hospitals, shops, and a clean, safe environment. The implementation of sustainable communities requires the investment of the government in urban renewal, housing, urban design, social service provisions and environment improvement.

The Local Government Act 2000 introduced Local Strategic Partnerships (LSP) and community strategies, aimed to improve the local quality of life. LSPs are intended to be cross-sector-agency, umbrella partnerships that include all sectors of society, including public, private, community and voluntary. An LSP is a single body that brings together at a local level the different parts of the public sector as well as the private, business, community and voluntary sectors so that different initiatives and services support each other and work together. It is a non-statutory partnership that provides a single overarching local co-ordination framework within which other partnerships can operate (Department for Communities and Local Government, 2008a; 2009). It is responsible for developing and driving the implementation of Community Strategies and Local Area Agreements and, in areas receiving Neighbourhood renewal funding, is responsible for agreeing the allocation of this funding and helping to "narrow the gap".

Funded by the Neighbourhood Renewal Fund, an LSP ensures that:

- the membership and methods of consultation and engagement are balanced and inclusive;
- difficult decisions are addressed and resolved, not just the easy ones; and
- the partners properly resource and support the LSP (Department for Communities and Local Government, 2009).

Under the Department for Communities and Local Government, there are a variety of units that aim to promote community building.

The Neighbourhood Renewal Unit targets deprived neighbourhoods with extra-funding allocation on neighbourhood renewal strategies and initiatives (Department for Communities and Local

Government, Neighbourhood Renewal website; 2008b). Primarily it operates three programmes:

- New Deal for Communities (NDC): This targets multiple deprivation in the most deprived neighbourhoods with extra resources through intensive and coordinated efforts. Problems in each of the NDC areas are unique, but all partnerships tackle five key themes of poor job prospects, high levels of crime, educational under-achievement, poor health and problems with housing and the physical environment.
- Neighbourhood Management: This involves working with local agencies to improve services at neighbourhood level through better management of local environment; increasing community safety; improving housing stock; working with young people; and encouraging employment opportunities.
- Neighbourhood Warden Teams: Introduced in areas with high crime rates, they work closely with residents and police to tackle deprivation and anti-social behaviour and foster social inclusion and caring for the environment (Department for Communities and Local Government, 2008b).
- "Together We Can": This is the government campaign to bring government and people closer together, encouraging public bodies to do more to enable people to influence local decisions. The website provides information about resources in order to provide easy access to government policy documents, programmes and initiatives being promoted by government departments and their partners (Department for Communities and Local Government, together we can website).

To facilitate the sharing of good practice on community cohesion, the Community Cohesion Unit and the Local Government Association have collated a range of good practice examples which have been placed on the website at: www.communitycohesion.gov.uk. There is also a movement to encourage community-based organisations to manage local redundant buildings, including schools, shops, offices, warehouses, and town halls. Such management experiences offer the opportunity of learning by doing.

The UK 2006 White Paper on local government, *Strong and Prosperous Communities* (Department for Communities and Local Government, 2006), outlined the importance of responsive services and empowered communities, accountable and responsible local government, local government strategic leadership in promoting local partnership, and encouraging community cohesion. In general, community building focuses on community engagement to prevent crime, improve race relations and religious harmony, integrate migrants and refugees, and avoid extremism and social disturbance.

V. Community Building in Hong Kong

Under the governing model of a minimal state, the role of the former Hong Kong colonial government in social welfare and community building, particularly before the 1970s, was largely limited and residual. In fact, the legitimacy of the government was seldom challenged and threatened. Community participation was not perceived as necessary or promoted by the government.

Early studies on community can be traced back to the analysis of the traditional community organisations, namely the District Watch Committees (Lethbridge, 1978) and the Kaifong Associations (Wong, 1972, 1995). In addition to the provision of public and social services, they were the main citizen consultative institutions related to district affairs. Not surprisingly, the support of the government for these community organisations was both ambivalent and piecemeal. With a sense of distrust and suspicion towards community organisations, the government adopted the basic policy of providing cautious support and limited recognition only to selected pro-government groups. On the other hand, the Hong Kong people, influenced by traditional Chinese culture, did not perceive that the government had the obligation to provide assistance to their needs. In a way, the government and the people tried to keep their distance from each other. In a sense, the social capital or mutual trust between the people and the government during the early colonial rule was low.

The 1966 and 1967 riots challenged the complacency and legitimacy of the government. To improve the communication between the government and the community, the City District Officer Scheme was launched in 1968. This initiative represented a significant move of the government to encourage and sponsor community participation. In the 1970s, the government began to show commitment to establish a more comprehensive social welfare system, particularly with the publication of the White Paper on Social Welfare in 1973. In addition to taking up the full responsibility of social assistance, the government also began to expand heavily subsidised universal education, public health care, and public housing programmes.

With increasing numbers of people living in new public housing estates, there were studies on community relations or neighbourliness. Findings indicated that there were already significant decline in neighbourliness due to the new housing design and changing way of life (Kan, 1974).

Through the rapid expansion of social welfare services, particularly in youth and community work, social welfare services, staffed by professionally trained social workers had increased tremendously. Youth services were primarily provided to prevent juvenile delinquency and community centre facilities were provided mainly in physically deprived districts through the provision of community centres, community welfare buildings and community halls, and in pockets of deprived areas, the Neighbourhood Level Community Development Projects. Community development services aimed to promote the social integration of the residents and fill the gaps of mainstream welfare services. Community centre facilities were established in public housing estates in the early 1960s and expanded in the 1970s to encourage the "amalgamation of divergent groups and the formation of more coherent communities, fulfilling the quasi-political function of integrating migrants from China into the Hong Kong society, inducing a sense of community and maintaining social stability" (Director of Social Welfare, 1967).

In the early 1970s, community-based social movements were inspired and led by community social workers working in physically deprived neighbourhoods, such as the squatter areas, old public housing estates and temporary housing areas. Community work practice by social workers was dominated by the Alinsky's paradigm of forming "people's organisations" through organising the residents living in deprived areas to seek improvements in housing and environment provisions. Pressure groups, as described by the government were "characterised by the use of group mobilisation and propaganda to highlight government deficiencies in order to press for changes in government policies" (Home Affairs, 1980). Pressure groups and social movement organisations often lack the effective mobilisation power to put pressure on the government, except in some short-lived social issues. These piecemeal actions did not facilitate establishing and sustaining large membership-based residents' organisations.

Pressure groups often depended on their leaders, acting as the advocate or champion, and mass media support, rather than direct disruptive and confrontative protest actions. In other words, the use of "civil disobedience" or "non-violence resistance", with the deliberate and active refusal to obey certain laws, demands and commands of the government, was not the dominant paradigm. The government, business and traditional community groups were identified by community workers more as "enemies" than as partners.

As Hong Kong did not have a system of local government, the colonial government introduced a system of community participatory and consultative structure in the 1970s, namely the three-tier structure of city district committee, area committee and mutual aid committee. "Community building" – building a society where there is mutual care and responsibility – was introduced by Governor Maclehose in 1976. Echoing the cherished governing principle of "government by consultation and consent", the community-based consultative structure eventually evolved to become the District Board in the 1982 and later the District Council (DC). These structures were primarily advisory with no political and management responsibilities. They received financial allocation from the government for district-based activities and can scrutinise public policies and services affecting the local community.

The community building policy established a system of community-based participation and consultation, facilitating vertical political communication or partnership between the government and the citizens, and at the same time, counteracting the thriving activities of community-based pressure groups. As the government was basically suspicious of the pressure group activities of community organisations, the promotion of horizontal relationships or partnerships among different community organisations was in fact discouraged. The government apparently was afraid that federations of community organisations could turn into pressure or political groups demanding representative democracy (Leung, 1994). In other words, the policy emphasis of the government was on promoting "linking social capital", the communication between the government and the local resident groups, rather than on "bridging" and "bonding" social capital.

Based on the Green Paper on District Administration published in 1980, District Boards (renamed District Councils in 2000) were established in 1982. District Administration aimed to achieve better coordination of government activities, responsive policy to local needs and promote public participation in district affairs. Without a system of local government, district boards/DCs were primarily community-based advisory organisations.

In a sense, the introduction of the District Administration in the 1980s was politically driven. This served to introduce the notion of popular election of community representatives before the return of Hong Kong to China in 1997. As such, election and committee politics eventually reduced the use of protest actions to redress grievances. As a result, many pressure groups either evolved to become political groups or were co-opted into the consultative structure. Despite their formidable image, pressure groups which took the government and traditional community organisations as the target of "criticisms", were short-lived, isolated and loosely organised. Pressure groups initially gained significant electoral success in district council elections. DC members, including those pro-government members, have learned to use advocacy and critical comments on government policy to gain the trust of the local residents. Increasingly, local residents can turn to DC members to redress their grievances rather than to rely on the organisation of community social workers. In contrast with community social work practice, DC members tended to take leadership and act on behalf of the residents rather than encouraging the residents to work on their own issues.

In the 1980s, DCs were reformed gradually with elected chairmanship, withdrawal of government officials as members, increased proportion of elected members (in 1994, appointed seats were abolished), regular briefing sessions on government policies and initiatives. Thereafter, DCs assumed a pivotal role to scrutinise the planning and provision and delivery of district services, and the government would seek consultation on local community and territory-wide issues. Since the withdrawal of the government district officers as the chairperson of the DC, however, the role of the district officers had become less prominent in district affairs, and its ability to coordinate efforts of different departments was eroded. After the return of Hong Kong to China in 1997, local district issues involving cross-departmental responsibilities had to move up to higher authorities for resolution. Petitions and protests involving community issues have continued to target government headquarters, bureau chiefs and the Chief Executive. In other words, the centre for policy debates has moved to the legislative council.

In his 2005–06 Policy Address, the Chief Executive stated (Tsang, 2005, p. 19):

> The Government will allow each DC to assume responsibility for the management of some district facilities, such as libraries, community halls, leisure grounds, sports venues and swimming pools. The executive departments will follow the decisions of the DC in managing such facilities, within the limits of their existing statutory powers and resources available.

In this way, a new and strengthened model of community engagement has been proposed. Accordingly, DCs will have more authority and resources to involve in the management of district facilities, namely leisure and sports facilities, community halls, and libraries, and promote community involvement activities. Meanwhile, the coordinating function and role of district officers to provide cross-departmental district services and to enhance the communication between the government and the DCs will be strengthened. Overseeing the coordination work of the district offices is a Steering Committee on District Administration, chaired by the Secretary of Home Affairs, comprising members from heads of relevant departments. It serves to resolve inter-departmental district management issues. In addition, heads of departments are expected to seek regular face-to-face consultation with DCs. So far, the reforms have received wide support from the community. DC members are looking for the further extension of the management responsibility to cover other district facilities. Moreover, in recent years, more DC members have been appointed to a wide range of advisory and statutory bodies which provide advice on government policies (Home Affairs Bureau, 2006).

On the other hand, DCs have become important bases for political parties to obtain resources, mobilise support, and nurture emerging politicians. DC elections have become more competitive, which can attract the participation of professionals and younger candidates to compete for the positions.

Overall, DCs are basically advisory bodies, with no constitutional authority and mandate to monitor government performance. They receive the power delegated to them from the government. Ideally, they can work together as partners with equal power. According to the intention of the DC reform, the executive departments are required to follow the decisions of the DC as far as possible. This has serious implications for the operational mode of the government departments and the culture of the civil servants. The real test of the reform is to what extent the "delegated power" of the DC can be "respected" in operation not only by the Home Affairs Department, but by other related government departments as well.

Further reforms of the DCs include whether DC members should be included in the election committee for the chief executive; further expansion of management responsibilities beyond local facilities provided by the Leisure, Culture and Sports Department; changes in the composition of DCs (adjustments of elected seats according to population changes, appointed members); strengthening administrative support to DCs; and capacity building of DC members and DCs.

Statistics show that there are certain communities/districts where there is a high concentration of vulnerable people, such as the new arrivals, single parents, old people, the unemployed, social assistance recipients, and low-income families (Commission on

Poverty, 2007). The situation may be aggravated in some new and remote communities where social and public services are not fully developed. Affected by the poor local economy, local residents in remote areas, far away from the city centres, may have difficulties of seeking employment. The situation of Tin Shui Wai is a typical example of such a community.

The establishment of the Community Investment and Inclusion Fund (CIIF) in 2002 demonstrates the determination of the government to promote social capital at the community level, through reinvigorating the mutual help support networks or creating new ones in the neighbourhoods. In social welfare, the community dimension has received more focus. The re-engineering of the family service centres in 2004 has transformed the traditional casework oriented approach to a service which is actively in search of community involvement and partnerships with other services and community organisations (Department of Social Work and Social Administration, The University of Hong Kong, 2001, 2004). In the care of the older people, the concept of "ageing in place" or "ageing in community" has become the cornerstone of the government's elderly care policy. It is believed that older people with caring needs should be as far as possible be provided with community-based support to live at home, rather than receiving residential care. Under the direction of "active ageing", older people should actively participate in community life as ordinary citizens. In domestic violence, the need to strengthen district coordination of key stakeholders has been highlighted in the report studying the family tragedy in Tin Shui Wai (Review Panel on Family Services in Tin Shui Wai, November 2004).

The re-structuring of the District Social Welfare Offices (DSWO) in 2002 has attempted to enhance the coordination and effectiveness of welfare services at the district level. More importantly, it has succeeded in extending participation in the implementation of welfare service delivery beyond NGOs to include other government departments, the DC and community organisations (Department of Social Work and Social Administration, The University of Hong Kong, September 2003).

Community activism continues to thrive. Studies are often limited to social movements in relation to democratisation, student, labour, and the environment (Chiu and Lui, 2000; Butenhoff, 1999). In relation to the community, social movements have been more linked to housing issues (Ho, 2000a, 2000b). With significant improvements in public housing provisions and pressure group activists being co-opted into the Housing Authority, social conflicts related to housing provisions have been reduced significantly. Community issues, with a wider base of involvement, have become more diversified to focus on social issues such as welfare rights, employment and wages, social service provisions and environmental and heritage protection.

Meanwhile, social worker activism at the community level has been largely reduced. Housing pressure groups have become less conspicuous. The rapid development of election politics have further turned pressure groups into political groups and reduced the use of aggressive protest actions (Lai, 2000). DC members are more interested in acting as champions of local interests rather than as builders of extensive community networks for mobilisation. In addition, the common use of legal challenges to government policies has in a way reduced the need for mass mobilisation. Evidently, the use of protest actions has proliferated, and more people from different strata have learned to use protest actions to redress their grievances. However, their actions have been limited to the use of petitions, marches, sit-ins and press conferences. These actions have become somewhat "institutionalised" and "routinised". In fact, most protest actions centred on the use of dramatic behaviours and rational evidence to appeal the attention, coverage and support from the mass media. They largely rely on the pressure from the "third party" rather than direct disruptive and crippling tactics causing harm to the opponents. As most community activists and their groups have operated within the polity rather than outside, they have in fact functioned more as interest groups, receiving access to and recognition among political authorities. Noteworthy is the fact that some recent protest actions have shown increased use of resistance action challenging the police and the law. However, it is difficult to envisage protest actions in Hong Kong turning into disorganised street violence and social disturbance.

Besides political and democratisation issues, public governance has seldom been seriously challenged by sporadic, piecemeal and short-lived protest actions. Unlike many developed countries, Hong Kong has been spared from the frequent turmoil and instability that have plagued other countries. As such, studies of social conflicts and social movements have rarely been the subject of inquiry among academics (Leung, 1996). Yet the most challenging research question is why the conditions in Hong Kong, despite lacking a western type of democratic political system, and aggravated by widened income disparities and insufficient social security provision, can still maintain a rather socially cohesive society, without a strong threat of social disturbance and instability. In a sense, Hong Kong people still seem to trust the government.

The community-based approach signifies the importance of community engagement and flexibility in providing more responsive and effective solutions to local social issues (Kwok, 2006; Commission on Poverty, 2007). The government is committed to providing an environment facilitative to these developments. DCs can become more active in taking actions and leadership to address local social issues, rather than simply focusing on the organisation of social, recreational and cultural activities.

VI. Conclusions

In many countries, government interventions to promote social capital, community engagement and community cohesion are aimed at maintaining social stability and cohesion through having responsive public services and shared responsibility. In the United Kingdom and Singapore, community cohesion efforts are targeted at improving racial relations (Cantle, 2005). Community engagement is pivotal to strengthen governance at all levels. Most governments are attempting to decentralise administration to the local level by giving the local community more opportunities and responsibility to manage their own affairs and communicate their views. In essence, all area-based initiatives should be developed and owned by local people and community organisations. Partnership, based on mutual trust, is the key working structure at the community level to bring people with competing interests and values together to address cross-cutting issues. Simply put, "bridging social capital" is the foremost ingredient for cross-sector partnerships.

Because of the colonial heritage, public policy formulation in Hong Kong, even after becoming a Special Administrative Region, has been heavily influenced by the UK experience. The community social capital building efforts in the UK have served to complement the local administration and governance, with specific government-funded area-based initiatives, targeting those deprived communities, whereas in China and Singapore, community building has focused more on overall community governance structures. In all these examples, government leadership has been vital to activate and facilitate cross-sector partnership building. In Hong Kong, long-term strategic planning and additional resource commitment targeting deprived communities have not been seriously considered. More importantly, community engagement involving key stakeholders is pivotal to re-invigorate the economy and improve the quality of life of deprived communities.

Hong Kong has always enjoyed rather harmonious racial, religious and social relations. Social disturbance in the form of violent protest actions has been rare. Yet community life has become more diverse, with more community groups having different and competing interests and values. How to bring these community stakeholders together for joint efforts will be a formidable challenge for the government. These key stakeholders include government departments, DC members and politicians, community leaders, community organisations, young people, faith groups, ethnic minorities, and NGOs.

The key issues relevant to Hong Kong are:

- Without a system of local government, to what extent can the DCs, primarily advisory bodies, have more authority to manage their own affairs?
- As the community becomes more diverse with competing interests, can different community stakeholders work together for the benefits of the "whole-of-the-community"?
- Are the communities equipped with the capacity to take up the responsibility of self-management?

References

Auspos, P. (2006). Community-focused efforts to increase employment: Strategies, theories of change, outcomes, and measures. In K. Fulbright-Anderson and P. Auspos (Eds.), *Community Change: Theories, practice, and evidence*. The Aspen Institute, Roundtable on Community Change, http://www.aspeninstitute.org.

Baron, S., Field, J., and Schuller, T. (Eds.) (2000). *Social capital. Critical perspectives*. New York: Oxford University Press;

Blunkett, D. (2003). *Building Civil Renewal: A Review of Government Support for Community Capacity Building and Proposal for Change*, Civil Renewal Unit, Home Office.

Briggs, X. (2002). Community building: The new politics of urban problem-solving. Faculty Research Working Paper Series, January 2002. John F. Kennedy School of Government, Harvard University;

Bruhn, J. (2007). *The sociology of community connections*. New York: Kluwer Academic and Plenum Publishers.

Butenhoff, L. (1999). *Social movements and political reform in Hong Kong*. Westport, CT: Praeger.

Cantle, T. (2005). *Community cohesion: A framework for race and diversity*. New York: Palgrave Macmillan.

Chaskin, R., Brown, P., Venkatesh, S., and Vidal, A. (2001). *Building community capacity*. New York: Aldine De Gruyter

Chiu, S., and Lui, T. L. (Eds.) (2000). *The dynamics of social movement in Hong Kong*. Hong Kong: University of Hong Kong Press.

Civil Renewal Unit (2006). *Community Assets – The benefits and costs of community management and ownership*. London: Department for Communities and Local Government.

Commission on Poverty (2007). *Report of the Commission on Poverty*. March 2007. Hong Kong: Government Printer.

Community Cohesion Unit (2003). *Community Cohesion: A report of the Independent Review Team*. Home Office of the UK Government, www.homeoffice.gov.uk/docs2/comm_cohesion3.html.

Community Development Council, http://www.cdc.org.sg.

Daly, G., and Davis, H. (2002). Partnerships for local governance: Citizens, communities and accountability. In C. Glendinning, M. Powell and K. Rummery (Eds.), *Partnerships, New Labour and the governance of welfare*. Bristol: The Policy Press.

Dekker, P., and Uslaner, E. (Eds.) (2001). *Social capital and participation in everyday life*. London: Routledge.

Department for Communities and Local Government, sustainable communities, http://www.communities.gov.uk/communities/sustainablecommunities.

Department for Communities and Local Government, neighbourhood renewal, http://www.neighbourhood.gov.uk/page.asp?id=10.

Department for Communities and Local Government, Together we can, http://togtherwe can.direct.gov.uk/about-us.

Department for Communities and Local Government, community cohesion, http://communitycohesion.gov.uk.

Department for Communities and Local Government (2006). *Strong and prosperous communities, the local government white paper,* London: HM Government.

Department for Communities and Local Government (2008a). *Working with local strategic partnerships and local area agreements: Some lessons from the New Deal for communities programme.* London: HM Government.

Department for Communities and Local Government (2008b). *Neighbourhood Management – Beyond the Pathfinders: A National overview.* London: HM Government.

Department for Communities and Local Government (2009). *Planning Together: Updated practical guide for local strategic partnerships and planners.* London: HM Government.

Department of Health (1998). *Modernising social services – Promoting independence, improving protection and raising standards.* Department of Health, UK Government, www.doh.gov.uk/scg/execsum.htm.

Department of Social Work and Social Administration, The University of Hong Kong (2001). *Meeting the challenge: strengthening families.* Hong Kong: Government Printer.

Department of Social Work and Social Administration, The University of Hong Kong (September 2003). *Building community strategic partnerships: The report of the study to evaluate the effectiveness of Social Welfare Department's enhanced district social welfare office functions,* Hong Kong: Social Welfare Department.

Department of Social Work and Social Administration, The University of Hong Kong (2004). *The steps forward: The formation of integrative family service centres,* Hong Kong: Government Printer.

Dickens, W. (1999). Rebuilding urban labor markets: what community development can accomplish. In R. Ferguson and D. William (Eds.), *Urban problems and community development.* Washington, DC: Brookings Institution Press.

Director of Social Welfare (1967). *Annual department report.* Hong Kong: Government Printer.

Field, J. (2005). *Social capital and lifelong learning.* Bristol: The Policy Press;

Hardin, R., Body-Gendrot, S., and Gittell, M. (Eds.) (2003). *Social capital and social citizenship*. Lanham, MD: Lexington Books;

Ho, K. L. (2000a). The rise and fall of community mobilisation: The housing movement in Hong Kong. In S. Chiu and T. L. Lui (Eds.), *The dynamics of social movement in Hong Kong*. Hong Kong: University of Hong Kong Press

Ho, K. L. (2000b). *Polite politics: A sociological analysis of an urban protest in Hong Kong*. Aldershot: Ashgate.

Holzer, H. (1996), *What employers want: Job prospects for less educated workers*. New York: Russell Sage Foundation

Home Affairs Branch (1980), *Information paper for Chief Secretary's Committee, monitoring of pressure group activities*, Mimeograph copy.

Home Affairs Bureau (2006), *Consultation document on review on the role, functions and composition of district councils*. Hong Kong: Government Printer.

Home Office (2001a). *Building cohesive communities: A report of the ministerial group on public order and community cohesion*. London: HM Stationary Office.

Home Office (2001b). *A report of the independent review team*, London: HM Stationery Office.

Home Office (2003). *Civil renewal: A new agenda*, CSV Edith Kahn Memorial Lecture, given by the then Home Secretary David Blunkett MP, 11 June. http://www.communities.gov.uk/publications/communities/civilrenewal.

Home Office (2004), *Firm foundations. The government's framework for community capacity building*. Civic Renewal Unit, Home Office, London: HM Stationery Office, London.

Hooghe, M., and Stolle, D. (Eds.) (2003). *Generating social capital: Civil society and institutions in comparative perspective*. New York: Palgrave Macmillan.

Gittell, R., and Vidal, A. (1998). *Community organizing – Building social capital as a development strategy*. Thousand Oaks, CA: Sage.

Jochum, V., Pratten, B., and Wilding, K. (2005). *Civil renewal and active citizenship: A guide to the debate*. The National Council for Voluntary Organisations, http://www.ncvo-vol.org.uk/publications/showall.asp?id=1512.

Kjaer, L. (2003). *Local partnerships in Europe – An action research project*. The Copenhagen Centre

Kan, A. (1974). *A study of neighborly interaction in public housing : The case of Hong Kong*. Chinese University of Hong Kong, Social Research Centre.

Kowk, A. (2006), *From welfare to self-reliance: District study on employment assistance*, Report for submission to Commission on Poverty, Hong Kong.

Lai, O. K. (2000), Greening of Hong Kong? – Forms of manifestation of environmental movements. In S. Chiu and T. L. Lui (Eds.), *The dynamics of social movement in Hong Kong*. Hong Kong: University of Hong Kong Press.

Lethbridge, H. (1978). *Hong Kong: Stability and change: A collection of essays.* Hong Kong: Oxford University Press.

Leung, B. (1996), *Perspectives on Hong Kong society,* Hong Kong: Oxford University Press.

Leung, J. (1994), Community participation: Past, present and future, in B. Leung (Ed.), *25 years of social and economic development in Hong Kong.* Hong Kong: Centre of Asian Studies, the University of Hong Kong.

Leung, J. (2000). Community building in China: From welfare to politics, *Community Development Journal,* 45.4: 425–427.

Lin, N., Cook, K., and Burt, R. (Eds.) (2001). *Social capital theory and research.* New York: Aldine De Gruyter.

Local Government Association (2002), *Guidance on community cohesion,* December, Office of the Deputy Prime Minister.

Local Government Association (2003), *Building a picture of community cohesion – A guide for local authorities and their partners,* June, Office of Deputy Prime Minister.

Local Government Association (2004), *Community cohesion – An action guide: guidance for local authorities.* November, Office of the Deputy Prime Minister.

Local Government Association (2007). *An action plan for community empowerment: building on success.* Department for Communities and Local Government, http://www.communities.gov.uk/publications/communities/communityempowermentactionplan.

Lund, B. (2007), State welfare. In M. Powell (ed.), *Understanding the mixed economy of welfare.* Bristol: Policy Press.

Means, R., Richards, S., and Smith, R. (2008). *Community care.* Houndmills: Palgrave Macmillan.

Ministry of Civil Affairs (2009). *Civil Affairs Development Report 2009.* Beijing: Ministry of Civil Affairs.

Montgomery, J., and Inkeles, E. (Eds.) (2000). *Social capital as a policy resource.* Boston, MA: Kluwer.

Norris, P. (2002). *Democratic phoenix: Reinventing political activism.* Cambridge: Cambridge University Press.

OECD (2001). *The well-being of nations: The role of human and social capital.* Paris: OECD.

OECD (2003). *Open government: Fostering dialogue with civil society.* Paris: OECD; OECD (2005), *Modernising government: The way forward.* Paris: OECD.

OECD (2005), Public sector modernization: Open government. *Policy Brief,* February, Paris: OECD.

Office of Deputy Prime Minister (2003), *New deal for communities: annual review,* http://www.neighbourhood.gov.uk/docs/NDC_Ann_Review_2001-2.pdf.

The National Economic and Social Forum (2003). *The policy implications of social capital.* Forum Report no. 28, June, Ireland, http://www.nesf.ie.

People's Association, http://www.pa.gov.sg.

Performance and Innovation Unit (2002). Social capital – A discussion paper. April 2002, UK Government, Cabinet Office, http://www.cabinetoffice .gov.uk.

Putnam, R. (2000). *Bowling alone: The collapse and revival of American community.* New York: Simon & Schuster.

Putnam, R. (Ed.). (2002). *Democracies in flux: The evolution of social capital in contemporary society.* Oxford: Oxford University Press.

Review Panel on Family Services in Tin Shui Wai (November 2004), *Report of review panel on family services in Tin Shui Wai,* Social Welfare Department.

Richardson, L. (2008). *DIY community action. Neighbourhood problems and community self-help.* Bristol: Policy Press.

Rogers, B., and Robinson. E. (2004). *The benefits of community engagement. A review of evidence.* Active Citizenship Centre, http://www.communities .gov.uk/communities/communityempowerment.

Snow, D.A., Soule, S.A., and Kriesi, H. (Eds.) (2004).*The Blackwell companion to social movements.* Malden, MA: Blackwell.

Togetherwecan. http://togetherwecan.direct.gov.uk/about-us.

Tsang, D. (2005). 2005–06 Policy Address, http://www.policyaddress.gov.hk/ 05-06/eng/p19.html.

Tsang, D. (2006), 2006-07 Policy Address, http://www.policyaddress.gov.hk/ 06-07/eng/p49.html.

Wang, Z. H. (2003). *Community politics.* Taiyuan: Shanxi People's Publishers.

Wong, A. (1972). *The Kaifong Associations and the society of Hong Kong.* Taipei: Orient Cultural Service; Wong, A. (1995). *The Kaifong (Neighborhood) Associations in Hong Kong.* Ann Arbor, MI: University Microfilm International.

6

Social Capital and Health

Albert LEE

I. Background:
Improvement of Population Health
from a Wider Perspective

Over the last few decades, factors such as income inequality, health inequities, other socio-demographic variables (ethnicity/race, age, gender and education) have been held accountable for health inequality. Health cannot be improved simply by the provision of health services focusing on particular diseases or organs. To improve the health of the population, one must put emphasis on reducing health inequalities and enhancing health protection and disease prevention, as well as early diagnosis and treatment of diseases. One needs to study how the cultural, social and political conditions enhance or reduce opportunities for populations to be healthy. The Ottawa Charter for Health has highlighted the importance of building a supportive environment. In 2005 the Bangkok Charter for Health also emphasised investment in sustainable policies, actions and infrastructures to address the determinants of health; capacity building for policy development and leadership; regulation and legislation; and partnership and building alliances with public, private, non-governmental and international organisations and civil society to create sustainable actions.

The determinants of health can be grouped into socio-political, environmental, cultural, and biological determinants, but they are inter-related. The determinants of health acting at the macro-level (upstream) focus on social systems and social change. It is concerned with the factors related to adoption of innovations within a social system (Roger, 1995). Interventions targeted at the determinants of health at the micro-level influence individual health actions (midstream interventions include lifestyle and behavioural modifications, and preventive measures; and downstream interventions such as diagnosis and treatment). It is the individuals who make decisions, and the sum total of their decision making ultimately forms societal actions. Based on the model of the human eco-system by Hancock and Perkin (Figure 1), interventions for health improvement need to act at, and across, different layers and different levels. Both primary health care and the "healthy setting" approach can tackle the determinants of health at both macro and micro levels. By strengthening community capacity and leadership in health promotion, human and social capitals can be further developed to meet the health challenges of this century.

Figure 1
Mandala of health: A model of the human ecosystem
(with kind permission from Dr Trevor Hancock)

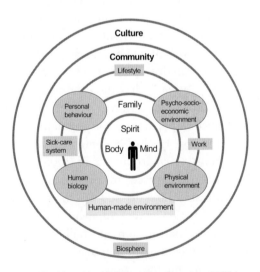

Source: Hancock and Perkins. *Health Education*, Summer 1985, pps-10.

II. Why It Is Important to Build Up Social Capital for Health Improvement

Improvements in the health of citizens require more than the availability of information and building up personal health skills. Health action is complex, so in the early 1970s Professor Keith Tones in England developed the Health Action Model (HAM) and identified major psychological, social and environmental influences on individuals adopting and sustaining health- or illness-related actions. There are four interacting systems that determine the likelihood of a given individual developing an intention to adopt a particular course of health- or illness-related action:

- beliefs
- motivation
- normative influences
- the self.

Apart from knowledge and skills, the availability of a supportive environment is needed to "make the healthy choice the easy choice". The enabling factors for motivation would be viewed as removing those psychological, behavioural and environmental barriers against people making healthy choices.

The normative system is the network of social pressures that would exert influence on an individual's intention to adopt or reject health actions (Tones and Green, 2004). It can be conceived as a hierarchical set of influences ranging from proximal impact of close family and friends to the increasingly distal effects of community and the further reaches of the social system. It is assumed that the effect of significant individuals, close family and friends will typically be more powerful than community pressures, which in turn will have more influence than national norms conveyed by mass media.

The self concept can be viewed from academic perspectives regarding actual achievement and competencies; or from the social perspective as viewed by peers, family and significant others; or self-presentation as a result of self-esteem and self-confidence and also self-image.

The health of the nation is determined by how the four interacting systems work together. Social scientists had explored the concept of social capital to explain the difference between societies. A recent literature review has documented two components of social capital; a cognitive component including "norms, values, beliefs and attitudes" and a structural component referring to social network or civic engagement (Islam, Merlo, Kawachi, Lindstrom and Gerdtham, 2006).

A wider perspective of capital needs to be considered to explain the difference of health in different societies. If one considers that "a nation's health is a nation's wealth", then it is not difficult to understand that the wealth of a nation means more than just its level of income. Wealth is not just economic capital, but includes three other forms of capital; social, natural and human capital. A healthy community is one that has high levels of social, ecological, human and economic "capitals", the combination of which is regarded as "community capital" (Hancock, 2001).

Human capital consists of healthy, well-educated, skilled, innovative and creative people who are engaged in their communities and participate in governance.

Social capital constitutes the 'glue' that holds communities together formally (social development programmes) and informally as a social network. The formal aspect also includes investment in social development so that citizens have equitable access to basic determinants of health.

Natural capital includes high environmental quality, healthy ecosystems, sustainable resources, nature conservation and biodiversity.

Economic capital refers to the level of prosperity that we need so we can feed, clothe and house everyone, provide clean water, proper sanitation, ensure universal education and provision of accessible health and social services. It should also create healthy jobs and equitable distribution of resources.

The challenge in the new millennium is to increase all four forms of capital. The World Bank acknowledged not only the existence but the importance of these four forms of capital in one of its research reports (World Bank, 1995). It was estimated that 20% of the world's total wealth was found in natural capital, another 20% in economic capital and the remaining 60% in the combination of social and human capital.

Social scientists have long wondered why some communities are prosperous and have effective political institutions and law-abiding and healthy citizens while other communities do not. Researchers have begun to turn to the concept of social capital as a possible explanation. Social capital has been defined as those features of social organisation – such as the extent of interpersonal trust between citizens, norms of reciprocity, and density of civic associations – that facilitate cooperation for mutual benefit (Coleman, 1990; Putnam, 1993; Kawachi and Kennedy, 1997). As mentioned above, it constitutes the "glue" that holds the community together.

Social capital has been claimed to be important for the enhancement of government performance and the functioning of democracy (Putnam, 1993), for the prevention of crime and delinquency (Sampson and Groves, 1984; Sampson Raudenbush and Earls, 1997), and, more recently, for the maintenance of population health (Kawachi, Kennedy, Lochner and Prothrow-Stith, 1997). A study by Kawachi, Kennedy and Glass (1999) found that states with low social capital also had higher proportions of residents who reported their health as being only fair or poor. Having higher levels of trust and feeling safe were consistently associated with low levels of psychological distress after adjusting for socio-demographic characteristics and other health conditions (Phongsavan, Chey, Bauman, Brooks and Silove, 2006).

Social capital may influence the health behaviours of neighbourhood residents by:

- promoting more rapid diffusion of health information (Roger, 1995);
- increasing the likelihood that healthy norms of behaviour are adopted (e.g., physical activity); and
- exerting social control over deviant health-related behaviour.

The theory of the diffusion of innovations (Roger, 1995) suggests that innovative behaviours (e.g., use of preventive services) diffuse much more rapidly in communities that are cohesive and in which members know and trust one another.

In fact, social and human development builds up economic

development. Business is more likely to be attracted to communities that have large numbers of well-educated people and that are stable, safe and have strong social networks (Hancock, 2005). Social development focuses on social collectiveness and building up social capital. Human development focuses on development of individuals building up human capital. Human capital can be regarded as the sum of the capacities of all individuals in the community – their level of intelligence, education, creativity and innovativeness, health and well-being, capacity for empathy and caring. Building up human capital is seen as a result of environmental, social and economic development as based on Hancock's model of healthy community (Hancock, 1993) placing human capital at the centre (Figure 2).

Figure 2. The four capitals model (Hancock, 1993)

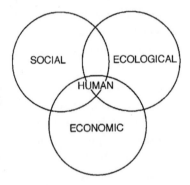

III. Effective Primary Health Care to Combat the Adverse Effect of Social Inequality on Health

Independent Effect of Primary Health Care on Health Improvement

In the past decade, there has been substantial literature that suggests a significant association between income inequality and mortality both in the US and elsewhere (Blakely, Lochner and Kawachi, 2002; Wilkinson, 1996; Kennedy, Kawachi and Prothrow-Stith, 1996; Lochner, Pamuk, Makuc, Kennedy and Kawachi, 2001; McLaughlin and Stokes, 2002; Subramanian, Blakely and Kawachi, 2003). From a social capital perspective, social relationships influence health either directly or through other phenomena. One postulated explanation is that more egalitarian areas are more socially cohesive, leading to less psychosocial stress and better health status. Kawachi and colleagues (1997 and 1999) have demonstrated that in areas where income differences are smaller, people are more trusting of one another and more likely to participate in communal activities, and this social cohesiveness is linked to lower overall mortality and better self-rated health. The relative income hypothesis proposes that the greater the gap in income between the rich and the poor in a given area, the worse the health status for the overall population of that area (Mellor and Milyo, 2001; Lochner et al., 2001; Kennedy et al., 1999; Wilkinson, 1997). However, the pathways through which income inequality might affect health are still unknown, and hypotheses include psychosocial and material pathways (Wilkinson, 1997). Other investigators have postulated that the political and policy context is itself a precursor to health inequalities (Kawachi et al., 1999; Navarro and Shi, 2001).

A study published by Shi, Starfield, Kennedy and Kawachi (1999) suggested an important role for health system factors, especially the role of primary care resources, in reducing the apparent adverse effects of income inequality. It was found that the supply of primary care services had an independent and positive impact on health indicators, and in multivariate analysis when demographic, income, and health system covariates were controlled for, a higher supply of primary care services actually reduced the magnitude of the deleterious impact of income inequality on health outcomes. Using a multi-level model including individual, community, and state-level variables, Shi and Starfield (2000) found that even when they controlled for all covariates, an increase of one primary care physician per 10 000 population was associated with a 2% increase in the odds of reporting excellent/good health.

There is strong theoretical and empirical evidence for the association between strong national primary care systems and improved health indicators (Macinko, Starfield and Shi, 2003; Starfield, 1992; Starfield and Shi, 2002). Better health outcomes were found in states with higher primary care physician-to-population ratios after sociodemographic measures (elderly populations, urban residents, minority populations, education, income, unemployment, pollution) and lifestyle factors (seatbelt usage, obesity, and smoking) were controlled for (Farmer, Stokes and Fisher, 1991). Individual-level and state-level measures of primary care resources were also significantly associated with lower heart disease and cancer mortality rates (Shi, 1994; Kawachi and Kennedy, 1999; Shi, Starfield, Politzer and Regan, 2002).

Primary health care addresses the most common problems in the community – how to maximise health and well-being. It integrates care where there is more than one health problem, and deals with the context in which illness exists and influences the responses of people to their health problems. It organises and rationalises the deployment of all resources, basic as well as specialised, directed at promoting, maintaining, and improving health. Primary care resources might be one strategy to help remedy the poorer-than-expected health profile seen in communities that suffer from income and other social inequalities.

Using state-level data from the USA from 1990, a significant association was found between the supply of primary care physicians and reduced mortality, increased life expectancy and improved birth outcome, even after controlling for income inequality and population sociodemographic characteristics. Similar findings were noted using US metropolitan areas as the unit of analysis (Shi and Starfield, 2001) and in mixed-level analyses (Shi and Starfield, 2000; Shi et al., 2002).

Another study by Shi and colleagues (Shi, Macinko, Starfield, Politzer and Xu, 2005), is unique in having examined the independent relationship between income inequality and mortality, and assessing the extent to which primary health care might mediate this association. By using 11 years of data, they are able to examine the relationship among the variables of interest in more than one period, thus improving the robustness of their findings to changes over time. A set of nested models was designed to examine the independent effect of primary health care and income inequality on mortality and the extent to which the addition of primary health care to the statistical model attenuates the association between income inequality and mortality. In Model 1, only income inequality was used as a predictor of mortality. In Model 2, mortality is predicted by both income inequality and sociodemographic characteristics of the population. Model 3 includes primary health care along with the other covariates included in Model 2. Both primary health care (inversely) and income inequality (positively) are significantly associated with total mortality ($p<0.01$ for primary care and $p<0.05$ for income inequality). In Model 2, the effects of both income inequality and sociodemographics on mortality are examined. In Model 3, the inclusion of primary care reduces the magnitude of all sociodemographic regression coefficients. Primary care is independently and inversely associated with mortality. An increase of one primary care doctor per 10 000 population is associated with a reduction of 1.44 deaths per 10 000 population, after taking into account the effects of income inequality and the sociodemographic correlates of mortality.

This study confirmed earlier findings that primary health care was associated with lower mortality and health improvement partially mediated the association between socioeconomic variables and mortality (Shi et al., 1999; Shi and Starfield, 2000; Shi et al., 2002; Shi, Starfield, Xu, Politzer and Regan, 2003). These findings are significant because they provide more robust evidence of a relationship between primary health care physicians and lower mortality in the state population. Primary health care remained significant after including income inequality and socio-demographic covariates of mortality, indicating thereby that primary health care is likely to be independently associated with lower population mortality. The unique features of primary health care, such as continuous, longitudinal, and person-focused care, may also work to reverse some of the negative health effects of social inequalities by "short-circuiting" the ability of long-term stressors to produce chronic ailments.

Similar findings have also been observed in Hong Kong. A study by Lee and colleagues has shown that children with regular family physicians (FPs) have better health behaviours and psycho-social health (Lee, Wong, Lam, Fung, Kan, and Leung, 2007). When all possible sociodemographic variables such as income, education level of parents, types of accommodation, employment status of parents, and any subsidy or social security, were entered as independent variables together, having their own family doctors still demonstrated as a statistically significant independent associated factor for better health behaviour. FPs in Hong Kong have demonstrated their willingness to discharge their duties and ability to adapt during the SARS period in 2003, despite worries for the safety of themselves and their families (Wong, Lee, Tsang and Wong, 2004). Many FPs in the private sector were involved in community health programmes to empower the community to fight against SARS and they served as important medical resource persons in the community (Lee and Abdullah, 2003). After the SARS outbreak, many FPs began to form networks in different districts to strengthen their capacity to handle any future health crisis.

Millennium Development Goals and Primary Health Care

During the UN Millennium Summit in 2000, 147 heads of state gathered and adopted the Millennium Development Goals (MDGs) to address extreme poverty in many dimensions such as income poverty, disease, lack of adequate shelter, education, gender inequality and environmental sustainability. The lives of hundreds of millions of people could be dramatically improved and millions of dollars would be saved every year if the MDGs were achieved. For example, there are known packages of effective and generally low cost interventions in the area of public health that could make a decisive difference to child survival if the poor would and could have access to those services (Black, Morris and Bryce,,2003; Jones et al., 2003; Bryce et al., 2003). Increased financing linked to effective governance structures in low income countries can produce dramatic results. The scaling-up of interventions and policies required to meet the MDGs will need long-term investments in management systems, training and retention of human resources, and infrastructure. A functioning district-level health system will be required to achieve and sustain many of the health goals. However, there can be quick gains for the health sector to make a profound difference to survival and quality of life such as:

- The training of large numbers of village workers in health, farming and infrastructures to ensure basic expertise and services in rural communities.

- Elimination of barriers to using basic health services.
- Expansion of access to special health services such as sex and reproductive health.
- Expansion of use of proven effective drugs combinations for different types of infectious diseases such as tuberculosis, malaria, and AIDS.
- Preventive measures for vector-borne diseases.

Poor countries tend to lack large numbers of scientific and technological personnel, and scientists and technological experts also tend to emigrate to developed countries for better employment opportunities. The development of a good primary health care system with adequate provisions of essential health services would be a quicker and more sustainable solution to improve health. The findings of an independent effect of primary care on reduced mortality are particularly relevant as it represents a specific mechanism for addressing at least some of the health impacts of growing social inequalities.

The promotion of primary health care may serve as a more feasible and less expensive strategy for combating mortality and for reducing socioeconomic disparities in health, compared with either social policy that addresses sociodemographic determinants of health or behavioural modifications. Improving primary health care resources would also lead to improvements in both material conditions and better management of conditions and behaviour associated with increased psychosocial stress in countries with high levels of social inequalities. Therefore, from a policy point of view, promotion of primary health care would serve as strategy for health improvement combating the adverse impact of income inequality and other socio-economic determinants of health.

IV. Healthy Setting Approach in Capacity Building

Apart from the availability of quality primary health care, the services need to be widely accessible, particularly by disadvantaged groups. The issue of equity is essential to ensure that those with greatest needs would receive the appropriate services. Universal approach might not fully address the questions of inequity as it might not necessarily benefit the economically disadvantaged groups. There is also a gap for preventive services across different socio-economic groups despite universal availability of the services. It is important to develop a strategy that the essential services for healthy development would be integrated into their daily lives. The "Healthy Setting" approach ensures that the ethos of the setting and all the activities are mutually supportive and combine synergistically to improve health and well-being of those who live or work or receive care there. It integrates health promotion into all aspects of the setting, including all those coming into contact with that setting. This helps to bring those disadvantaged groups into contact of essential primary health care service. It helps to create the cultural for health improvement and organisational and policies changes for supporting the population to promote and improve their health.

The fundamental requirement of education for health improvement is to enable individuals or groups to have easier access to information, and to facilitate their understanding of health improvement concepts. The opportunities afforded by different settings for gaining entry to the individuals and groups therein, are of paramount importance. Green, Poland and Rootman (2000) draw a critical theory to provide a broader conceptualisation of setting, compared to the WHO (1998) definition of a setting as a place which people actively use and thus create or solve problems related to health. A setting can normally be defined as having physical boundaries, a range of people with defined roles, and an organisation. Green et al. (2000) expanded the meaning of the term to include the arenas of sustained interaction, with preexisting structures, policies, characteristics, institutional values, and both formal and informal social sanctions on behaviour. The Healthy Setting approach, such as healthy schools, healthy cities and healthy workplaces can address the determinants of health particularly the social, cultural and political aspects and facilitates organisations and institutions to create a culture for health improvement.

A positive culture for health would facilitate a higher level of health literacy within communities, leading to a collective deeper understanding of social, environmental, organisational and political factors that impact on health. Improvements in health literacy can help individuals tackle the determinants of health better as they build up the personal, cognitive and social skills which determine the ability of individuals to gain access to, understand and use information to promote and maintain good health (Nutbeam, 2000). Community members are likely to be more empowered to engage in debates around local health issues, and more enabled to collaborate with others in advocating for change at community and government level, thus supporting the original intent of the Ottawa Charter.

V. Case Studies Demonstrating How Different Healthy Setting Approaches Could Strengthen Social Capital

Healthy City

The approach of the "Healthy City Programme" (HCP) is based on the philosophy and assumption that enhancement of health (in its broadest sense) can be achieved through improvements in certain social, cultural and economic conditions, together with changes in human attitudes; initiatives in improvement of personal and environmental health. A high degree of participation and control by the public over the decisions affecting their lives, health and well-being is an important characteristic of a "Healthy City" (Tsouros, 1993; WHO, 1997). HCP would be one alternative way to solve public health problems which result from complex social, economic, political, biological, genetic and environmental causes.

Healthy City project in developing countries

The HCP strategy advocates intersectoral approaches to health development with a strong focus on determinants of health (environmental, social and economic) and puts health issues onto the urban agenda. A study by Harpham, Burton and Blue (2001) reported the first evaluation of five cities (Cox's Bazaar, Bangladesh; Dar es Salaam, Tanzania; Fayoum, Egypt; Managua, Nicaragua; and Quetta, Pakistan) based on the WHO's HCP approach (WHO, 1995):

- Political mobilisation and community participation in preparing and implementing a municipal health plan
- Increased awareness of health issues in urban development efforts by municipal and national authorities, including non-health ministers
- Capacity of municipal government in management of urban problems and partnership with communities and community-based organisations (CBOs) in improving living conditions, and
- Network establishment.

The main activities selected by the projects were awareness-raising and environmental improvement, particularly solid waste disposal. Two cities used the "setting approach" of the healthy city concept effectively. Markets and schools were targeted. There was also evidence that understanding of environment-health links was increased across stakeholders. Most projects of the cities achieved effective inter-sectoral collaborations.

Task forces based on settings have been found to be an effective way of facilitating intersectoral collaboration in implementation. In Cox's Bazaar, an action plan was implemented through six task forces; land development and infrastructure, environment, poverty alleviation, education, health and tourism. Many sectors were represented in more than one task force so lateral coordination could be more feasible.

In Dar es Salaam, sectors had come together in different settings such as schools and markets. All departments of the City Commission and relevant ministries, NGO, CBO, and WHO and other partners, participated in the consultation to produce thematic papers on the following topics:

- development context,
- environment profile,
- housing and health,
- food safety,
- school health,
- water, sanitation and health,
- health profile,
- healthy hospital, urban life and mental health, and
- the key players in the area of health.

In Fayoum, the HCP developed early linkages with other government institutions (education, agriculture, transport, sanitation, production and social) as activities carried out required greater associations with local planning units, community development societies and the communities. HCP also aims to reduce inequalities in health by focusing on improving the health and environmental conditions of the poor.

From the preliminary analysis of the evaluation of HCP in the five cities, good progress was made to build up human and social capitals. The project created a group of skilled, innovative and creative people who are now engaged in their communities and participate in governance. The HCP has also been successful in "gluing" the communities together both formally with inter-sectoral collaboration and informally through a strong social network. The strong human and social capitals can lead to strong community capitals which can build the capacity of the community to improve the health of the population.

Healthy City project in Hong Kong

In Hong Kong, the Haven of Hope Christian Service (HOHCS), a non-governmental organisation based on its service foundation of more than forty years coupled with the commitment to the local community, initiated in 1997 the development of Tseung Kwan O (TKO) New Town into the first "Healthy City" in Hong Kong. This was later incorporated into the Sai Kung District Council in 2002, which represented the transfer of ownership to the community. This bottom-up approach, while a stark contrast from most Healthy Cities in other parts of the world, bears the strategic advantage in building up inter-sectoral partnership with different stakeholders in the community. The stakeholders range from the district council, government departments, corporations, non-governmental organisations, schools, housing estates, commercial enterprises, community bodies to local people. They are engaged first through publicity events, a website and regular newsletters; then, participation at in different programmes addressing health needs identified through community diagnosis; and further on, collaborating with the scheme to plan, implement and evaluate health-promoting campaigns conducive to shared ownership of the "Healthy and Safe City" movement. The project addressed the social, economic and environmental determinants of health.

Community diagnosis was conducted in 2000 to identify health needs and set priorities for actions. A follow-up community health survey was conducted in 2006 to assess the impact of interventions under "Healthy City" and shed light on the way forward. The results of evaluation of the interventions show:

- Over 65% perceived their health status as very good or quite good in both surveys
- Increase in awareness in more physical activity and healthier diet ("five-a-day"), though still not meeting optimal level in behaviour terms
- Over 80% perceived family relationships as very good or quite good in both surveys
- Significant improvement in neighbourhood relationships: 61% rated very good or quite good in 2006 as compared with 51% in 2000
- More people showed concern for local affairs (24% in 2006 as compared with 19% in 2000) and participated in volunteer services (42% in 2006 as compared with 30% in 2000)
- Significant rise from 19% to 35% of respondents knowing about "Healthy City".

The bottom-up approach facilitates flexibility in building intersectoral partnerships and encourages innovations in implementing local solutions to address local problems by pooling local resources among stakeholders. The incorporation of "Healthy City" into the Sai Kung District Council signified the transfer of ownership of the movement to the community so as to encourage participation from all parties. While a great deal of effort has gone into making the environment more conducive to better physical health of the local people in the earlier years, interventions for the psycho-social dimensions of health should follow so that the holistic health of the local people and community can be realised in the long run. It is important that people feel a strong sense of belonging to the community for them to want to participate and contribute in its best interests.

Healthy Workplace

Healthy workplace provides all members of the workforce with physical, psychological, social and organisational conditions that promote health and safety. It enables the workforce at different levels to increase control of their own health and to improve it (WHO, 1999). In return a more stable, committed and productive workforce can be established. Health protection and promotion of health are two important concepts to the achievement of healthy workplace. A healthy workplace offers the ideal setting for introducing health promotion programmes and also the non-occupational factors as determinants of health of workers. It also helps to link families and communities together.

Healthy workplace project in China

The Shanghai Health Education Institute, the Ministry of Health and WHO launched a model healthy workplace project in four enterprises between 1993 and 1995 (WHO, 1999). The project aimed to implement a comprehensive approach with objectives to create healthy work environments, encourage healthy lifestyles and reduce the incidence of occupational diseases and industrial accidents.

Three surveys were conducted during the study period. The first survey established baseline data and guided the development of an action plan, the second measured mid-term progress and the last evaluated the project outcomes. Using data collected from the baseline survey and focus group discussions, the factories developed multifaceted work plans focused on promoting healthy lifestyles (smoking and drinking behaviours), controlling common diseases (hypertension, ulcers, laryngitis and cervical erosion), reducing occupational health risks (exposure to noise, carbon monoxide, silica and cotton dust), improving the general work environment (e.g. better garbage disposal, expanded green space) and strengthening basic and occupational health care services.

The occupational health strategy attempted to control the hazards at the source through purchase and use of new equipment and reorganisation of work processes. In addition, the use of hearing protection and dust masks markedly increased following a labour union mandate and intensive health education. Among the outcomes were:

- Reduced smoking rates and increase in physical exercise among males
- Decreased noise and dust levels
- Development of health-promoting policies (e.g. smoking, occupational protection and diet)
- Reduced salt content in canteen food
- Improved health services (e.g. hypertension management programme)
- Cleaner environment (e.g. improved toilet facilities and waste disposal)
- Decreased prevalence of target diseases (e.g. ulcers, laryngitis)
- Integration of health promotion and protection into ongoing management practices.

The project experience has been shared with professionals in healthy workplace development in Shanghai and other cities in China. The four initial enterprises continue to host visitors to share their experience of healthy workplace development.

Health Promoting School

The school is a fundamental institution not only in building educational outcomes, but also creating opportunities for improving the health status of students and enabling them to be active participants in their communities (St Leger, 2001). Health Promoting School (HPS) is one pathway to achieve these aims. The essential elements of HPS include improvement in the school's physical and social environment, active promotion of the self-esteem of all pupils by demonstrating that everyone can make a contribution to the life of the school, development of the health promoting potential of the school health services beyond routine screening towards active support for the curriculum, and development of good links between the school, home and the community. HPS can help to ensure sustained positive changes and encourage the schools to address the intertwined social, educational, psychological, and health needs of school children. A study by Lee, Tsang, Lee and To (2001) has shown that students of the prevocational schools (PVS), known as alternative high schools, were at higher risk for most categories of health risk behaviours than mainstream schools when adjusted for the demographic factors. The findings suggested that the school environment is an influential factor on lifestyle behaviour of the students.

HPS and Healthy Schools Award (HSA) schemes have been developed in several European countries. They provide a structured framework for development as well as a system of monitoring and recognition of achievement (Rogers, 1998). Positive award-related changes in terms of children's health behaviour, and the culture and organisation of the school have been demonstrated (Moon, 1999). Promoting health during adolescence through the concept of HPS is one of the most important investments that any society can, and should make for positive youth development (Lee, 2004).

Health Promoting Schools (HPS) project in Macedonia

Children in communities exposed to rapid changes such as a war or refugee crisis are forced to learn quickly, and more quickly than children in stable environments. They become more receptive and skilful in recognising and dealing with changes. A "Safe Schools in a Community at Risk" was initially designed to reduce a general feeling of insecurity in the children and their teachers, and to restore the lost trust of the multi-ethnic school and community faced with the crisis. The project was carried out in the northwest of Macedonia, a region characterised by a rich multicultural tradition which is a key part of the Macedonian concept of HPS (Kostarova, 2005).

The project was highly participatory, democratic and multi-level in its approach to the problem. The project started with networking and cooperation amongst teachers, school heads, and students. The subject of "violence" was initially regarded as a taboo and was gradually introduced in a sensitive way into the schools' activities.

The children's personal experiences of action, expressed through their numerous performances as creators or leading characters, no doubt fostered the development of children's own significance and an awareness of their new roles. They could be recognised as an attempt to address the challenges of transforming a dangerous environment and threats into experiences shaping their own well-being and the well-being of the community. The project demonstrated that the health promotion approach to the crisis, in which parents and other adults recognised and utilised the potential and energy of children, would help to transform the community into a landscape that nourished development and health for all.

Health Promoting Schools (HPS) project in Hong Kong

The Centre for Health Education and Health Promotion of the Chinese University of Hong Kong launched the Hong Kong HSA (HKHSA) in 2001, building on the concept of HPS to encourage educational achievement and better health (Lee, 2002). The HKHSA scheme also aims to promote staff development, parental education, involvement of the school community and linkage with different stakeholders as a way of improving the health and well-being of the pupils, parents, staff and the broader community. This concept is very much in line with the research literature on school effectiveness and improvement. The indicators examined to evaluate the success of the HKHSA reflect outcomes related to both health and education and are not limited to changes in population health status. The early results demonstrated significant improvements in various aspects of student health and also improvement in school culture and organisation. Differences were observed when data from the pre- and post-surveys of the students attending schools which reached a certain level of HPS standard, as indicated by the HSA, were compared with students whose schools did not receive the award (Lee, Cheng, Fung and St Leger, 2006). Students' satisfaction with life improved if their schools adopted the HPS concept comprehensively. The results suggest that comprehensive implementation of HPS would contribute to differences in certain behaviours and self reported health and academic status. Results generated from those studies provide valuable data about how the health promoting school approach can enhance the health and well-being of all school users.

VI. Health and Social Capital: Mutually Interactive

The case studies discussed above have provided evidence to suggest the important role of primary health care in health improvement by a more holistic and comprehensive approach. The benefits of good primary health care for socio-economically disadvantaged people have also been shown.

The case studies in Section 4 have demonstrated how Healthy City, Healthy Workplace and Healthy School projects have led to positive changes in health. These improvements range from changes of individual health behaviour and health status to changes in policies, organisational practice, culture and environment (physical and social) becoming more conclusive for health. Healthy setting shifts away from specific health behaviour towards creating the conditions that are supportive of health and well-being. It shifts the focus from risk factors and population groups to organisational change. The organisation change would ensure sustainability of the system.

The case studies from good primary health care and healthy setting have also shown how interventions there would build up human capital as they also increase social, natural and economic capital as well. Pre-requisite for health needs to eliminate range of adverse factors such as poor housing, inadequate food, limited education, prolonged unemployment, poor access to primary health care and few opportunities for leisure and recreation. If primary health care were to work hand in hand with different healthy settings, it would remove hindrance factors and provide the enabling factors for better population health.

The interconnectedness of primary health care and healthy setting can tackle prevention at primary, secondary and tertiary levels effectively and efficiently. At primary prevention level, the primary health care team can be very useful resource personnel in empowering the community to prevent them exposing themselves to health risk factors and to adopt a healthy lifestyle. At secondary prevention level, screening programmes can be implemented successfully for different age groups if different settings can strengthen the educational perspectives of different screening programmes for their respective client groups. At tertiary level of prevention, it is even more important that the primary health care team members need to work closely with different settings so those with health problems can be managed in their natural environment. Primary health care can be highly effective if management of health problems can take place where they live and/or work or study. The healthy setting approach can create an environment conducive to health and facilitate care in people's natural environment. This would adjuvant recovery and rehabilitation of people with chronic health conditions.

Healthy setting is acting at macro-level of health improvement. It cannot be fully successful if there is nothing at micro-level or individual level. The changes of organisational practices and policies on their own will only facilitate changes but health improvement will not happen without individual actions. However, if individuals are only working on their own, they will face many barriers for health improvement as many factors are beyond control of individual and even the health care sector.

Primary health care services can serve to bridge the gap between macro and micro levels and also pull the community resources together for efficient use. Primary health care serves individuals and families but also the neighbourhood communities. The synergistic effect of effective primary health care and the healthy setting approach can serve as a new model of health improvement and building up human and social capital in meeting the challenges of health as result of rapid urbanisation and globalisation.

Acknowledgements

This chapter is based on the Thematic Paper "Improving Health and Building Human Capital through an Effective Primary Care System and Healthy Setting Approach" for the Knowledge Network on Urban Settings of WHO Kobe Centre for Health Development and submitted to WHO Commission on the Social Determinants of Health in 2006. I would like to thank Dr. Andrew KIYU Dr. PH, the then Deputy Director, Sarawak Health, Malaysia, Dr Helia Molina Milman, Pontifica Universidad Catolica de Chile, and Dr Jorge de la Jara, Pontifica Universidad Catolica de Chile for their expert inputs for the thematic paper.

References

Black, R. E., Morris, S.S., Bryce, J. (2003). Where and why are 10 million children dying every year? *Lancer, 361*, 2226–2234.

Blakely, T. A., Lochner, K., and Kawachi, I. (2002). Metropolitan area income inequality and self-rated health – a multi-level study. *Social Science & Medicine, 54*, 65–77.

Bryce, J., el Arifeen, S., Pariyo, G., Lanata, C. F., Gwatkin, D., Habicht, J-P., and the Multi-Country Evaluation of IMCI Study Group (2003). Reducing child mortality: Can public health deliver? *Lancet, 362*, 233–241.

Coleman, J. S. (1990). *The foundations of social theory.* Cambridge, MA: Harvard University Press, pp.300–321.

Farmer, F. L., Stokes, C. S., and Fisher, R. H. (1991). Poverty, primary care and age-specific mortality. *J Rural Health, 7*, 153–169.

Green, L. W., Poland, B., and Rootman, I. (2000). The Settings Approach to Health Promotion. In B. Poland, L.W. Green and I. Rootman (Eds). *Setting for Health Promotion: Linking Theory and Practice.* Thousands Oaks, CA: Sage.

Hancock T. (1993). Health, human development and the community eco-system: three ecological models. *Health Promotion International, 8 (1)*, 41–47,

Hancock T (2001). People partnership and human progress: building community capital. *Health Promotion International, 16(3)*, 275–280.

Harpham, T., Burton, S., Blue, I. (2001). Healthy city projects in developing countries: the first evaluation. *Health Promotion International, 16(2)*, 11–125.

Islam, M. K., Merlo, J., Kawachi, I., Lindstrom, M., Gerdtham, U. G. (2006). Social capital and health: Does egalitarian matter? A literature review. *International Journal for Equity in Health, 5*:3.

Jones, G., Steketee, R. W., Black, R. E., Bhutta Z. A., Morris. S. S. and Bellagio Child Survival Study Group (2003). How many child deaths can we prevent this year? *Lancet, 362*, 159–164.

Kawachi, I., Kennedy, B. P., and Glass, R. (1999). Social capital and self-rated health: A contextual analysis, *Am J Public Health, 89(9)*, 1187–1193.

Kawachi, I., and Kennedy, B. P. (1997). Health and social cohesion: Why care about income inequality? *BMJ, 314*, 1037–1040.

Kawachi, I., Kennedy, B. P., Lochner, K., and Prothrow-Stith, D. (1997). Social capital, income inequality, and mortality. *Am J Public Health*, 87,1491–1498.

Kennedy, B. P., Kawachi, I., and Prothrow-Stith, D. (1996). Income distribution and mortality: cross sectional ecological study of the Robin Hood index in the United States. *BMJ*, 312(7037), 1004–1007.

Kostarova, L. (2005). Empowering children for risk-taking-children's participation as a health promotion strategy in the "Safe Schools in a Community Risk" project. *Promotion and Education, X11*(3–4), 142–143.

Lee, A. (2002). Helping schools to promote healthy educational environments as new initiatives for school based management: The Hong Kong Healthy Schools Award Scheme. *Promotion and Education*, Suppl 1 (Special issue for the Symposium on Health Education, December 2001), 29–32.

Lee, A. (2004). Helping students to adopt healthy lifestyle and positive youth development through school setting: Hong Kong experience of Health Promoting Schools. *HK Journal of Paediatrics, 9*, 325–328.

Lee, A., and Abdullah, A. S. M. (2003). Severe Acute Respiratory Syndrome: Challenge for public health practice in Hong Kong. *Journal of Epidemiology and Community Health, 57*, 655–658.

Lee, A., Cheng, F., Fung, Y., and St Leger, L. (2006). Can Health Promoting Schools contribute to the better health and well being of young people: Hong Kong experience? *Journal of Epidemiology and Community Health, 60*, 530–536.

Lee, A., Tsang, K. K., Lee, S. H., To, C. Y. (2001). A YRBS at alternative high schools and main stream schools in Hong Kong. *J School Health, 71*(9), 443–447.

Lee, A., Wong, J., Lam, C., Fung, Y., Kan, W., and Leung, P. (2007). Children with regular family doctors have better psycho-social health and health behaviours. *Australian Family Physician, 36* (3), 180–183.

Lochner, K., Pamuk, E., Makuc, D., Kennedy, B., and Kawachi, I. (2001). State-level income inequality and individual mortality risk: A prospective, multilevel study. *Am J Public Health, 91*, 385–391.

Macinko, Starfield, & Shi (2003). The contribution of primary care systems to health outcomes within Organisation for Economic Cooperation and Development (OECD) countries, 1970–1998. *Health Services Research, 38*, 831–865.

McBride, N. (2000). The Western Australian School Health Project: Comparing the effects of intervention intensity on organizational support for school health promotion. *Health Education Research, 15*(1), 59–72.

McLaughlin, D. K., and Stokes, C. S, (2002). Income inequality and mortality in US counties. Does minority racial concentration matter? *American Journal of Public Health, 92*, 99–104.

Mellor, J. M., and Milyo, J. (2001). Re-examining the evidence of an ecological association between income inequality and health. *Journal of Health Politics, Policy and Law, 26*, 487–522.

Moon, A. M., Mullee, M. A., Rogers, L., Thompson, R. L., Speller, V. and Roderick, P. (1999). Helping schools to become health-promoting environments – an evaluation of the Wessex Healthy Schools Award. *Health Promotion International, 14*, 111–122.

Social Capital and Health

Navarro, V., and Shi, L. (2001). The political context of social inequalities and health. *Social Science and Medicine, 52(3),* 481–491.

Nutbeam, D. (2000). Health literacy as a public health goal: a challenge for contemporary health education and communication strategies into the 21ˢᵗ century. *Health Promotion International, 15*(3), 259–267.

O'Malley, A. S., Forrest, C. B., Politzer, R. M., Wulu, J. T., and Shi, L. (2005). Health Center Trends, 1994–2001: What do they portend for the Federal Growth Initiative? *Health Affairs, 24,* 465–472.

Phongsavan, P., Chey, T., Bauman, A., Brooks, R., Silove, D. (2006). Social capital, socio-economic status and psychological distress among Australian adults. *Social Science & Medicine, 63,* 2546–2561.

Putnam, R. D. (1993). *Making democracy work. Civic traditions in modern Italy.* Princeton, NJ: Princeton University Press.

Rogers, E. (1995). *Diffusion of Innovations.* 4th edition, New York, NY: The Free Press.

Rogers, E., Moon, A. M., Mullee, M. A., Speller, V. M. and Roderick, P. J. (1998). Developing the "health-promoting school" – a national survey of healthy school awards. *Public Health, 112,* 37–40.

Sampson, R. J., and Groves, W. B. (1984). Community structure and crime: Testing social-disorganization theory. *Am J Sociol, 94,* 774–802.

Sampson, R. J., Raudenbush, S. W., and Earls, F. (1997). Neighborhoods and violent crime: A multilevel study of collective efficacy. *Science, 277,* 918–924.

Shi, L. (1994). Primary care, specialty care, and life chances. *Journal of Health Care for the Poor and Underserved, 24,* 431–458.

Shi, L., Macinko, J., Starfield, B., Politzer, R., and Xu, J. (2005). Primary care, race, and mortality in US states. *Social Science and Medicine, 61,* 65–75.

Shi, L., Regan, J., Politzer, R. M., and Luo, J. (2000). Community health centers and racial/ethnic disparities in healthy life. *Int J Health Serv. 31,* 567–582

Shi, L., and Starfield, B. (2000). Primary care, income inequality, and self-rated health in the United States: a mixed-level analysis. *Int J Health Serv. 30,* 541–555.

Shi, L., Starfield, B., Kennedy, B., and Kawachi, I. (1999). Income inequality, primary care, and health indicators. *J Fam Pract, 48,* 275–284.

Shi, L., Starfield, B., Politzer, R., and Regan, J. (2002). Primary care, self-rated health, and reductions in social disparities in health. *Heath Services Research, 37,* 529–550.

Shi, L., Starfield, B., Xu, J., Politzer, R., and Regan, J. (2003). Primary care quality: Community health center and health maintenance organization. *South Med J, 96,* 787–795.

St Leger, L. (2001). Schools, health literacy and public: possibilities and challenges. *Health Promotion International, 16*(2), 197–205.

Starfield, B., and Shi, L. (2002). Policy relevant determinants of health: An international perspective. *Health Policy*, 603, 201–218.

Starfield, B. (1992). *Primary care: Concept, evaluation, and policy.* New York, NY: Oxford University Press.

Subramanian, S. V., Blakely, T. A., and Kawachi, I. (2003) Income inequality as a public health concern where do we stand? Commentary on "Is exposure to income inequality a public health concern?". *Health Services Research*, 38, 153–167.

Tones, K., and Green, J. (2004). *Health Promotion: Planning and strategies.* London: Sage.

Tsouros, A. (1993). *World Health Organisation Healthy Cities Project: A project becomes a movement.* Milan: SORGRESS.

WHO (1995). *School Health Promotion Series 1: Report of the Workshop on School Health Promotion Sydney.* Manila: World Health Organisation.

WHO (1997). *Twenty steps for development of a Healthy Cities project.* World Health Organisation, Regional Office for Europe.

WHO (1998). *The WHO approach to health promotion: Settings for health.* Geneva: World Health Organisation.

WHO (1999). *Healthy Settings: Regional guidelines for the development of Healthy Workplaces.* World Health Organisation, Regional Office for the Western Pacific.

Wilkinson, R. G. (1996). *Unhealthy societies: The afflictions of inequality.* London: Routledge.

Wong, W., Lee, A., Tsang, K. K., and Wong, S. (2004). How did general practitioners protect themselves, their staff and their families during the Severe Acute Respiratory Syndrome epidemic in Hong Kong? *Journal of Epidemiology and Community Health*, 58, 180–185.

World Bank (1995). *Monitoring Environmental Progress (MEP). A report on work in progress.* Washington, DC: The World Bank.

7

The Relationship Between Gangs and Social Capital in Hong Kong

Tina L. ROCHELLE,
Tit Wing Lo
and Sik Hung NG

Social capital refers to "the institutions, relationships, and norms that shape the quality and quantity of a society's social interactions . . . social capital is not just the sum of the institutions which underpins society. It is the glue that holds them together." (World Bank, 2005). This widely cited definition and other similar ones (Bourdieu, 1986; Coleman, 1988; Putnam, 1993) assume that social capital is a positive societal good. Yet social capital also has its dark side: it can go wrong leading to "negative" social capital. For example, although bonding social capital (see below) can do good to group members through close relationships and mutual support, it has the potential of them becoming intolerant of individual diversity (Baum, 1999). Further, as Putnam (2000) has acknowledged, if bonding becomes too strong, it has the unintended consequence of excluding outsiders, dividing and polarising society, and becoming negative. Such adverse effects constitute the "dark" side of social capital (Office for National Statistics, 2001).

The bright and dark sides of social capital referred to above are practised legally. Social capital is also practised underground, for good or ill, by nationalist resistance movements, religious sects, gangs, mafias, terrorists, and similarly subterranean groups. The present chapter is about the social capital of gangs. By linking gangs with social capital, the present chapter will show, first, the usefulness of a social capital perspective for understanding gang behaviour, structure and culture. For this purpose key concepts of social capital will be introduced. Second, research on gangs in Hong Kong and elsewhere will be summarised to illuminate how gangs build social capital in ways that may lie hidden in the existing social capital literature that has conventionally been focused on "non-deviant" institutions, relationships, and norms that glue society together. The present chapter will focus on a series of topics dealing with gangs and Triads in Hong Kong, gangs' structural social capital and their cognitive social capital.

I. Social Capital and Gangs:
Introduction and Key Concepts

Greatly influenced by the early work of Cloward and Ohlin (1960) and Thrasher (1963), modern gang research strives to understand the interactions between gangs and the macro social and community environment. Marginalisation and the lack of social capital in communities are often seen as important causes of gang formation. Putnam (2000) and others (e.g., Weerman and Decker, 2005) have argued that in neighbourhoods with weak social capital, where youths are poorly integrated into wider social networks, they are inclined to create their own forms of social capital in the form of gangs. The early study by Whyte (1943/1993) provides a vivid account of how low social capital in a slum contributed to the emergence of gangs that in turn had developed their own forms of social capital. It should be noted that low or declining social capital above ground is neither a necessary nor a sufficient condition for the formation of gangs, although such a condition tends to be highly correlated with gangs.

Gang research has observed the increasing prominence of economics in the genesis and functioning of modern gangs in recent decades. Researchers have noted that the nature of gang activity has evolved as a result of economic restructuring in urban areas, and gangs in many instances have subsequently turned into vehicles of individual economic gain. In other words, gangs have become primarily economic entities in the illegitimate economy instead of strictly delinquent groups, and consequently, gang membership has also taken on an economic character. As such, gang participation can no longer be considered solely as merely delinquent behaviour, but should also be considered as a form of economic action (Pih, de la Rosa, Rugh and Mao, 2007). This is particularly so in the case of the informal sector, or on the margins of the organised economy, or in sprawling urban slums or shanty towns, or in rural-urban peripheral areas. Labour mobilisation at a large scale has often been carried out with the help of gangs, for example, human trafficking, fishermen for high-seas expeditions, railway construction projects, and so forth.

It is no easy task to conduct economic activities that are highly organised. This is doubly challenging for gangs because their illicit activities put them on the wrong side of the law. To be successful a gang must have developed an enabling organisational structure along with norms for internal control, and forged alliances with other gangs and with legal operators for greater control over society. Those structures, norms and alliances that enable gangs to survive and thrive can be considered as forms of social capital.

Specifically, many of the features of structural and cognitive social capital (Krishna and Uphoff, 2002) that are normally associated with societal good, for example, mutually beneficial networks and associations, as well as trust and reciprocity, are being religiously practised by gang members underground for their own illicit or anti-social purposes (Elliot, 2001). How this is carried out will be discussed in the sections that follow.

In addition to structural and cognitive social capital, the concepts of bonding, bridging, and linking social capital are also useful for understanding gangs. Bonding capital refers to interpersonal relations among members of the same group. The group's relations with similar other groups constitute bridging capital. At a still more macro level of relationships, different sectors are involved, for example between NGOs and businesses, or between gangs and the government. These cross-sector linkages are referred to as linking capital. In recent years, Hong Kong Triads (see below) have become adept at adjusting themselves to a changing environment. Chu (2005) reports three general trends in Triad activities. First, Triad members from different gang societies tend to group together to run profitable criminal projects. Second, they will team up with legitimate entrepreneurs to monopolise a newly developed market. Lastly, Triads are reported to be increasingly investing in legitimate businesses. However, the extent of their involvement is not known.

II. Gangs and Triads in Hong Kong

Hong Kong society is experiencing increasing problems with youth gangs, their crime and their unemployment (Cheng, 2005; Wong, 2000). The mass media have done much in recent years to publicise shocking crimes committed by youth gangs (Hong Kong Standard, 1999; SCMP, 1999; SCMP, 2007), and there is general concern about juvenile group violence (China Daily, 2007). Public concern also centres on the involvement of youths in local organised crime, and the exploitation of youths in Triad organised crime.

The word "triad" means the unity of three essential elements of existence: heaven, earth and humanity (Zhang and Chin, 2003). Rooted in historical events in China and in keeping with international Chinese migration, Triads as a criminal subculture evolved in many parts of the world initially as mutual help groups, clans or associations (Lee, Broadhurst and Beh, 2006). The fact that Triads initially emerged as mutual-help groups demonstrates the links between gangs and structural and cognitive capital, features which will be discussed below.

The Chinese Triads have gained notoriety over the years, much of which is related to the way in which they are portrayed in sensational media reports and films eulogising gangs (Chu, 2005). Triad societies are alleged to be the largest, most dangerous and closely organised criminal entities in Hong Kong. According to the Hong Kong Police, there are around 50 Triad groups and many of their members are minor localised gangs comprising delinquent youths (Hong Kong Police, 2007). The number of Triad members is reported to be quadruple that of the Hong Kong Police Force (Lo, 1992a). Although Triads as a whole are no longer believed to be very cohesive, they have become modernised, internationalised and commercialised (Choi and Lo, 2004). Triads are known to attract police attention at the lower levels of their activities where their involvement in criminal activities is primarily through youth and street gangs (Ip, 1999). The survival of Triad societies is thought to accelerate the formation of juvenile gangs (Choi and Lo, 2004), and Triad-sponsored youth gang relations are known to be an established problem in Hong Kong (Hong Kong Police, 2007; Hong Kong Standard, 1998).

Triad societies are reported to be involved in illegitimate enterprises such as gambling, prostitution and drugs, as well as legitimate businesses (Chu, 2000). Triad activities are not limited to Hong Kong and its adjacent regions, such as Macau and mainland China. Reports from Southeast Asia, North America and the UK in recent years demonstrate that Triad activities, such as extortion, gambling, drug trafficking and immigrant smuggling, are on the rise (Dubro, 1992). Triad gang problems are therefore a global issue and not merely a regional issue.

Triads and other traditional crime groups, such as the Italian mafia, place much emphasis and importance on factors such as group identity, loyalty, and familial relationship to create a sense of belonging and secure personal commitment to sustain gang activities. Consequently, Triad societies have developed various levels of organisational obligations such as rules, rituals, oaths, codes of conduct and chains of command (Zhang and Chin, 2003).

Triads are a menace to Hong Kong society, thriving on public fear through their notorious mystery and intimidation. However, not all organised crime in Hong Kong is committed by Triads. According to the Hong Kong Police, in the past decade only 3–4% of criminal cases were related to the Triads. In 2004, a total of 81,315 crimes were reported in Hong Kong, however, only 2.9% of these were Triad-related cases (Chu, 2005).

Lee and Lo (1994) have identified Triad domination in public housing estates in Hong Kong, and a significant relationship between youth gang subculture and Triad societies. Involvement in gang activities is thought to weaken the social bonding between young people and conventional institutions, thus leading these individuals to commit crime (Wong, Lee and Lo, 1995). Another study conducted in Hong Kong found that Triad subculture is a big influence on secondary school students; in addition to this it has been observed that there has been a sharp increase in teenage girls' involvement in gang activities (Hong Kong Federation of Youth Groups, 2005).

The rapid development of new towns in Hong Kong has also become a breeding ground for gangs of delinquents. Research has observed that, concomitant with population increase and rise in commercial activities in new towns, more youth gangs are emerging and the juvenile crime rate has increased. Triad societies have been observed to take root as soon as residents have moved into the new towns, with Triad societies recruiting young people as gang members. Gang activities are not limited to public housing estates, however, and have been reported to occur over entire new towns (Hong Kong Federation of Youth Groups, 2000).

For many young people in Hong Kong, joining a gang is a common experience. Young gang members often live in the same neighbourhood, are childhood friends or classmates. Predominant reasons for younger individuals to join gangs are to make friends and have company. Many individuals derive satisfaction and a sense of heroism and security from gang activities. While prior to gang involvement, individuals may feel excluded from society, or from the community in which they live, gang involvement often leads to feelings of solidarity, inclusion in the group and a sense of belonging. These and other benefits of gang membership are discussed in more detail in the following section in relation to the links between gangs and the creation and sustainability of structural capital.

Gangs and Structural Capital

There are a number of links between gangs and components of the structural social capital. Structural capital consists of regulated networks that foster mutually beneficial relationships and gangs can be seen as one example of a network that fosters mutual beneficial relationships for both gang members and those individuals who choose to interact or do business with gangs. This section will further explore the relationship between the structural capital and gangs, looking at how gangs can be exploited as a source of support, friendship and shared values as well as a source of protection, and how the gang can come to represent an alternative form of family.

Looking at the relationship between gangs, delinquency and lack of social recognition, it has been reported that when the family is incapable of providing guidance and protection for its younger members, the latter will look to friends and the street environment for relationships of trust and understanding. This can be seen in youths who, lacking in family bonds, construct surrogate relationships in order to protect themselves and to stave off loneliness. Research conducted by McCarthy, Hagan and Martin (2002) among homeless youths in Canada reveals the importance of having a social nucleus one can trust; a group with whom to establish relationships, which can be exploited as a resource when necessary. The gang can therefore be perceived as offering benefits, advantages and protection.

When a boy joins a gang, the likelihood of him becoming a victim of violence diminishes since he can rely on fellow gang members to protect him against danger. In this respect the gang becomes an alternative form of social organisation, a substitute for the legitimate institution, the family. Research conducted by Gatti, Angelini, Marengo, Melchiorre and Sasso (2005), looking at Genoese youth gangs in Italy, concluded that youth gangs appear to constitute a form of social relationship that makes up for the shortcomings of the family. Rather than being used solely as a protection against danger, however, this relationship seems to be exploited as a source of support, friendship, shared values, and acceptance in an environment in which esteem is often viewed as difficult to achieve. These benefits are mutual with advantages for both the individual and the gang as a whole.

Social capital research typically distinguishes familial relationships from other associations and assumes that these ties are generally closer than others, or that they represent a unique type of relationship (Lin, 2001). However, gangs and their associations can also resemble an additional or surrogate family, described in studies of inner-city life such as that of Gatti et al. (2005). Like conventional families, surrogate families, in the form of gangs, may generate interactions that provide greater access to an array of valued outcomes, such as protection from harm, feelings of kinship, sense of belonging and identity, as well as economic gain from illicit gang ventures. Gang relations include associations based on being part of the same group, being from the same area etc.

The Hong Kong Federation of Youth Groups (1993) has observed that young people in Hong Kong join gangs as a result of wanting to meet ordinary youth needs, such as having fun, seeking protection, and meeting new friends. A Hong Kong-government commissioned study on the risk factors of gang associations found that youth gang members were more susceptible to peer pressure and exposed to more negative peer and family influences, had a higher level of sensation-seeking tendency and more adverse family relations, as well as used more passive and internal coping styles. In addition, youth gang members were found to exhibit more negative school behaviour, misdemeanours and delinquency, such as fighting with, or collecting protection fees from classmates, recruiting gang members in school, threatening classmates and teachers, playing truant and committing minor offences (Tang and Davis, 1997).

Gang research in Hong Kong suggests that gang attachment begins at the pre-teen or teenage stage (Lee and Lo 1994; Lo 1984; 1992b) with youths who believe that society is treating them unfairly ready to express their dissatisfaction by means of deviant activities mainly as a result of boredom and frustration with their school work. This observation is in line with Downes' (1966) conception of dissociation. In view of the perceived boredom and hardship of school life coupled with a lack of autonomy and involvement in work, Downes argued that gang delinquency is not rooted in the "anti-social" context, but in an "anti-study" and "anti-work" context. As such, gang involvement is suggested to be a "leisure solution" not a "delinquent solution" and a way to assert self-agency and a form of group-valued identity amongst peers. The benefits and consequences of gang membership are discussed in more detail in the following sections looking at the links between gangs and the creation and sustainability of structural capital.

Social Solidarity and Inclusion

In studies conducted in Hong Kong over the last two decades[1], youths have spoken directly about their gang relationships. A

---

1 Lo, T. W. (2008). CityU Gang Research Database 1992–2008. Hong Kong: City University of Hong Kong (unpublished).

number of youths described being childhood friends with some of their fellow gang members, thus implying that the development of a gang can often be an unintentional, or as one Hong Kong gang youth described, a *"natural"* development of a collection of childhood friends from the same neighbourhood or community into a gang. Individuals begin by *"hanging out"* in their neighbourhoods while the gang begins to take form and begins to play a larger role in the lives of the individuals. One individual describes how he and his fellow gang members *"live in the same building . . . we're all about the same age and we like to hang out together"*, another respondent described how gang activities often consist of *"just spending time together and doing nothing . . . we joke and fool around with each other... or we just talk nonsense"*. Another individual went on to comment about the improvement in his mood since joining a gang: *"I am happy now because I have company"*. This demonstrates how individuals bond and how feelings of solidarity and inclusion are developed in the gang through participation in regular activities such as group members spending time with one another.

While gang members initially bond as a result of having similar backgrounds in that they are from the same neighbourhood, this enables the natural development of the gang eased by the level of trust amongst these individuals, who are from similar backgrounds and have known each other for some time. This promotes feelings of inclusion and solidarity amongst gang members who are from similar backgrounds, or those who have known one another for some time. The importance of trust is emphasised further in one respondent's comments, describing fellow gang members as *"brothers"* and *"sisters"*, reflecting the trust and importance of gang relationships among some respondents. Equality among gang members was also emphasised in the following: *"There is no power difference between us . . . .we are all equal"*.

Mutual Assistance and Reciprocity

Some individuals interviewed recognised that being part of a gang was advantageous to them in numerous ways. Several respondents described how being part of a gang offered a form of protection. While for some, being involved in a gang is a natural development of group friendships, other individuals have specific motivations for joining a gang. The subject of needing to protect one another and of feeling secure was often mentioned, as one individual explained: "*I was proud of myself after I joined the gang; I can bully others and don't have to worry about being bullied by others because I have someone to back me up when I am in trouble*". Another individual mentioned: "*As a group we're more powerful, especially when we quarrel or fight*", while another respondent described feeling happy because "*no one will bully me anymore*". This illustrates that some individuals derive a sense of security and feelings of heroism by being part of a gang, and that individuals trust their fellow gang members and will look to rely on them if they are in trouble.

These comments by Hong Kong gang members suggest that part of being in a gang for some individuals is related to delinquent behaviour in so much that, if an individual is involved in trouble, there will be fellow gang members there to support and defend him. In this sense, respondents recognised that being part of a gang helps them in numerous ways, such as if they want to fight, knowing that they will have individuals willing to defend them, or protect them. However, being in a gang is not just related to the importance of having protection when in times of trouble. As one respondent commented, "*If I have no money, my big brother will give me some money to buy some food*". While another respondent described, "*My big brother will give me money. We'll feast and he will pay for it. He told me that I can ask him for help if I have any problems*", demonstrating that gang members offer support and assistance, not just in physical terms, but also in emotional and financial terms.

Social Exclusion and Negative Impact

Social exclusion from society is often a pre-requisite of inclusion into a gang. For some respondents, having someone or a group of people to rely on was important, particularly for those individuals who were from dysfunctional backgrounds. Some gang members described a lack of support from their families: "*my family don't care*", "*my dad doesn't care*". This suggests that being involved in a gang was more important to some gang members, particularly those with a lack of familial support, almost as if the gang was family, or a form of substitute family in some respects, as McCarthy et al. (2002) have described, a "street family".

Some respondents expressed feelings of resentment for being blamed for things they did not do on the assumption that as a gang member they must be up to no good. This was particularly so for younger gang members still attending school. One gang member described: *"teachers think that we are all bad people"*. Another individual mentioned that, *"the school treats me bad...they blame me for things I haven't done"*. While another respondent commented, *"teachers tell us that it would be great if we dropped out"*. This sort of reaction against young gang members can lead to resentment of educational establishments, in addition to a response of rebelliousness from some individuals, such as becoming involved in delinquent behaviour with fellow gang members in defiance of authority, feeling that perhaps if they are being blamed for things they have not done then they may as well become involved as they have nothing to lose. This in turn creates a heightened sense of solidarity among fellow gang members and potentially leads to a deepening sense of commitment and involvement in gang life.

Individuals belong to relationships that they believe are characterised by trust and other social capital attributes (McCarthy et al., 2002). For example, gang members interviewed described their assumptions about what relationships with fellow gang members would offer in terms of benefits, such as provision of food or money when in need, or protection from harm if necessary. However, respondents also talked of the costs of joining gang life. They talked of noticing changes in themselves in terms of being influenced by other fellow gang members and exposure to new experiences, perhaps experiences to which they would not have been exposed had they not been involved in gang life. One respondent talked of a positive change in outlook since joining a gang: *"The environment is different now. I see new stuff"*, another respondent mentioned, *"I'm much smarter now"*. However, not all individuals felt that involvement in gang life was a good experience, one respondent was quick to acknowledge that negative bonding in relation to gang life exacerbated bad habits: *"I smoke more often, I swear too much, I spend more money. I may not go home for 3 or 4 days. My temper has grown worse. When I'm with my friends I will take drugs which make me confused."*. This emphasises the negative impact that joining a gang can have on individuals. While these individuals may not be forced to behave in the way they do when they are in the gang, the influence of social pressure to join in activities should not be underestimated.

A negative impact of gangs is that they are seen as significant facilitators of crime. American research has demonstrated that gang members are disproportionately arrested and that they are likely to be significantly more delinquent than non-gang youths, and that delinquency levels increase once youths have entered a gang. Bradshaw (2005) has demonstrated that youths in gangs are more delinquent than those individuals who had delinquent friends who are not involved in a gang. Being a gang member facilitates delinquent behaviour and research has shown that delinquent behaviour adversely affects individual transition to adult status. On the assumption of social network theory, gang membership is expected to have an independent effect on the likelihood of disorderly transitions, over and above the impact of delinquent behaviour (Thornberry, Krohn, Lizotte, Smith, and Tobin, 2003). As an important and powerful social network, the gang constrains the behaviour of its members, limits access to pro-social, legitimate networks which may act as social capital artefact in facilitating adult transitions, and increases the criminal stronghold of its members. All of these characteristics combine to cut the individual off from conventional pursuits and increase the likelihood of deviant behaviour in adult life.

III. Gangs and Cognitive Capital

The gang subculture that operates underground in Hong Kong has its own language code, values and social norms, as well as requirements for winning and granting trust. From a social capital perspective that has been described earlier, these sub-cultural elements constitute cognitive capital. The language code can be illustrated by "Triad slang", a kind of foul language widely practised by members of youth gangs in Hong Kong. Some gang members believe that they should use such language because they deem it as appropriate to their identity as a Triad gangster. Some sub-groups within gangs will also create their own language in order to exchange or disseminate information or to make fun of people who do not understand them. Youth gang members also like to make fun of each other's flaws while exaggerating their own strengths. Moreover, they often use nicknames which may have derived from their pet names or names that others called them when they were in school, as well as those from their own personality, appearance or performance in the gang.[2]

The following norms of delinquent gangs reflect the essence of sworn brotherhood and loyalty of Triad societies. Some of the norms, such as "no cheating" and "remaining loyal", can be regarded as normal if they belong to legitimate social groups. However, as Triad societies are criminal rackets that use youth gangsters to work for them in illegal operations, the norms serve as a means to control their behaviour in the course of committing crimes. In this respect, these norms, listed below, should be regarded as socially undesirable.

1. Don't "cal dai" (don't join other gangs)
2. Don't be "yee ng tsai" (no squealing)
3. Don't "po wong" (do not report anything to the police)
4. Obey Triad leaders
5. "Bong tall" (help gang members in fights)
6. "Chow kei" (give financial help to gang members in times of trouble)
7. Don't "ngau dai" (don't be scared of committing crime)
8. No cheating on gang members
9. Don't "tuk pui chek" (do not speak ill of gang members behind their back or spread disadvantageous information about them) (Lo, 1984).

Youth gangs seldom resolve problems through legitimate means but rather by violence or evasion, indicating that gang members believe that violence can solve problems. A popular pastime for

---

2   Lo, T. W. (2008). CityU Gang Research Database 1992–2008. Hong Kong: City University of Hong Kong (unpublished).

gangs or a way to have fun is to use drugs. Substance abuse is particularly popular among youth gang members in Hong Kong. Gang members tend to believe in fate and most are also superstitious. For example, gang members may believe in the psychic, visit shamans or fortune tellers, or wear amulets or jewellery that are believed to bring them luck. They also believe in other spiritualistic or superstitious fads such as horoscopes and psychological tests reported in youth magazines.[3]

There is not much variation in how gang members spend their leisure time. Gang members only engage in activities that they deem as appropriate to their own gang culture. Common activities include gambling, going to drug parties, hanging around in fast-food shops, reading comic books, and joining activities with which they are familiar such as video games, karaoke, movies, and so on. Although other activities (e.g., football and basketball) may be "in", gang members will not be interested unless they consider them appropriate. Tattooing is also common and is enjoyed by most gang members who may want to have a (new) tattoo whenever they have the money or may even pay for other members. They also enjoy discussing tattoo styles with each other.

Patriarchal values are dominant values for Triad gangs. Female members believe that they should listen to their men. Males are central to the gang while females are treated as "accessories" or even sexual objects. Sexual relationships will not increase male members' sense of responsibility towards "their" women. Contraception, conception, and even abortion are solely the responsibility of females. Female gang members are therefore under intense psychological stress. Most male members who are married expect their wives to stay at home, particularly after they have children. The traditional roles of men and women are still highly regarded among gang members, although some women may have paid employment outside the gang (Lo, 1984).

One central ingredient of cognitive capital is trust. Trust is also an important value for gangs. In the case of Triads, given the power

---

3   Lo, T. W. (2008). CityU Gang Research Database 1992–2008. Hong Kong: City University of Hong Kong (unpublished).

distance between older leaders, known as "dai lo" or "big brother", and subordinates (normally the younger members), trust is asymmetrical. Subordinates need to win the trust of the "dai lo" through involvement in criminal activities in order to become a trusted member of the gang. Initially such involvement among subordinates will be minimal; however, over time, with increased involvement in gang activities and after building up relations with their "dai lo", younger subordinates become more committed and more involved in the gang and criminal activities, reinforcing their sense of belonging to the gang.

IV. Conclusions

A social capital approach to gangs provides important insights. This chapter has explored the links between gangs and social capital, specifically looking at the relationship between structural and cognitive capital and gangs. It hopefully contributes to a new understanding of gang behaviour from a larger social perspective.

It is noted that gangs and other criminal societies are often adept in building their own social capital despite the pressure and restrictions of social control. Social capital is needed not only for their survival but also for recruiting new members and transmitting their subculture to other gangsters. For mainstream society, the gangs' social capital is a form of "negative" social capital harmful to law and order. It is costly to fight against, and even more costly if it were ignored and allowed to grow.

Lest this chapter may appear to be one-sided in its preoccupation with "negative" social capital, we shall conclude with a statement on how correctional services may help to reduce recidivism and enhance the re-integration of ex-gangsters into mainstream society. Conventional wisdom has rightly stressed the importance of shifting ex-gangsters from their gang subculture to mainstream culture, of unlearning their old ways of satisfying their psychological, social and economic needs and relearning new ways, and so forth. A social capital perspective that recognises "positive" and "negative" elements points to a different approach. The adept skills of ex-gangsters in building (negative) social capital deserve recognition, and may be further developed but channelled in the right direction and for the right purpose (BBC, 2008; Bowman, 2006;). It would be both interesting and useful to look at ways the community could become more actively involved in the transference of gang members' skills in a positive direction.

References

Baum, F. (1999). Social capital: Is it good for your health? Issues for a public health agenda. *Journal of Epidemiology & Community Health, 53*(4), 195–196.

BBC (2008). Gang warning for city youngsters, 17 January 2008. Available online at: http://www.news.bbc.co.uk/2/hi/uk_news/england/london/7192736.htm.

Bourdieu, P. (1986). The forms of capital. In J.G. Richardson (Ed.) *The handbook of theory and research for the sociology of education* (pp. 241–258), New York: Greenwood.

Bowman, J. C. (2006). Faith-based approaches to combating gang involvement. Available online from Education Public Policy & Consulting Global Management: http://www.eppcmanagement.com/ArticlesDetail.asp?id=14.

Bradshaw, P. (2005). Terror and young teams: Youth gangs and delinquency in Edinburgh. In S.H. Decker and F.M. Weerman (Eds.), *European street gangs and troublesome youth groups* (pp. 193–218). Oxford: Altamira Press.

Cheng, H. C. H. (2005). Effectiveness of services to youth-at-risk: The case of outreaching social work. In F.W.L. Lee (Ed.), *Working with youth-at-risk in Hong Kong*. Hong Kong: Hong Kong University Press.

China Daily (2007). Juvenile criminal cases rising. *China Daily*, 5 December 2007, P03.

Choi, A., and Lo, T. W. (2004). *Fighting youth crime: A comparative study of two little dragons*. Singapore: Marshall Cavendish International.

Chu, Y. (2000). *The Triads as business*. London: Routledge.

Chu, Y. K. (2005). Hong Kong Triads after 1997. *Trends in Organized Crime, 8*(3), 5–12.

Cloward, R. A., and Ohlin, L. E. (1960). *Delinquency and opportunity*. New York: Free Press.

Coleman, J. (1988). Social capital in the creation of human capital. *American Journal of Sociology, 94*, S95–S120.

Downes, D. M. (1966). *The delinquent solution: A study in subcultural theory*. London: Routledge & Kegan Paul.

Dubro, J. (1992). *Dragons of crime: Inside the Asian underworld*. Markham, Ontario: Octopus.

Elliot, I. (2001). *Social capital and health: Literature review*.Institute of Public Health in Ireland. Unpublished report.

Gatti, U., Angelini, F., Marengo, G., Melchiorre, N., and Sasso, M. (2005). An old-fashioned youth gang in Genoa. In S.H. Decker and F.M. Weerman (Eds.), *European street gangs and troublesome youth groups* (pp. 51–80), Oxford: Altamira Press.

Hong Kong Federation of Youth Groups (1993). *The push & pull factors of joining juvenile gangs*. Hong Kong: Hong Kong Federation of Youth Groups.

Hong Kong Federation of Youth Groups (2000). *A study on youth gangs in New Town developments*. Hong Kong: Hong Kong Federation of Youth Groups.

Hong Kong Federation of Youth Groups (2005). *A study on girls in gangs*. Hong Kong: Hong Kong Federation of Youth Groups.

Hong Kong Police (2007). Available online from: http://www.info.gov.hk/police/hkp-home/english/history/history_08.htm.

Hong Kong Standard (1998). Triad-linked boys "leading teenage girls into crime". *Hong Kong Standard*, 26 March 1998.

Hong Kong Standard (1999). Youths jailed for gang rape, *Hong Kong Standard*, 17 March 1999, A05.

Ip, P.F.K. (1999). Organised crime in Hong Kong. Presented at the first seminar on "Organised Crime and the 21st Century", The University of Hong Kong, 26 June 1999.

Krishna, A., and Uphoff, N. (2002). Mapping and measuring social capital through assessment of collective action to conserve and develop watersheds in Rajasthan, India. In C. Grootaert and T. van Bastelaer (Eds.) *The role of social capital in development: An empirical assessment*. Cambridge: Cambridge University Press.

Lee, K. W., Broadhurst, R. G., and Beh, P. S. L. (2006). Triad-related homicides in Hong Kong. *Forensic Science International, 162*, 183–190.

Lee, W. L., and Lo, T. W. (1994). *Report on the study of youth problems in the Southern District*. Hong Kong: Southern District Board.

Lin, N. (2001). *Social capital: A theory of social structure and action*. New York: Cambridge University Press.

Lo, T. W. (1984). *Gang dynamics*. Hong Kong: Caritas.

Lo, T. W. (1992a). Law and order. In Y. S. Cheng and C. K. Kwong (Eds.) *The Other Hong Kong Report 1992*. Hong Kong: Chinese University of Hong Kong.

Lo, T. W. (1992b). Groupwork with youth gangs in Hong Kong. *Groupwork*, 5(1), 58–71.

McCarthy, B., Hagan, J., and Martin, M. J. (2002). In and out of harm's way: Violent victimization and the social capital of fictive street families. *Criminology*, 40(4), 831–866.

Office for National Statistics (2001). *Social capital: A review of the literature.* London: Office for National Statistics

Pih, K. K. H, de la Rosa, M., Rugh, D., and Mao, K. R. (2007). Different strokes for different gangs? An analysis of capital among Latino and Asian gang members. Unpublished report, California State University.

Putnam, R. (1993). *Making democracy work: Civic traditions in modern Italy.* Princeton, NJ: Princeton University Press

Putnam, R. (2000). *Bowling alone: The collapse and revival of American community.* New York: Simon & Schuster.

SCMP (1999). Teenager chopped to death in barbeque row, *South China Morning Post*, 28 October 1999.

SCMP (2007). Teenagers jailed for merciless attack. *South China Morning Post*, 16 June 2007, CITY4.

Tang, C., and Davis, C. (1997). *An exploration of the risk and protective factors of juvenile gangs and runaway youths in Hong Kong.* Hong Kong: Chinese University of Hong Kong.

Thornberry, T. P., Krohn, M. D., Lizotte, A. J., Smith, C. A., and Tobin, K. (2003). *Gangs and delinquency in developmental perspective.* New York: Cambridge University Press.

Thrasher, F. (1963). *The gang.* Chicago: University of Chicago Press

Weerman, F. M., and Decker, S. H. (2005). European street gangs and troublesome youth groups: Findings from the Eurogang research program. In S.H. Decker and F.M. Weerman (Eds.), *European street gangs and troublesome youth groups* (pp. 287–310). Oxford: Altamira Press.

Whyte, W. F. (1943/1993). *Street corner society: The social structure of an Italian slum*, 4th edition. Chicago: University of Chicago Press.

Wong, D. S. W. (2000). Juvenile crime and responses to delinquency in Hong Kong. *International Journal of Offender Therapy & Comparative Criminology*, 44(3), 279–292.

Wong, S. W., Lee, W. L., and Lo, T. W. (1995). *A study of youth behaviour and values in Tuen Mun: An analysis of the road to deviance.* Hong Kong: Tuen Mun District Board.

World Bank (2005). Social Capital, Available online from: http://www .worldbank.org/poverty/scapital/index.htm.

Zhang, S. and Chin, K. L. (2003). The declining significance of Triad societies in transnational illegal activities: A structural deficiency perspective. *British Journal of Criminology*, 43, 469–488.

8

"Saying Hello Everyday":
Towards the Enhancement of Social Capital Among Lonely and Isolated Older People in Modern Cities

Steven M. Shardlow, Barbara Walmsley,
Martin Johnson and Julia Ryan

Active ageing is the process of optimising
opportunities for health, participation and security
in order to enhance quality of life as people age.
It applies to both individuals and population groups.
WHO, *Active ageing: A policy framework* (2002)

I. Introduction:
Demography, Ageing Well and Social Capital

World demography is changing; in many nation states and modern cities the number of older people is set to increase dramatically both absolutely and as a proportion of the total population. In Hong Kong this has been termed the "Grey Wave", as a large population cohort ages and is followed by a much smaller cohort. Ageing, we would like to stress, is not of itself a problem. Nonetheless, many nation states and modern cities around the world face a range of social issues that arise in respect of their older populations some are generic and some culturally specific. In respect of Hong Kong, there are particular issues that arise from these demographics, as Chow comments:

> Hong Kong is also placed in a very special situation, in regard to the ageing of her population. Our system of

supporting the elderly, especially in terms of the provision of formal services, has basically been adopted from the West, with an emphasis on professionalism and modernisation. However, our value towards the elderly has remained unchanged, stressing the importance of a harmonious, rather than egalitarian relationship between generations. Hence, while we may offer the elderly the widest choice of professional services, we have yet to establish that the elderly have a right to use them. (as reported by Kwan, 2002, pp. 3–4)

Hence, the provision of services for older people must respond to their actual and perceived needs. Models of service provision cannot merely be transposed, they must take account of the cultural context in which they are provided. Most importantly, the *degree of satisfaction that the individual experiences*, as they progress through the ageing process, both of the process of ageing and also of the social support provided within their own cultural context, must be taken into account. How then can the experiences of older people be understood through the dominant conceptualisations about ageing?

- **Successful ageing**, as a concept, is usually attributed to Havighurst (1961), who argued that life should be added to extra years from which the older person should gain satisfaction. Recent discussion of successful ageing takes Rowe and Kahn's seminal (1987) paper as a pivotal initial perspective. Rowe and Kahn propounded the notion that researchers should concentrate their attention on those who demonstrate successful patterns of ageing – as identified by low morbidity; the capacity for independent living; and high levels of engagement with social activity and the joys of life – in order to identify lessons that could be applied to those who are "less successful agers".
- **Active ageing**: the originators of this concept are usually taken to be Lemon, Bengtson and Peterson (1972). [1] Literature about the components that lead to active ageing

---

1 Somewhat naively, activity theory is sometimes taken to be summed up by the aphorism "be active and live long."

has several elements. Leaving aside, for present purposes, discussion about physical health (see, for example, Chi and Leung, 1999) the most pertinent is a substantial body of material about volunteering and its impact on the individual and as a contribution to the community (see, for example, in respect of Hong Kong, Chi and Chow (1999)). Active ageing has become a key concept in government policy and is associated with the need to combat social exclusion in later life and to increase social capital often underpinned by removing full stop economic imperatives. The word "active", from a contemporary policy perspective, carries the connotation of participation in civic society (WHO, 2002, p. 122). An important development derived from the notion of active ageing has been the more specialised notion of "productive ageing" (Morrow-Howell, Hinterlong and Sherraden, 2001).

One core aspect of "good" ageing, whether constructed through either of the above conceptualisations, is the engagement of the individual in the social networks within the community. Irrespective of the individual's capability and capacity to use the potential of the community, the strength of that community can be quantified, at least at a theoretical level, through proxies that identify and measure the extent of social capital. Harpham, Grant and Thomas (2002), following Bain and Hicks, comment that social capital can be disaggregated:

> . . . into two components: structural and cognitive. The structural component included extent and intensity of associational links or activity, and the cognitive component covers perceptions of support, reciprocity, sharing and trust. At the simplest level, these two components can be characterized as what people "do" and what people "feel" in terms of social relations. (Harpham et al., 2002, p. 106).

Gittell and Vidal (1998) introduced a further useful distinction that has had a deep impact on debates about social capital – the distinction between *bonding* and *bridging* forms of capital. Bonding social capital is that which cements the connection *within* a social group, bridging social capital is that which makes connections *across* more disparate social groups. A further form of social capital is sometimes identified as *linking* social capital, capital that concerns "connections with people in positions of power and is characterised by relations between those within a hierarchy where there are differing levels of power" (Office for National Statistics, 2003). These three categories of social capital are used in the case study that follows and emphasis is placed upon the way that people feel about their social networks. There is not a great deal of evidence about older people and their networks, especially from the point of view of the older person. Bowling (2007) comments that the notion of what is regarded as successful ageing is to a large extent determined by the academic or professional discipline in which the investigator is theoretically located and, moreover, that too few attempts to define successful ageing explore the views of those who are experiencing the ageing process themselves. Similarly, Bowling and Stafford assert that "evidence of the enabling influence of neighbourhood-level factors on social or physical functioning is sparse or conflicting for older populations" (Bowling and Stafford, 2007, 2535), citing the work of Kavanagh, Goller, King, Jolley, Crawford and Turell (2005) and Walters, Breeze, Wilkinson, Price, Bulpitt, and Fletcher (2004) as justification. What knowledge has been gained about older people and social capital is largely confined to Western and developed economies (Yip, Subramanian, Mitchell, Lee, Wand and Kawachi, 2007).

II. A European Case Study

In the study that follows, the strongest emphasis is placed upon the feelings that older people have about their response to loneliness and isolation and how these responses can be understood using social capital theory. Much of the evidence that was found indicates that amongst the older people in the study population "bonding" social capital was the most prevalent. "Saying Hello Everyday" was a three-and-a-half-year project completed in July 2007, that was funded by the Big Lottery and jointly conducted by Age Concern, Wigan Borough Council and the Institute of Health and Social Care

Research at the University of Salford. A range of methods was employed to investigate the strategies used by older people to challenge loneliness and isolation. These included individual and group interviews and personally written narratives to produce rich data from 149 respondents living in Wigan, an urban area in the north-west of England. It represents the largest qualitative study of how older people manage loneliness and isolation in England to date. One of the most unusual features of the project was that some twelve older people were recruited and trained as researchers.

The essence of the study was to understand an aspect of life often experienced by older people, loneliness and isolation, and how some older people successfully overcome the challenges these present.[2] There is a significant and voluminous body of literature about the experience of loneliness and isolation, both of which may be defined objectively or subjectively. Research in the Netherlands has identified three important indicators of loneliness; it means an absence of a person's social relations, it is a feeling that differs from being alone, and it is unpleasant and depressing (Walker, 2005). Second, Victor, Bowling, Bond and Scrambler (2001) distinguished between "social isolation", the (lack of) integration of individuals (and groups) into the wider social environment, and 'loneliness', how individuals feel about the nature, extent and quality of social contact and engagement with the wider world. The focus here is not upon the nature or the experience of loneliness and isolation *per se* but rather upon how older people deal with the challenges presented and how their ability to deal with these challenges is shaped by the various forms of social capital (bonding, bridging and linking). If loneliness and isolation are significant problems at some point in many older people's lives, an exploration of how people manage these experiences should provide information about successful and active ageing and reveal the extent to which residual or new

---

2   It is difficult to establish the incidence of these phenomena: in the UK, the site of the case study, the evidence is contested. A recent study by Help the Aged (2007, p. 4) reported a significant increase in the extent of reported loneliness amongst older people, whereas, Victor, Bowling, Bond and Scrambler (2001) reported that the incidence of loneliness and isolation had shown little change in the past 50 years.

accumulation of social capital are factors in successful negotiation of these challenges.

The study directly connects with current debates about the constituents of successful ageing by investigating and highlighting the experience of older people who are more successful at negotiating loneliness and isolation, and providing a detailed case study of how older people demonstrate the ability to use a range of strategies to challenge loneliness and isolation. In part this ability is dependent upon the strength and vibrancy of the individual's social networks. Using social capital theory provides a conceptual tool that enables a better understanding of existing social networks and how these contribute to the individual's ability to challenge loneliness and isolation. What makes such a case study particularly interesting from the perspective of theorising about social capital is that "older age" is characterised, for many people, by partial or in some cases complete loss of social networks, through death of lifelong partner or friends, loss of role (e.g. as an employed person), loss of physical capacity and loss of capability for action. It is therefore a point at which an individual's social capital reserves may be significantly pressurised. Having made an analysis of older peoples' abilities to challenge loneliness and isolation, deficits and remedies can be presented as policy drivers that impact on the real world using social capital theory to achieve change and improvement and thence to promote active ageing.

III. Bonding Social Capital

In the study, two main examples of bonding capital emerged; networks with family and with friends.

First, the family, where the network picture is complex. A naïve assumption may be made that those older people that experience regular contact with members of their family are more socially integrated and enjoy a pattern of more successful ageing. Conversely, those that do not are less successful. The reality is more nuanced. Many respondents recognised and valued the importance of family and the majority were satisfied with the nature and quality of their intergenerational networks. However, as a respondent commented:

Having a loving supportive family that's the most important thing [in having happy life] but later stated anxiously: I don't want to be a nuisance to anybody, that's, that's my worry, I don't want to be a nuisance to anybody, oh please (gasps), I don't want to be a nuisance to my family or anybody.

It is not merely the existence of family networks but their quality and texture that is relevant. Often older people reported that they were made to feel dependent and as if they were being cared for – which may or may not be the case – rather than that they were involved in a reciprocal relationship in which they felt confirmed as making a contribution. Older people can and do provide significant levels of support particularly to their children who had grown up, for example; care for children, gardening, household chores (cleaning, shopping and so on) and household maintenance. A key area in which older people can make a contribution is through caring for grandchildren. For example, Clark and Roberts (2003) found that two- thirds of grandparents see their grandchildren every week, as one respondent commented:

Well there are many, many things. When I first retired I had two daughters who had just got married, so I spent a lot of time helping them, I went round helping them. I went round doing gardens for about five people, my mother and all these people. After about twelve months they asked me to go back to work, which I did for about three months, then someone asked me to go as a consultant [. . .]. And then on top of that over the years I got four grand children, so for the past eight years I mean it's been a full time job childminding.

For a very significant number of respondents such contacts were not possible due to the geographical dispersal of family members. Some older people expressed the view that they were taken for granted and that, apparently perversely, the engagement in *bonding* activities within a proximate family network restricted their ability to engage in wider social networks, in other words, their contribution could be "taken for granted".

Second, friendship networks, where friends were seen as providing both practical and emotional support. Many regarded friendships as being more significant than family support; friends of the same age cohort shared experiences, providing both practical and emotional support. Respondents felt themselves to be understood by friends. For example one male respondent who had never married commented:

> We are soul-mates . . . it's that person who you can go to and say, "Look, I need to speak". He goes on to describe how, when he was having problems, he could call at night . . . and they would say, "We'll be over in twenty minutes, get your gear . . . we're coming to pick you up . . . ". We've got a tight friendship, I think.

The possession of a wide circle of differentiated friendships (age and gender) was highly valued; their importance in helping to challenge loneliness and isolation was placed above that for family – there were more comments to that effect from respondents. Having at least one good friend was seen as highly important:

> I think basically you need a good partner, a good friend really. I mean even if it's only one person. I mean to me a few good friends are far better than knowing a million people.

A particular issue for older people is that the extent of an individual's friendship network is likely to reduce in size over time due to the death of some members; this factor may account for the importance attached to maintaining friendships and establishing new ones. Perhaps surprisingly, the majority of recipients found no greater difficulty in establishing new friendships in later life than they had at earlier life stages. Although some did experience difficulty:

> Definitely, for me especially. I can't make new friends. Well there's no-one of my age, I go to church they're all in pairs sixties, seventies, they're not my age group. They don't want old folk hanging round. They don't want "Ooo the olden days". They don't want that,

they'll get the violin out you see, play the old tunes
(laughs).

Notable among many respondents was the impact upon their
lives when they did not have sufficient *bonding* forms of social
capital – either though family or friendship networks. This may be
the result of life events, such as the death of a partner or an
increasingly common phenomenon in modern cities where families
can be helpful and supportive, but they may be geographically
dispersed, living in different regions or countries. However, the
really significant finding is the emphasis placed on friendship
networks rather than family networks. Family is an attribute that it
is difficult to change whereas friendships are built throughout life
and can be renewed and extended – they are a form of social capital
that the individual can influence or that social structures can
enhance.

IV. Bridging Social Capital

The nature of the community in which older people live has a
profound impact upon their stock of bridging social capital whereby
they are enabled to build bridges with others less proximate than
family or friends, or not so enabled. In the study, there was a mixed
pattern of community engagement; there were differences in terms
of how individuals experienced the community, reflecting their
personal stock of social capital. Some in the study had a "residual"
notion of community as a feature of their lives that was always
available in the background, rather like background music in a
shopping mall: something that you do not really notice unless you
choose to listen. In the mall, when you actively listen to the music
you may find it is not of the quality that you imagined! So it may be
with the community. It may be that the *idea* of community is
comforting and supportive, but the reality when accessed may be
found wanting. A key feature that may provide confidence in the
strength and nature of community networks is that of having a
shared sense of common history, as one respondent commented:

> Although we don't see each other every (day), we know
> everybody's there, and if we're having any problems we

> can go anywhere. Because on, on this road where I am,
> this side of the road here [. . .] we're all the same
> neighbours that moved in young.

It is the sense of being a part of a networked community,
however infrequently accessed, that is crucial. For some, however,
the sense of history generated a sense of loss. As one respondent
commented:

> When I think back to, say, when I was a child, where I
> lived, I knew all the families across the street, because I
> probably grew up with some of their sons and
> daughters.

The community in which she now lived was no smaller in extent
than her community of childhood but her community of active
reference was only four families. Whether the childhood perceptions
are correct is irrelevant, they may or may not be accurate. The key
issue is that the respondent's beliefs about the nature of the present
community are shaped by beliefs about the past. For some there was
a better past when the community was more open and networked
and that provided "bridges to people".

> There was never a more working class area [. . .] we just
> used to go into people's houses and we'd not a clue who
> they were.

If this sense of loss for a different type of community (in this
case a change of social make up) is pervasive, then it suggests the
need to engage in significant community networking programmes
that purposively develop linking social capital. Some older people
may be resistant to such approaches, however:

> There are you know sort of community associations in
> some areas, who would possibly try and involve people.
> But most people, they keep themselves to themselves
> and if someone knocks at your front door and you
> don't want to answer it you don't [. . .] I think a lot of
> older people get like that [. . .] well it's part of the
> make-up sometimes.

This reflects an attitude that might be shared by many, but the
very nature of community may have changed. Opportunities for

interaction may be reduced by the changing nature of modern cities, as one responded commented:

> People don't walk past your house. I mean how many people have walked past this house while you've been sitting there? Nobody. No cars have gone past. So you never see anybody really.

The changing nature of communities, often a response to increasing affluence, may introduce behavioural changes that weaken the social bonds within communities. An example is increased use of cars as a form of transport, which "cocoons" the individual in their own social space and actively prevents interaction with others. Hence, a journey does not provide an opportunity for interaction with others but is undertaken with functional precision.

Volunteering was a significant strategy used by some respondents to remain involved in society, for making oneself valuable and indicating the imperative to maintain or develop a personal stock of social capital. Voluntary work provided the opportunity of turning a negative situation into a positive one; this strategy used the social self as a means to acquire self-esteem. Respondents were engaged in a range of activities, and some were very active:

> I have got a set pattern as far as dancing and voluntary work goes, I am the organiser this year. I'll keep myself busy, I just don't like to sit around and watch TV.

Others adopted a "comfortable ageing" approach exemplified by the comment of this respondent:

> I'm waking at 7 am but I just rest and lie. I love music and jigsaws late at night, nobody bothering you [. . .] I think I have not got enough hours in the day.

Respondents used a variety of creative mechanisms other than volunteering to establish contacts with other people. Many of these were unlikely to lead to established social networks. They provide transitory satisfaction for the individual but do not lead to the development of enduring social capital; for example, one woman would take a bus not with the intention of going to any particular place but to strike up a casual conversation with someone else:

> I had a friend, a man friend, he didn't live with me or anything and he died and I were so bereft because he died suddenly. We used to get on the bus at Upsale Lane and I'd go Wigan, stop on't bus, give him me ticket, go back, go into Manchester and then come back and I'd been out all afternoon and I were ready for me tea then, and if you do that long enough, you'll not be lonely cause you meet people and you can say "'ello" to them on the next trip, if it's a man or a women, you say "'ello, nice day" or if it's raining or what have yer and then you start talking and I don't think there's few people that won't talk to yer, old or young, if you're on a bus. I mean, I don't complain about teenagers because them I come in contact with, when I am with 'em, I go back to what they are, little kids.

If she had (had) a wider social network she may not have felt the need to establish social contacts with others in this way. This approach nevertheless requires confidence and is an innovative and purposive strategy to challenge loneliness and isolation. This evidence poses for policy makers questions about how to promote substantive rather than transitory opportunities for the development of lasting "bridges" to other older people – rather than transitory encounters. One obvious way is for governmental authorities to ensure that public spaces are able to be used by older people. Many expressed fear of being in public spaces and that these had been colonised by the young. These various accounts prompt the need for discussion about how those who make policy in modern cities can promote opportunities for the development of bridging social capital.

V. Linking Social Capital

The study demonstrated that respondents lacked linking social capital. A good illustration is the responses provided about formal services. Perhaps surprisingly, formal health services did not play a very significant part in the provision of "links" between older

people. Their expectations of services were to some extent limited
and perfunctory. These views were not critical nor were they
resigned – just expressed in a rather matter of fact manner; these
were to travel to a particular place receive a service and then depart.
Major concerns were expressed about how to access these services
through appropriate transport. Many respondents expressed similar
views about social services; thus neither formal health nor social
services were seen as primarily sites for social or networking
experiences. However, this was not always the case; one respondent
was concerned about losing the opportunity to attend a day centre:

> I am a service user at [. . .] Centre.[3] I have been here
> twice a week for three years and have tried to help the
> lonely people I have met here. I have only one leg and
> am very old, but have all my faculties. The centre is
> closing down and we are all being scattered and I shall
> most likely lose contact with all my friends I have made.
> I try hard to make us all laugh and I feel better for it. I
> have not been my usual self since we got the notice to
> quit because the staff here are marvellous and it is
> central for a lot of us.

Here a central facility, a traditional day-care centre has provided
both links with older people who live in different parts of the urban
area and bridges between older people and those who provide
services – this centre was valued by those who use it. Nonetheless,
the overall perception by respondents was that social and health
care services did not enhance their social experiences, or develop
social capital. This raises a question about the function of those
services. Should they have as a secondary function the development
of linking social capital? Possibly staff who work in these services
would wish to qualitatively enhance the lives of service users, but
perhaps the expectations on these services are too great.

---

3   The centre name has been removed to maintain participant's anonymity.

VI. Discussion

Active Ageing

Figure 1

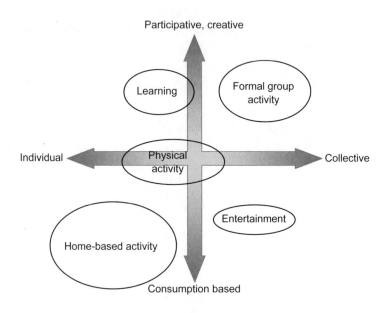

This figure is an interpretation of Figure 22, Range of Participative Activities, in Office of the Deputy Prime Minister (2006, 63). This figure is derived from work by Cowling (2005).

The purpose of Figure 1 is to illustrate the extent to which older people are involved in participative and collective activities, and that such activities are socially inclusive, have benefits for social capital accumulation and maintenance, and are in keeping with policy aspirations for active ageing. The magnitude of circles/ovals in the diagram provides a rough indication of the range and prevalence of activities in which "Saying Hello" participants were engaged, the larger the circle/oval the more prevalent the activity. The activities that older people engage in to challenge loneliness and isolation can be categorised into those that are predominantly: entertainment (for example, bingo, cinema, theatre, and all forms of enjoying entertainment that do not involve social engagement/participation, but that are individual not community oriented); home based (daily chores; cooking, cleaning and the like); participative and creative (such as reading and study); and those that are collective (participation in groups either formally or informally). In our study, home-based activities seemed to be most prevalent. Whilst being busy and doing things are important, people stressed that activity has to have some meaning, it has to be interesting, stimulating, challenging and valuable. Some respondents filled their time with activity of a routine type, such as preparing meals or going to places where there were people (for example, shopping malls).

This is not active and engaged ageing. Many of the activities reported were indicative of the existence of forms of social capital that promoted "bonding" among peers. In other words older people were interacting with other older people through social networks and structures set up for that purpose, the main exception being the family. Where family attachments were strong, older people were well integrated and respected and often had a social role within the family that was fulfilling. Whether the residual levels of social capital evident in the study location were sufficient or whether enough had been done by central government, local government or NGOs to build and enhance social capital remains an open question. There is much less evidence of the existence of "bridging" social capital that, for example, connected different age groups together, or "linking" social capital. A significant number of participants indicated that for them a more limited sphere of influence was desirable and they were content with home life and a slower pace of life. Supporting older people to maintain habits and routines that are valued by them is a way of maintaining quality of life. Low level support services would help an older person to retain "mastery" over their home environment and enhance self-esteem.

Absence of Social Capital

There were very clear examples amongst the respondents of people who possessed little if any personal social capital, and their responses to this lack are instructive and informative. When talking about these issues, respondents' mood was lowered and often resigned. Some attended sporting or social events, notably bingo[4], not because they enjoyed the activity but because it was an opportunity for social interaction. Despite these attempts at networking there was an underlying sadness in the responses of many of the respondents as one commented: "*You just try and fill your time – I have learnt to live with loneliness*". Another recognised explicitly that there is no cure for loneliness, it is something that you just have to live with. There was an acceptance of a declining quality of life as a result of ageing, as one respondent commented:

> It's a bit like a graph that goes up and then settles down [. . .] it's actually been on a downward spiral, I am thinking where the hell is this going [. . .] and I don't know the answer.

There may be significant gender differences in the experience of an absence of social capital. One man commented that having given up work he had nothing else to do, and did not want to have to spend the entire day engaged in recreational activity. One of the most poignant accounts was provided by a man who took a bus journey each day to sit on a bench for several hours. Before their deaths he had sat on the same bench with three of his friends. When he described how he spent his time it was not with sorrow but with a serene contentment. Objectively, to the external observer, it may appear that this behaviour represents a morbid engagement with the past, however, this was not how this person regarded the situation. For him he was still connecting with his social networks. This raises the intriguing possibility of "historic social capital" that is still meaningful to the individual. For others the rituals of domestic tasks or indeed the home itself provided an alternative to the lack of social capital; the home is valued as a place where the individual can be in control and is valued by older people as such (Office of the Deputy Prime Minister, 2006; Windle & Woods, 2004). The significance of an absence of personal social capital is great, absence of a confiding relationship increases the incidence of depression (Chappell and

---

4   A gambling game played in a large hall.

Badger, 1989), more generally the absence of social support increases the incidence of depressive symptoms evident in individuals (Jang, Haley, Small and Reynolds, 2000; Newsom and Schulz, 1996).

Implications for Hong Kong

As stated previously much of the evidence about social capital and ageing has been derived from non-East-Asian studies (Yip et al., 2007). The study discussed here adds to that body of non-East-Asian work. However, it does provoke and intensify the request for replication or similar studies to be undertaken in modern cities such as Hong Kong. Nonetheless, the findings of this study do invite immediate questions as to whether the experiences of older people living in Hong Kong would be similar or different. The very nature of the city itself, combined with the unique cultural context identified in the opening paragraphs of this chapter, suggests that much may well be different. A key finding to be tested is the emphasis given by older people to friendship networks over and above family networks. If this is the case in Hong Kong and other modern cities, then policy makers have the potential/possibilities to develop opportunities for social capital construction. Whereas, if there is greater emphasis on the family, which given Chou's comments in the first paragraph of this chapter may well be the case, the replacement of "lost" social capital or enhancement of personal social capital may be problematic.

References

Bowling, A. (2007). Aspirations for older age in the twenty-first century: What is successful aging? *The International Journal of Aging and Human Development, 64*(3), 263–297.

Bowling, A., and Stafford, M. (2007). How do objective and subjective assessments of neighbourhood influence social and physical functioning in older age? Findings from a British survey of ageing. *Social Science & Medicine, 64*(12), 2533–2549.

Chappell, N. L., and Badger, M. (1989). Social isolation and well-being. *Journal of Gerontology, 44*(5), 169–176.

Chi, I., and Chow, N. W. S. (1999). *A study on the volunteering aspirations of retired or retiring professionals in Hong Kong.* Hong Kong: YWCA and Department of Social Work and Social Administration.

Chi, I., and Leung, M. F. (1999). Health promotion for the elderly persons in Hong Kong. *Journal of Health and Social Policy, 10*(3), 37–51.

Clarke, I., and Roberts, C. (2003). *Grandparenthood: Its meaning and contribution to older people's lives.* Swindon, UK: Economic and Social Research Council.

Cowling, J. (2005). *Mapping culture and civil renewal.* London: IPPR.

Gittell, R., and Vidal, A. (1998). Community organizing: Building social capital as a development strategy. Thousand Oaks, CA: Sage.

Harpham, T., Grant, E., and Thomas, E. (2002). Measuring social capital within health surveys: Key issues. *Health Policy and Planning, 17*(1), 106–111.

Havighurst, R. J. (1961). Successful aging. *The Gerontologist, 1*(1), 8–13.

Help the Aged. (2007). *Spotlight on older people in the UK.* London: Help the Aged.

Jang, Y., Haley, W. E., Small, B. J., and Reynolds, S. L. (2000). Psychosocial resources as predictors of depressions among older adults in Korea: The role of sense and mastery, social network and social support. *Hallym International Journal of Ageing, 2*(1), 26–35.

Kavanagh, A. M., Goller, J. L., King, T., Jolley, D., Crawford, D., and Turell, G. (2005). Urban area disadvantage and physical activity: A multilevel study in Melbourne, Australia. *Journal of Epidemiology and Community Health, 59*, 934–940.

Kwan, A. Y.-H. (Ed.). (2002). *Aging Hong Kong. Issues Facing an Aging Society.* Hong Kong: Cosmos Books.

Lemon, B. W., Bengtson, V. L., and Peterson, J. A. (1972). An exploration of the activity theory of aging: Activity types and life satisfaction among in-movers. *Journal of Gerontology, 27*, 511–523.

Morrow-Howell, N., Hinterlong, J., and Sherraden, M. W. (Eds.). (2001). *Productive Aging: Concepts and Challenges.* Baltimore, MD: John Hopkins University Press.

Newsom, J., and Schulz, R. (1996). Social support as a mediator in the relations between functional status and quality of life in older adults. *Psychology and Ageing, 11*, 34–44.

Office for National Statistics. (2003). Social Capital: Measuring networks and shared value. Available online from http://www.statistics.gov.uk/CCI/nugget.asp?ID=314. Accessed 28 March 2008.

Office of the Deputy Prime Minister (2006). *A Sure Start to later Life. Ending inequalities for older people. A social exclusion report.* Final Report. London: ODPMo.

Rowe, J. W., and Kahn, R. L. (1987). Human aging: Usual and successful (Physiological changes associated with aging). *Science, 237*(July 10), 143–147.

Victor, C., Bowling, A., Bond, J., and Scrambler, S. (2001). Loneliness, social isolation and living alone in later life, from www.shef.ac.uk/uni/ projects/gop/index.html.

Walker, A. (Ed.). (2005). *Growing older in Europe.* Maidenhead, UK: Open University Press.

Walters, K., Breeze, E., Wilkinson, P., Price, G. H., Bulpitt, C. J., and Fletcher, A. (2004). Local area deprivation and urban-rural differences in anxiety and depression among people older than 75 years in Britain. *American Journal of Public Health, 94,* 1768–1774.

Windle, G., and Woods, R. (2004). Variations in subjective well-being: The mediating role of a psychological resource. *Ageing and Society, 24*(4), 583–602.

WHO (2002). *Active Ageing: A Policy Framework* Geneva: World Health Organisation.

Yip, W., Subramanian, S. V., Mitchell, A. D., Lee, D. T. S., Wand, J., and Kawachi, I. (2007). Does social capital enhance health and well-being? Evidence from rural China. *Social Science & Medicine, 64*(1), 35–39.

Part III

Social Capital

and Social Enterprise

9

Social Capital, Social Enterprise and Social Work – Social Capital for Enterprising Social Workers

Steven M. SHARDLOW

I. Introduction – Is Social Work Necessary?

This chapter provides an exploration of a possible future for social work; a future social work that could be conceptually located within a theoretical framework that is bounded by notions of social capital and social enterprise. To the extent that the argument is speculative and future orientated it is open to question. Engaging in the exploration of possible or hypothetical futures may not be seen by some to be a legitimate or respectable activity for members of academe – perhaps it is best left to the soothsayer or shaman! However, if academe is not engaged with the future then its contribution to the betterment of human society is restricted to the enhancement of historical understanding, which is hardly promising. There is another danger here, that the exploration of a possible future is of itself a component in the realisation of that *particular* future – for Marx this was certainly not a problem – and that the purpose of academe was not just to understand but also to influence and change events in the material world. The intention behind this exploration of a possible future social work is both to illuminate emergent trends and to generate discussion and hypotheses about the viability of a future that entwines social work with social enterprise leading to the enrichment of social capital. The location of these developments is modern cities, primarily Hong Kong, which has often been a bridge between past and future (Lee, 1994) to begin to understand the future, it is necessary to delve a little into the past.

There is no "iron law"[1] that specifies that social work is a necessary service in modern cities. The social welfare problems with which social work purports to deal are by no means restricted to modern societies. Pre-modern societies provided forms, albeit of limited scope, of care for vulnerable individuals, usually through faith-based organisations legitimated by the dominant religion.[2] At the core of these early forms of welfare are beliefs about the nature of obligations owed to others, which are dependent upon perceptions about the individual's relationship both to the state and to others within the society. Mutual obligation may derive from a range of imperatives: a pragmatic need to survive in adversity (such as may have been found in the earliest human social groups); religious belief about the duty owed to a deity (as is found in pre-modern societies); the need to have a fit and healthy army and workforce (an imperative that drove the construction of welfare states): the fear of social breakdown and the desire to enhance social cohesion (possibly derived form a fear of global terror or the development of social unrest through economic pressure) and so on. Modern cities have an increased imperative to address similar issues, often through forms of social work, as increased social interdependence is intensified in large urban sites.

II. Social Work Paradigms

Classifying social work approaches that address identified social problems is less than straightforward; nonetheless, perhaps

---

1 Lassalle (1863) is often credited with the first use of the term "Iron Law" to denote a set of fixed economic or social rules.
2 Exemplified: In Confucism, by the pursuit of Jen: for example, to be a well-established person it is necessary to help others to be established (Analects vi 28); in Christianity, by the tale of the Good Samaritan – where a man is under a duty to help his enemy (Luke 10:30-35); in Islam by the belief that those who alleviate the suffering of others in this life will have their sufferings alleviated in the next life (An-Nawawi's Forty Hadiths).

somewhat simplistically, taking an historical view, three broad paradigms can be discerned. Frequently, the origins of modern social work are traced to the last quarter of the nineteenth century, specifically to the United States and the United Kingdom "settlement movement", so called because settlement buildings were established in parts of major cities where deprivation was rife (Younghusband, 1981). The first professional paradigm embodied within this early emergent social work (often driven by religious imperatives), can be defined within a paradigm of *rescue* and *education*. The aim was to rescue people from poverty or criminal behaviour by providing models of how to behave differently and through education to provide alternatives and opportunities. A second paradigm, *care and protection*, is embodied in the idea of the welfare state that emerged in the post Second World War period in various parts of Europe. This paradigm affirms that social work provides *care and protection* for vulnerable and marginalised populations. Different types of welfare states provided different levels of social care and assistance (Esping-Andersen, 1990, 1996). During the post-colonial period, since the major European empires disintegrated, in societies where day-to-day survival, generally rural and economically undeveloped, cannot be taken for granted, social work, to the extent that the profession exists, has been centrally concerned with ensuring the *security of necessities of life* – a third paradigm. Key concerns within this paradigm are to ensure the security of water and food supplies combined with the adequate provision of shelter and medical assistance. Once these basic needs have been met (Maslow, 1943), then and only then can social work address other social concerns if sufficient economic resources are available. This paradigm draws upon social development theory – social work and social development are often conceptually indistinguishable in such contexts. These three different paradigms are not necessarily inconsistent with each other and do co-exist worldwide.

The breadth and diversity of activities across the globe that fall within the purview of social work is well illustrated by the differences between social work as part of a welfare state and as a vehicle to ensure the basic necessities of life. This rich texture of social work has been captured by the definition of social work (IFSW, 2000) developed by International Federation of Social

Workers (IFSW) and the International Association of Schools of Social Work (IASSW).

DEFINITION
The social work profession promotes social change, problem solving in human relationships and the empowerment and liberation of people to enhance well-being. Utilising theories of human behaviour and social systems, social work intervenes at the points where people interact with their environments. Principles of human rights and social justice are fundamental to social work.

COMMENTARY
Social work in its various forms addresses the multiple, complex transactions between people and their environments. Its mission is to enable all people to develop their full potential, enrich their lives, and prevent dysfunction. Professional social work is focused on problem solving and change. As such, social workers are change agents in society and in the lives of the individuals, families and communities they serve. Social work is an interrelated system of values, theory and practice.

[. . .]

PRACTICE
Social work addresses the barriers, inequities and injustices that exist in society. It responds to crises and emergencies as well as to everyday personal and social problems. Social work utilises a variety of skills, techniques, and activities consistent with its holistic focus on persons and their environments. Social work interventions range from primarily person-focused psychosocial processes to involvement in social policy, planning and development. These include counselling, clinical social work, group work, social pedagogical work, and family treatment and therapy as well as efforts to help people obtain services and resources in

the community. Interventions also include agency administration, community organisation and engaging in social and political action to impact social policy and economic development. The holistic focus of social work is universal, but the priorities of social work practice will vary from country to country and from time to time depending on cultural, historical, and socio-economic conditions.

This definition illustrates the range of activities that currently comprise social work, as specified by the international social work community. The definition does not include as one of the aims of social work the development of social capital nor is social enterprise mentioned: certainly there is no mention of partnership with the business community. However, the section of the definition that describes current forms of practice could accommodate emergent forms of social work that include social enterprise. It is likely that this definition will require modification in light of emergent developments in modern cities.

III. Social Capital Theorisation and Social Work

The notion of *social capital* is not well conceptualised either as a theoretical construct that informs the discipline of social work nor as distinctive approach to professional practice. Some examples of theoretical literature pertinent to social work have been published, for example, two systematic reviews of social capital and particular service user groups can be identified by searching the ISI Web of Knowledge[3]: Ferguson's (2006) review of 22 studies that focus on social capital and children's well-being; De Silva, McKenzie, Harpham, and Huttly's (2005) systematic review of 21 studies of mental illness and social capital (14 of which measured social capital levels at the individual level and seven ecologically). In addition, there appear to be a larger number of explorations of social capital

---

3 Correct as of March 2008.

that have relevance for professional social work practice with specific service-user groups, for example, in respect of: children and Sure Start (Bagley, Ackerley, and Rattray, 2004); older women in a disadvantaged community (Boneham and Sixsmith, 2006); those with a disability (Kitchin, 1998); welfare recipients (Tang and Cheung, 2007), and so on.

Despite the apparent theoretical pre-occupation of social work with the individual and the family group, the discourse around the discipline has at various times demonstrated an engagement with professional approaches that are collectivist rather than solely individualist, which have through promotion of the idea of *community* challenged the exclusivity of individualist approaches in theoretical debate about social work. Notable among these collectivist theoretical discourses is the so-called *radical social work* movement that attained some prominence in the United Kingdom (Langan and Lee, 1989) and United States (Galper, 1980) in the 1970s and early 1980s.[4] See, for example, the work of the English writer Simpkin (1983), who argued that social workers should take collective action through the trade unions to further the interests of their clients. Rather less subversively, the government of the United Kingdom sponsored a report, the Barclay Report (1982), which advocated the adoption of community social work. Community social work was, in part, about local residents being able to have easy access to a network of health and social work services, hence the report may have encouraged the formation of social capital through formal provision of services, to the extent that it was implemented. Similarly, pre-figurative discourses can be found in the United States. Of particular significance are the theoretical debates that have developed around the notions of system theory and ecological theory. System theory entered social work discourse through the work of Pincus and Minahan (1973), which located the person seeking help within a series of interlocking systems; family, work, employment, community and so on. This approach to professional practice designated the social worker as a "change

---

4   An expression of the revolutionary *Zeitgeist* in the aftermath of the riots in many European cities during 1968.

agent" who would intervene to achieve change in the most appropriate system at the most appropriate locus for intervention. Systems theory morphed into ecological social work, which is built upon the notion that human beings are constantly being shaped by and shaping their own physical and social environment (for a debate on the value of the ecological approach, see Greif, 2003; Ungar, 2002, 2003).[5] These examples illustrate that social work discourse has exhibited strands that are in the broadest sense collectivist or concerned with community. However, while these few examples illustrate the existence of such a discourse; they do not of themselves reveal the weight given to these ideas at the level of theory or professional practice. However, the purpose here is not to provide an historical overview of social work ideas but merely to demonstrate the existence of collectivist thinking albeit of a different character to that embedded in the notion of social capital.

Whatever the extent of theorising about *community* within social work discourse the content of that discourse has not been framed to any great extent within a contextual framework that draws richly upon notions derived from social capital studies. There are many reasons for this, possibly because in recent years social work theorising has been seduced by post-modern preoccupations that counterpoise a profession increasingly dominated by managerial constraint over professional freedom and discretion – at least in many of the world's modern cities. That being the case, it is essential to lay out key features of theorising about social capital that are pertinent and relevant to social work. Here, it is essential to delineate how a social work practice located within a social capital framework might be different from other forms of social work practice.

It is conventionally accepted that social capital "theory", in so far as it can be taken as a coherent body, was derived initially from

---

5 Ungar (2002), drawing upon the work of Naess (1989), derives eight principles for a new ecology in social work practice. One of these in particular, "Structured alliances between communities and the services that provide for them must act to increase the diversity of resources that are directly available to individuals and families to help them help themselves" (2002, 488) has clear resonances with social capital theory.

a fusion of ideas drawn from the work of three core thinkers, two of whom were the sociologists Bourdieu (1985) and Coleman (1988) and the third was the policy analyst Putnam (1993) whose later work, *Bowling Alone* (Putnam, 2000), has become a seminal text in the field. A large body of social capital literature has developed. As evidence of the extent of this literature a search of ISI Web of Knowledge generated 2083 hits on the term "social capital" appearing in titles of journal articles.[6] Moreover, the concept of *social capital* has attracted the attention of governments around the world. For example, the World Bank has produced the *Social Capital Assessment Tool* (SOCAT), a standardised measurement tool to identify levels of social capital (World Bank, 1999); the European Union has established the European Observatory on the Social Situation and Demography, which reports on the accumulation of social capital or otherwise across members states (European Commission, 2008); in the UK, the Office for National Statistics has produced a definition that summarises other work, and includes an approach to measurement and a discussion of policy implications (2003); while in Hong Kong, the SAR Government Labour and Welfare Bureau has introduced the Community Investment and Inclusion Fund specifically to enhance social capital development (CIIF, 2007). At a theoretical level, Boix and Posner (1998) comment on the effect of the idea of social capital on government action, while the review by Evans comments on findings of five other papers in the same edition of the journal *World Development* that explored the synergy between state and society, concluding that: "Creative action by government organisations can foster social capital" (Evans, 1996, 1130). This may be contrasted with Pinnock (2007) who delineated and reviewed what he terms the "thirteen theses of social capital" (2007, pp. 346–7) and comments:

> Modern social capital theory has had little effect on public policy so far (though a lot on political rhetoric which might be mistaken for policy) because it fails to connect with the bricks-and-mortar world actually

---

6   Correct as of March 2008.

inhabited by policymakers. It is a classic bridging problem. (Pinnock, 2007, p. 349)

Disputes continue about the extent of the application of social capital theory to the real world and about the nature of the concept: see, for example, the theoretical discussion about the nature of social capital and public health (Stephens, 2008, pp. 1174–7). Others comment about the scope of social capital theory, for example, Healy, Haynes and Hampshire (2007) comment that much emphasis has been paid to theorising aspects of social capital that relate to "political participation and social support [. . . but] far less to attention has been paid to the gender dimensions of the topic" (Healy, Haynes and Hampshire, 2007, pp. 110–11). Nonetheless, the kernel of thinking about social capital that is central to social work is relatively easily grasped. The notion of "social capital" can be understood as a social consequence, a result, and a by-product of social networks (whether purposive or desired or not), whether familial or located within the wider community, as the World Bank has famously stated:

> Social capital refers to the institutions, relationships, and norms that shape the quality and quantity of a society's social interactions . . . Social capital is not just the sum of the institutions which underpin a society – it is the glue that holds them together. (World Bank, 1999)

Social capital, is then, at its simplest, a product of the individual's participation in the human relationships that bind society together. Through participation in these relationships, individuals develop reciprocal and mutual obligations to each other and to the wider community, which in turn generates trust between individuals. As Coleman states:

> If physical capital is wholly tangible, being embodied in observable material form, and human capital is less tangible, being embodied in the skills and knowledge acquired by an individual, social capital is less tangible yet, for it exists in the relations among persons. Just as physical capital and human capital facilitate productive

activity, social capital does as well. (Coleman, 1988, pp. S100–1)

From these comments about social capital, it is evident that central to an individual's well-being is the extent, nature and quality of his or her social networks, and the ability to use and exploit those networks for purposive activity. Such an understanding permits the theoretical possibility of developing an index that will provide a measure of the extent of social capital at individual, community and state level using proxies such as the nature or extent or networks. For example, van Oorshot and Arts (2005) used an eight-scale measurement model.[7] This potentiality for measurement, albeit by proxy, could have considerable significance for the development of a social work that is grounded in social capital theory (see below). In addition, the increased emphasis on "measurement" and review has the potential to increase the scientific nature of social work – long a matter of debate (Karpf, 1931).

The primary focus of professional social work to date has *not* been the promotion of "social networks and the norms of reciprocity and trustworthiness that arise from them" (Putnam, 2000, 19). However, a core – but not sole – function for social work *could* both become the enhancement of existing social networks, the promotion and development of new social networks and also to work with individuals to maximise their skills in network use. If, social work is securely located within a theoretical framework that requires network development, then this approach may provide a theoretical underpinning for the development of social care structures, independent of the state, which are particularly suited to modern cities such as Hong Kong. For example, an older person who is well located within the community may find that people are willing to help with tasks that they are unable to manage – because through participation in networks a sense of trust and reciprocity develops that leads to the expression of help though mutual obligation. The idea of "networks" is broad and to be professionally useful in social work it requires honing into a more precise form.

---

7 These were: trustworthiness; trust in institutions; interpersonal trust; passive participation; active participation; friends; family; political engagement.

The Office for National Statistics (UK) have produced a helpful summary of considerable theoretical discussion, see the box below.

What are networks?

Formal and informal networks are central to the concept of social capital. They are defined as the personal relationships which are accumulated when people interact with each other in families, workplaces, neighbourhoods, local associations and a range of informal and formal meeting places.

Different types of social capital can be described in terms of different types of networks:

Bonding social capital – describes closer connections between people and is characterised by strong bonds, e.g., among family members or among members of the same ethnic group; it is good for "getting by" in life.

Bridging social capital – describes more distant connections between people and is characterised by weaker, but more cross-cutting ties, e.g., with business associates, acquaintances, friends from different ethnic groups, friends of friends, etc.; it is good for "getting ahead" in life.

Linking social capital – describes connections with people in positions of power and is characterised by relations between those within a hierarchy where there are differing levels of power; it is good for accessing support from formal institutions. It is different from bonding and bridging in that it is concerned with relations between people who are not on an equal footing. An example would be a social services agency dealing with an individual, e.g., job searching at the Benefits Agency (Office for National Statistics, 2003).

This categorisation or typology of social capital provides an opportunity for nuanced social work interventions that address deficits of particular types of social capital or that seek to enable those lacking in skills to use social capital to be able to maximise their use of opportunities. Theory of this type directly applied to social work is lacking at present but could be developed through reflexive dialogue with the rich developments occurring in the real world where actual practice is in advance of theoretical understanding – at least for social work in this field. The next section explores some of these real world developments.

IV. Two Variants of a Social Work Infused by Notions of Social Capital

It is postulated in this chapter that new forms of social work are emerging, forms that draw either implicitly or explicitly upon theorisation about social capital. These forms fall into two distinct types. The first are forms of social work that use conventional social work methodologies but which embrace the development of social networks as a key objective for social work intervention – this form may be termed social networking. These are distinct from innovative forms of social work that deploy methodologies that derive from business models – this form may be termed social entrepreneurship.

One example, responding to the social problem of homelessness, will serve to illustrate the nature of these emergent social works. Homelessness is a major problem for modern cities. The causes are complex and include: shortages in housing supply; poor quality housing and overcrowding; population migrations; urbanisation processes and a range of other health and social problems. Many who are homeless find temporary accommodation with family or friends or through social housing projects. Those who do not are the *roofless*, i.e., those live on the streets, "street sleepers" (Kwok and Chan, 1998). The social composition of the roofless suggests that significant numbers will have complex needs with a high incidence of alcoholism, substance abuse, mental illness, poor physical health, and so on (for discussion of Hong Kong, see, if somewhat dated: Chau, 1995; Lee, 1994). The interlocking complexity and intractability of problems experienced by many roofless people makes assisting individuals within this group to escape from their life on the streets extremely difficult. The conventional response to these problems is to provide care for the roofless from within a welfare paradigm, for example, the provision of emergency food kitchens or rough sleepers' hostels. Such services are designed to meet only the most urgent and pressing physiological hierarchy of human need (Maslow, 1943) and do not strive to build or develop an individual's social capital.

Social Networking

All too often homeless people are seen as not only "hard to reach" and therefore are not high priority for scarce social work resources. Nonetheless, responses to homelessness vary in type but often share a similar theoretical justification as the care and protection paradigm. One such example of a care and protection response is the Guadalupe Homeless Project in Los Angeles (founded in 1988), provided by a religious foundation, Proyecto Pastoral. This foundation provides a range of services to homeless men, primarily of the Latino community, including "shelter and meals; legal referrals; basic health care referrals; weekly onsite free medical clinic; tobacco, drug and alcohol abuse information; HIV, STD testing and counseling; ongoing ESL classes; how to access community services; classes in how to establish a savings plan" (Proyecto Pastoral, 2005). This project is not untypical of many projects in modern cities that respond to the problem of homeless people. The approach taken, evidently from the nature and range of services provided, is grounded in the provision of care through meeting some basic physical needs for shelter and food. Clearly, there is the potential for the development of bonding capital amongst the homeless project users, many of whom are likely to be socially isolated. Most importantly, there are opportunities for those who use the project to access and engage with different health and welfare groups, which provides potential for the development of *linking* social capital. The question is whether the opportunities are maximised by the project or whether all services are provided on an immediate and therefore transitory basis, and whether the theory of social capital development is embedded to any extent if at all in the approach taken. The nature of the theoretical orientation of this and similar projects depends on whether the project is primarily concerned with immediate rescue or attempting to establish a way for homeless men to become more integrated into society and to modify their life through the development and use of their personal social capital. For example, Hawkins and Abrams' (2007) qualitative study of 39 co-morbid formally homeless individuals in New York found that they had very small social networks and therefore possessed little social capital. As a response they suggest:

> . . . a deeper assessment helps providers better understand their client's social interactions, but it provides insight into the client's personality, social abilities, and ways of re-integrating into the community and building new relationships or reconstructing those that could produce positive social capital. (Hawkins & Abrams, 2007, p. 2040)

There is a need for such projects to actively seek to build the social capital of those that they seek to help though a social networking approach. There are elements of this in the Guadalupe Homeless Project but they could be significantly enhanced. This example has illustrated a very important if conventional approach to the provision of help for homeless people.

Social Entrepreneurship

A radical approach to social work, drawing upon business models, that is centrally concerned with social capital could be developed. Moreover, there is evidence that such developments are underway, particularly in modern cities such as Hong Kong. Again taking the example of homelessness, consider the following approach taken by social entrepreneurs, which provides an exemplary example of a social enterprise. *The Big Issue* is a weekly magazine that was launched in London in 1991. Now the magazine is available through regionally produced editions in many modern cities across Australia, Japan, South Africa, Namibia and Kenya. The Big Issue is a commercial business, designed to make profit[8] – yet it also offers a

---

8   These profits are donated to The Big Issue Foundation, a charity that exists to provide further help to homeless people – they could just as legitimately be used to make money for shareholders.

"business solution to a social problem" (The Big Issue, 2008). The magazine is produced by professional journalists and is sold by authorised homeless people (sellers) who are required to attend a training session and adhere to a code of conduct concerning appropriate behaviour with the public. These sellers are allowed to keep over 50 per cent of the cover costs of each magazine that is sold. Several aspects of this social enterprise are structured to develop the social networks and skills of authorised sellers. The overall approach is designed to engender basic commercial skills and to build social networks with the organisation and beyond, including access to banking assistance and with the general public – with the intention that through an increased sense of dignity and self worth sellers will be given "a hand up, not a hand out" (The Big Issue, 2008). This approach purposively builds social capital for homeless people; close *bonds* are formed between sellers; *bridges* are formed between the wider public and homeless people. Because of the high regard in which *The Big Issue* is held members of the public are more likely to engage with sellers than they would with other homeless people, and those homeless who engage with The Big Issue are *linked* to a formal organisation which has the potential for other benefits. Whether explicitly or not, the approach behind The Big Issue is grounded in the creation of social capital.

The Big Issue is an example of social enterprise developed by a successful business entrepreneur. Could social workers develop similar, if perhaps more small-scale social enterprises? Kwok suggests:

> . . . social workers have to adopt a model shift to equip
> themselves with broad helping perspectives and
> multi-skills in order to become effective social capital
> builders and avail themselves as partners of all sectors
> of society in dealing with the challenges of modern
> times. (Kwok, 2004).

Similarly, Tan (2004) has argued that social workers should expand their current roles to become social innovators and to create social value through actions that promote the inclusion of marginalised groups in economic activity, and the enhancement of social participation. This may entail the adoption of the kind of approach to social problems adopted so successfully by The Big Issue in respect of homeless people. Not that all marginalised social groups should go onto the streets and sell magazines! Rather, social workers as social entrepreneurs should look for creative solutions that amalgamate business and social models as there is a need for:

> . . . people with the mission to create and sustain social value. These social change agents are not limited by resources currently at hand but pursue new opportunities to serve people, take calculated risks and engage in a process of continuous social innovation, adaptation and learning. Ultimately, social entrepreneurs have a sense of accountability to the constituencies served and for the outcomes. (Tan, 2004)

The type of social work that echoes the approach taken by The Big Issue suggests that social workers working as social entrepreneurs represents the emergence of a new theoretical paradigm for professional social work. This approach could be developed to fuse social work with social enterprise.

There is evidence in Hong Kong, one of the world's leading modern cities, that the social networking and social entrepreneurship approaches to social work represent the emergence of a new paradigm. These approaches are being actively developed through practical rather than theoretical development, for example, through the work of the government-sponsored Community Investment and Inclusion Fund (CIIF, 2007). Such a paradigm is being fashioned through the interchange of dynamic of continuing economic development and the emergence of a form of social work that "fits" with prevailing economic and social conditions (Ngan and Hui, 1996), just as there was a "fit" between the social work of the welfare state, *care and protection* and the economic systems and structures in the post-Second World War period in Europe.

What is being claimed is not that conventional or traditional models of professional practice are necessarily redundant. Rather that we may be witness to the birth of new models that have greater relevance for the emergent and dynamic economies such as are found in modern cities like Hong Kong. It may be that these new-models-based paradigms of social enterprise and social capital will influence social work globally and in many major developed economies and could eventually replace, to a substantial extent, more traditional forms of social work. Certainly, there is evidence of an increasing preoccupation with provision of forms of social help that promote the individual's engagement with employment. This approach is evident in Netherlands, for example (van der Laan, 2000), and is found to be generally applicable to Hong Kong (Cheng, 2007; Tang and Cheung, 2007b). The final section of this chapter explores in a preliminary manner the components of how a theory of social work that was based on social capital might be constructed.

V. Social Capital in Practice:
Developing Policies to Enhance
the Creation and Use of Social Capital –
An Emergent Model of Social Work

The rapid economic growth of several East Asian countries has promoted discussion about the emergence of new forms of welfare (Goodman, White and Kwon, 1998). In Hong Kong, there has been a long standing concern by successive governments that the provision of significant levels of welfare by the state would in some way contaminate the economic model through the emergence and subsequent dominance of a dependency culture (Yu, 1996). Hence, new paradigms of social work that do not compromise economic development and in fact work in harmony with the predominant economic ideological consensus, through the use of business models, are especially likely to find favour. These are being created through practice. There is a very real need to develop a theoretical underpinning for such an approach to social work. Such a new theoretical approach does not merely introduce a new theoretical paradigm for the delivery of social work. Rather it proposes a new set of functions, roles, skills and knowledge that social workers would need to acquire to implement such a model successfully. There can be no assumption that this would be a simple matter: illustrated in part by Schneider's study of civic engagement and social capital in community-based not-for-profit organisations appears to suggest that increased engagement does not of itself lead to an increase on the level of social capital (Schneider, 2007). This study is indicative of the need for a detailed and nuanced approach to the incorporation of social capital theory into social work. In other words it is not enough for social workers to conceptualise social capital as a method to promote instructed network construction in a community with the expectation that this will of itself resolve problems, unless those networks are systematically developed to achieve particular goals.

Thus, to develop a social work grounded in a theoretical understanding of social capital would require a close integration between business and community development models with social work theory. Such modes of thinking are not obviously part of the way in which social work is conceptualised in social work professional curricula (see, for example, Social Workers Registration Board, 2008). Currently, theoretical models of social work are firmly grounded in social science or health care theory. Hence, to fully incorporate social capital theory and to develop an "enterprising social worker" will require a significant paradigm shift.

Current emergent practice requires codification and incorporation into a robust framework that through an iterative process between the constructs of theory and the imperatives of practice will enable the generation of a new model of social work practice; a model for the enterprising social worker. When working with individuals social workers will need to develop a practice repertoire with precise professional tools that enable the following questions to be addressed:

1. How can the range and extent of an individual's social networks be identified?
2. How can the frequency and intensity of usage made of those networks by the individual be determined (this may suggest that "frequency" and "intensity" of usage are proxies for "quality"?
3. What mechanisms are available to conduct a review with individuals to determine if the characteristics of their social networks are sufficiently vibrant and strong so that key objectives may be achieved?

4. How can the social worker classify the types of existing social capital as bonding, bridging and linking to identify potential sites for intervention?

5. How can social workers help people to assess if they have sufficient skills in the use of their networks to be able to realise personal goals?

6. If the networks are agreed by the social worker and individual to be of insufficient calibre, then how to agree with the individual an action plan to develop and enhance the social networks that is targeted and goal focussed and takes account of different types of social capital?

7. If there is an identified skill deficit in the use of networks, then how to identify mechanisms for the individual to develop new skills either individually or through engagement in group activities.

The answers to these key questions will have to incorporate a business element. If this is not present then there is a real danger that the fundamentals of social capital would not suffuse the approach to social work in an integrated fashion but would rather be limited additions which might be described as "social work with networks".

However, the ability to conceptualise practice and theory from the point of the individual is one of the strengths of social work. However, a more radical approach would be to develop a theoretical paradigm in which social workers were primarily focussed on working at the community level to develop social capital through using or building social enterprises. This would be a highly innovative approach to social work and would require that social workers were able to:

1. Work with community groups and stakeholders (including business and NGOs) to undertake community profiling;

2. Develop an intervention strategy with key stakeholders to develop specific types of social capital within a particular community;

3. Promote intervention strategies that are sustainable, that use social enterprise models and do not rely on continuing state support for the maintenance of those forms of social capital;

4. Monitor effectiveness of the intervention strategy in the production of social capital.

Such an approach requires a creative fusion of social work, social capital and social enterprise models. A pragmatic approach to theory development would be to take examples of practice that incorporate elements of this approach, The Big Issue for example, and to subject these to rigorous single case study design evaluation to reveal the essential elements that could be replicated in other similar cases. This might reveal how social work could contribute to a collaborative partnership that generates creative solutions and how social workers would need to modify their practice. There is much more to be done to bring this illustrative outline of a paradigm for social work, grounded on social capital theory, to fruition – this can be no more than the roughest sketch. Nonetheless, it does allow the question to be posed as to whether such a paradigm might be more suited to the economics of modern cities generally and Hong Kong in particular. Might this also be the paradigm that will be adopted elsewhere in the world and displace traditional and existing paradigms of social work? That is where academe must allow the futurologist or fortune teller to begin their speculation.

Acknowledgements

This chapter draws upon ideas that were initially presented at the Fifth Annual Forum of the Community Investment and Inclusion Fund (CIIF), Hong Kong SAR, and at the Seminar for Staff and Graduate Students, City University of Hong Kong. I am grateful to Grace Ng and Sik Hung Ng who have been an invaluable source of comment as these ideas have developed, and Brahm Prakash whose gentle editing has improved the clarity of the chapter.

References

Bagley, C., Ackerley, C. L., and Rattray, J. (2004). Social exclusion, Sure Start and organizational social capital: evaluating inter-disciplinary multi-agency working in an education and health work programme. *Journal of Education Policy, 19*(5), 595–607.

Barclay, P. M. (1982). *Social Workers: Their role and tasks (The Barclay Report)*. London: Bedford Square Press.

Boix, C., and Posner, D. N. (1998). Social capital: Explaining its origins and effects on government performance. *British Journal of Political Science, 28(4)*, 686–693.

Boneham, M. A., and Sixsmith, J. A. (2006). The voices of older women in a disadvantaged community: Issues of health and social capital. *Social Science & Medicine, 62*(2), 269–279.

Bourdieu, P. (1985). The forms of capital. In J.G. Richardson (Ed.), *Handbook of theory and research for the sociology of education* (pp. 241–258). New York: Greenwood.

Chau, R. C. M. (1995). The functions of negative aspects of welfare in capitalist societies. A case-study of temporary accommodation for the homeless in Britain and housing policy for small households in Hong-Kong. *International Social Work, 38*(1), 87–102.

Cheng, T. (2007). How is "welfare-to-work" shaped by contingencies of economy, welfare policy and human capital? *International Journal of Social Welfare, 16*(3), 212–219.

CIIF (2007). Community Inclusion and Investment Fund. Available online, http://www.ciif.gov.hk/index.htm. Accessed on 15 October 2007.

Coleman, J. S. (1988). Social capital in the creation of human capital. *American Journal of Sociology, 94* Supplement, S95–S120.

De Silva, M. J., McKenzie, K., Harpham, T., and Huttly, S. R. A. (2005). Social capital and mental illness: A systematic review. *Journal of Epidemiology and Community Health, 59*(8), 619–627.

Esping-Andersen, G. (1990). *The three worlds of welfare capitalism*. Cambridge: Polity Press.

Esping-Andersen, G. (1996). *Welfare states in transition*. Cambridge: Polity.

European Commission (2008). European Observatory on the Social Situation and Demography. Available online at http://ec.europa.eu/employment _social/spsi/ european_observatory_en.htm. Accessed on 10 April, 2008,

Evans, P. (1996). Government action, social capital and development: Reviewing the evidence on synergy. *World Development, 24*(6), 1119–1132.

Ferguson, K. M. (2006). Social capital and children's wellbeing: a critical synthesis of the international social capital literature. *International Journal of Social Welfare, 15*(1), 2–18.

Galper, J. (1980). *Social work practice. A radical perspective.* New Jersey: Prentice Hall.

Goodman, R., White, G., and Kwon, H.-j. (Eds.) (1998). *The East Asian Welfare Model: Welfare Orientalism and the State.* London: Routledge.

Greif, G. L. (2003). In response to Michael Ungar's "A deeper, more social ecological social work practice". *Social Service Review, 77*(2), 306–308.

Hawkins, R. L., and Abrams, C. (2007). Disappearing acts: The social networks of formerly homeless individuals with co-occurring disorders. *Social Science & Medicine, 65*(10), 2031–2042.

Healy, K., Haynes, M., and Hampshire, A. (2007). Gender, social capital and location: understanding the interactions. *International Journal of Social Welfare, 16*(2), 110–118.

IFSW (2000). Definition of Social Work. Available online at, http://www.ifsw.org/ en/p38000208.html, accessed on 14 March 2006.

Karpf, M. (1931). *The scientific basis of social work.* New York: Columbia University Press.

Kitchin, R. (1998). "Out of place", "knowing one's place": Space, power and the exclusion of disabled people. *Disability & Society, 13*(3), 343–356.

Kwok, J. (2004). Social welfare, social capital and social work: Personal reflection of a Hong Kong social worker. *Journal of Social Policy and Social Work, 8*(March), 23–32.

Kwok, J., and Chan, R. (1998). Street sleeping in Hong Kong. *International Social Work, 41*(4), 471–784.

Langan, M., and Lee, P. (1989). Whatever happened to radical social work? In M. Langan and P. Lee (Eds.), *Radical Social Work Today* (pp. 1–19). London: Unwin Hyman.

Lassalle, F. (1863). Offnes Antwortschreiben an das Central-Comite zur Berufung eines Allgemeinen Deutschen Arbeitercongresses zu Leipzig (pp. 15–16). Zurich.

Lee, P. C. Y. (1994). Social-work in Hong-Kong, Singapore and Taiwan. Bridging tradition and modernisation. *Indian Journal of Social Work, 55*(3), 419–432.

Maslow, A. H. (1943). A theory of human motivation. *Psychological Review, 50*, 370–396.

Naess, A. (1989). *Ecology, community and lifestyle: Outline of an ecosophy* (D. Rothenberg, trans.). Cambridge: Cambridge University Press.

Ngan, R., and Hui, S. (1996). Economic and social development in Hong Kong and Southern China: Implications for social work. *International Social Work, 39*(1), 83–87.

Office for National Statistics (2003). Social Capital: Measuring networks and shared value. Available online at, http://www.statistics.gov.uk/ CCI/nugget.asp ?ID=314, accessed 28 March 2008,

Pincus, A., and Minahan, A. (1973). *Social work practice: Model and method.* Itasca, IL: F.E. Peacock.

Pinnock, A. (2007). The infrastructural aspect of social capital: Suggestions for a bridge between concept and policy. *Public Money and Management, 27*(5), 345–350.

Proyecto Pastoral (2005). Guadalupe Homeless Project. Available online at, http://www.proyectopastoral.org/prog-GHP.htm, accessed 2 November 2007.

Putnam, R. D. (1993). The prosperous community. Social capital and public life. *The American Prospect, 4*(13), 35–42.

Putnam, R. D. (2000). *Bowling alone. The collapse and revival of the American community.* New York: Simon & Schuster.

Schneider, S. J. A. (2007). Connections and disconnections between civic engagements and social capital in community-based nonprofits. *Nonprofit and Voluntary Sector Quarterly, 36*(4), 572–597.

Simpkin, M. (1983). *Trapped within welfare.* 2nd edition, Houndmills, Basingstoke: Macmillan.

Social Workers Registration Board (2008). Principles, Criteria and Standards for Recognising Qualifications in Social Work for Registration of Registered Social Workers. Available online at, http://www.swrb.org.hk/EngASP/criteria_e.asp, accessed on 10 April 2008.

Stephens, C. (2008). Social capital in its place: Using social theory to understand social capital and inequalities in health. *Social Science and Medicine, 66*(5), 1174–1184.

Tan, N.-T. (2004). Social entrepreneurship: Challenge for social work in a challenging world. *Asia Pacific Journal of Social Work and Development, 14*(2), 87–98.

Tang, K. L., and Cheung, C. K. (2007). Programme effectiveness in activating welfare recipients to work: The case of Hong Kong. *Social Policy & Administration, 41*(7), 747–767.

The Big Issue (2008). The Big Issue. Available online at, www.bigissue.com, accessed on 15 March 2008.

Ungar, M. (2002). A deeper, more social ecological social work practice. *Social Service Review, 76*(3), 480–497.

Ungar, M. (2003). A deeper, more social ecological social work practice – Reply. *Social Service Review, 77*(2), 309–311.

van der Laan, G. (2000). Social work in the Netherlands. In A. Adams, P. Erath and S. M. Shardlow (Eds.), *Fundamentals of social work in selected European countries* (pp. 83–102). Lyme Regis: Russell House.

van Oorshot, W., and Arts, W. (2005). The social capital of European welfare states: The crowding out hypothesis revisited. *Journal of European Social Policy, 15*(1), 5–26.

World Bank (1999). What is social capital? Available online at, http://www.worldbank.org/poverty/scapital/whatsc.htm, accessed 10 November 2007.

Younghusband, E. (1981). *The newest profession: A short history of social work*. Sutton, Surrey: Community Care/IPC Business Press.

Yu, S. W. K. (1996). The nature of social services in Hong Kong. *International Social Work, 39(4)*, 411–430.

10

A Case Study for Social Enterprise –
The Evolution of Mental-Care Connect Company Limited in Hong Kong

Stephen Yan-Leung Cheung
and Wai-Sing Chung

The Oxford Saïd Business School defines social entrepreneurship as "a professional, innovative and sustainable approach to systemic change that resolves social market failures and grasps opportunities".

Social entrepreneurship is typically adopted in the non-profit sector, predominantly as a strategy to employ business skills in response to shrinking resources. However, the basic concept of social entrepreneurship should not be confused with non-profit enterprises per se, nor should it be confined to businesses with an explicit social purpose. On the contrary, social entrepreneurship can be found in the public, private and third sectors alike. In spite of adopting an entrepreneurial model of work, social enterprises consider the overall impact of their work on society, rather than their profitability as the primary criterion for an evaluation of their performance and credibility of their assessment.

I. A Brief History
of Social Enterprises in Hong Kong

The phenomenon of social enterprise (SE) in Hong Kong is still in its preliminary stages, but one can observe its remarkable growth in recent years. As of January 2006, there were 46 non-governmental organisations (NGOs) assisting or undertaking 186 SE projects. SEs in Hong Kong have social goals and aim at encompassing: (1) work integration, (2) community empowerment, (3) service innovation, (4) sector-wide capacity building, and (5) enterprising philanthropic practices. They participated in 37 types of businesses. The establishment of the Social Enterprise Resource Centre (SERC) in early 2006, by the Hong Kong Council of Social Service, has further advanced SE growth in Hong Kong. The Centre offers an extensive range of support services to equip social entrepreneurs with the essential knowledge and skills to run SEs, including consultancy services (mentorship programmes, start-up assessment and evaluation services), training and learning programmes (workshops and training programmes on social enterprise operation and management, local and overseas study visits), and assistance in marketing and promotional ventures (social enterprise exhibitions, social enterprise market-place).

SEs in Hong Kong, as also globally, aim to enhance the self-esteem and employability of the disadvantaged sections of society. There are no formal statistics on the size of the SE sector in Hong Kong, partly due to very diverse backgrounds and mode of operations, and partly due to the lack of a common definition. SEs can broadly be classified under the following heads: (i) some SEs are subsidiaries of for-profit businesses, which run well-developed corporate social responsibility programmes alongside their business operations; (ii) some SEs are run by charities and non-profit organisations (either directly or through a subsidiary) which have become more entrepreneurial and integrated market operation approaches with some of their welfare programmes; (iii) some SEs stem from projects supported by seed funding from the government. Most of them have long-term financial self-sufficiency as the aim, while currently they are at various levels of cost recovery.

The most striking example of the last category of SEs is the "Enhancing Employment of People with Disabilities through Small Enterprise" project (a "seed money" project). This project aims to enhance the employability of people with disabilities (PWDs), though it has also generated employment opportunities for the able-bodied. Up to June 2005, 396 posts were created, which engaged 290 disabled and 106 able-bodied workers on the 31 social enterprises involved in the Project.

Although there is no commonly agreed definition of a social enterprise (SE) in Hong Kong, a SE nevertheless possesses certain essential characteristics. It aims to accomplish its social goals and mission by using enterprise strategies and therefore it combines both the "from Welfare to Work" and "Social Investment" approaches. The fundamental goal of the SE is to provide assistance and support to marginalised groups in the community by encouraging self-reliance, and therefore the issue of sustainability of the SE assumes paramount significance.

Increasing knowledge of the work of SEs in Hong Kong reflects a growing recognition of their positive contribution to social well-being. An integration of social and commercial purposes in goods and services delivery creates a real-work environment for disadvantaged groups, which proves extremely conducive to raising their skills levels and employability. The disadvantaged develop a progressive change in mindset, owing to the business approach incorporated in SEs. This greatly augments their capacity to embrace life's challenges and uncertainties, which is indispensable for ultimate and long-term self-reliance. The NGOs and community organisations develop a spirit of dynamism and innovation, because of the alternative income generated from service delivery to meet societal needs. As SEs grow, their growth is often accompanied by an increase of community networks and cross-sector partnerships. These go a long way in reducing the initial entry barriers for SEs, and are extremely advantageous from the perspective of nurturing social capital. The positive contribution of the SE sector has prompted governments and non-governmental sectors in many countries to pay increasing attention to facilitating SE development.

Like other business enterprises, some SEs tend to be successful; on the other hand, many start-ups fail. A critical success factor for the SEs is to possess a genuine enterprising spirit and a mentality to compete and operate like any other business enterprise. Other success factors include professional and business management, and community support. The long-term sustainability of a SE's operations is to a large extent determined by community support for its objectives and mission from both the neighbourhood and the private sector. For instance, some SEs offer low-skill personal and community support services and rely on neighbourhood networks and goodwill for business. Consequently, partnership with the private sector may turn out be a profitable means of providing a source of business and other modes of support (e.g., donations and soft loans to facilitate start-up and expansion, business connections and professional advice).

SEs also lead to resource mobilisation, as there is a change of status of those employed at the SE from unemployed to employed, from unwaged to waged, and from being disadvantaged to being a respected member of society. One of the most lasting and significant contributions of a SE would be empowerment of people with disabilities (PWD). The SE serves a "springboard function" to propel the PWD into the employment arena, thus leading to enhanced esteem and increase in self-worth, because of their employment status. Finally, SEs play an intermediary role between the government, private and third sectors, and thereby succeeds in forging strong tripartite relationships. One method of encouraging this partnership would be to organise forums to promote public knowledge and understanding of SEs, and to involve the business sector and the wider community in considering the latent possibility of using SEs to assist PWDs.

The government recognises the potential benefits of the development of SEs in enhancing the employability of the disadvantaged, particularly the PWDs. In spite of government recognition and support, SEs very often encounter difficulties or constraints in the initial stages of set-up. In Hong Kong, there is a lack of experienced personnel with the business background and the requisite business knowledge and skills to operate SEs in the NGO and welfare sectors, despite the escalating number of NGOs. This limits the development of successful SEs for it would take time to nurture such "social entrepreneurs". Besides, the challenge in human resources can also take the form of creating a change in mindset of people and then achieving a balanced ratio of normal and disabled workers in the SEs. As most social services are presently provided by NGOs, it appears that SEs would find it difficult to enter this market, and then generate a decent income for the disabled and disadvantaged employed by them.

Challenges in financial resources are encountered when SEs seek to mobilise the necessary financial resources to start up or support their enterprises. It is easier for SEs that employ disabled workers to obtain seed money or funding from the government than it is for SEs that seek to employ the able-bodied unemployed persons, which may have to seek start-up funding from other more difficult sources. Nevertheless, given the positive contribution of SEs and the successful experience overseas in extending the concept to the able-bodied, the government could give serious consideration to exploring how SEs may be further developed to help prepare the able-bodied for work and eventual self-reliance. SEs also face the problem of breaking even, as most of them receive their seed or initial funding from an NGO and then have to work hard to achieve profitability, in spite of all the constraints they encounter. They also face competition in the open market from bigger commercial players offering the same products or services that they offer. Many of their business activities, like retail, catering and cleaning services, tend to be very competitive fields.

Finally, a major constraint is that the tendering system for awarding of contracts tends to be unfavourable for the development of SEs. Some SEs operate in sectors where a contract's term is only for a period of two or three years. With the risk of non-renewal ever-present, the very survival and sustainability of the SE is at stake. Besides, it defeats the entire aim of the setting up of the SE, when the disadvantaged people that it employs face the risk of unemployment once again, with its closure on non-renewal of the contract. SEs may also encounter financial obstacles in the tendering system. Some of the tender bids for government renovation projects stipulate that potential bidders must possess cash reserves of HK$2 million and three years of experience to be eligible to bid for the tender. Many SEs are unable to meet this stipulation and therefore are unable even to bid for government contracts.

Notwithstanding the challenges and difficulties they encounter, SEs are expected to flourish in Hong Kong, as is evident from the Budget Speech of the Financial Secretary in February 2007:

The Enhancing Self-Reliance through Partnership Programme launched by the Home Affairs Department has so far provided funding to 41 social enterprise projects, which are expected to provide about 750 jobs. In order to nurture more management talent for social enterprises, the Hong Kong Council of Social Service and various tertiary institutions, with the support of the Commission on Poverty, will offer Hong Kong's first social enterprise management training course in the middle of this year. In collaboration with the business, social welfare and education sectors, we will continue our efforts to promote and facilitate the further development of social enterprises in Hong Kong.

II. Case Study
on Mental-Care Connect Company Limited

As a non-profit organisation providing for the needs of the mentally disabled, the Mental Health Association of Hong Kong (MHAHK) has been active in Hong Kong since 1954, when it started off as a study group with the primary objective of educating the public on mental health. It became a member agency of the Hong Kong Council of Social Service in 1968 and the Community Chest of Hong Kong in 1969. Incorporation under the Companies Ordinance took place in July 1970. The MHAHK has consistently striven over the years to adhere to the following objectives: (i) to promote the study of basic principles of mental health and their application in Hong Kong; (ii) to promote the advancement of a mental health programmes in Hong Kong in its broadest medical, social and recreational aspects, covering the needs of both the mentally ill and the mentally handicapped; (iii) to further the establishment of better human relations in all possible ways; and (iv) to establish and operate half-way houses, hostels, sheltered workshops, day training centres, social clubs or any such projects on a non-profit basis.

As the MHAHK gradually gained more experience in operating income-generating business ventures, it also realised the potential of providing long-term employment opportunities for the disabled. With its primary goal as work integration, Mental-Care Connect Company Limited (MCC) was incorporated in 2002, by the MHAHK, its parent non-profit organisation, as a limited company. In response to the "Enhancing Employment of People with Disabilities through Small Enterprise Project", which was launched by the Social Welfare Department in December 2001, the MHAHK established MCC as a subsidiary to (i) develop new business projects and (ii) restructure the existing business projects being operated by the MHAHK. Several years later, a well-established SE in Hong Kong, the business scope of MCC now encompasses convenience stores, "rehab shops", household goods shops, direct sales services and cleaning services. At present, the organisation has 96 employees, of whom 61 suffer from different disabilities.

The MHAHK established the first of its "Cheers Gallery" enterprises at the Jockey Club Building in 1997. Since then, nine more "Cheers Gallery" enterprises have been established by MCC. Using the brand name "Cheers Gallery", MCC now operates eight retail outlets (including four convenience stores and five outlets selling rehabilitation products), most of which are located within public hospitals, with a monthly total turnover of almost HK$1 million. The brand "Cheers Gallery" has become a source of pride among the disabled community. This paper seeks to discuss the development of MCC's Cheers Gallery with the application of the SE concept, and its impact on socio-economic development.

"Cheers Gallery" was established as a retail brand to set up diversified businesses, in order to create more job opportunities for the disabled by reducing the "labelling" effect (the stigma or branding effect) of people with disabilities in society and encouraging them to participate actively in their own business enterprises. Through MCC and its "Cheers Gallery" brand, the MHAHK advocates the development of "social enterprise", making it an integral part of the socio-economic system. It endeavoured to strengthen the cross-sectoral collaboration of MCC with government, business sectors as well as the general public and to build up a strong bond of partnership with these parties. Its final aim was to be a self-financing organisation, through profit gained from business expansion activities.

III. Project Overview

The development of "Cheers Gallery" has had three distinct stages: (i) the initial stage, (ii) the development stage, and (iii) the social expansion stage, the age of social enterprise.

Initial Stage (1998–1999)

In October 1997, the MHAHK formally declared open its new head- quarters, the Jockey Club Building at Kwun Tong. In the same year, MHAHK received a grant from the Hong Kong Jockey Club Charities Trust for a sum of over HK$1 million to be utilised towards setting up an integrated retail and service outlet comprising a café, gift shop, printing service and automatic vending machines. Immediately after the MHAHK's service units, training and employment services centre had moved to the new Jockey Club Building, MHAHK worked diligently towards establishing the outlet, named "Cheers Gallery". Hence, the first-ever "Cheers Gallery" integrated store began operations in March 1998.

Pre-vocational training enhances open employment of the disabled. The "Cheers Gallery" enterprises provide a broad spectrum of training; waitering, beverage mixing, cleaning, cashiering, sales techniques, printing, management of vending machines etc. The trainees learn a variety of customer services and job skills during the training periods, lasting from three months to a year, in a genuine working environment. More importantly, these PWD trainees gain a complete competitive work experience, wherein they inculcate discipline into their working habits, develop endurance skills, problem-solving skills and a wide range of social skills for work and responsibility. Although there is no guarantee that a trainee will find a suitable job at the end of his or her training period, this pre-vocational character building and soft-skills training helps greatly to promote their adaptability for a future job. Each year, "Cheers Gallery" trains about 30 to 40 PWDs, and their success rate in getting a job through the open recruitment market is about 30 per cent.

Cheers Gallery as a meeting point for community integration. Initially during the building phase of the MHAHK Jockey Club Building in Kung Lok Road, Kwun Tong there was a fear that there would be opposition to a centre being operated for ex-mentally ill or mentally handicapped people, for society as a whole still discriminates against people with special needs and disabilities. This can be traced largely to the fact that the general public on the whole lacks an inherent understanding about PWDs and may also to a certain extent be influenced by distinct negative experiences. The main goal of "Cheers Gallery", was thus to eliminate any misunderstanding in society about disabled persons, through promoting direct contact and dealings with them. Apart from PWDs serving clients within the building, 20 or 30 PWDs from the community visit "Cheers Gallery" daily to use various services. Not only did the staff that greeted clients, prepared food and catered to the various needs of clients have different disabilities, but some of the clients had disabilities too. This kind of integration in a daily congenial environment, went a long way towards giving the general public a better understanding of the abilities of the disabled and a more positive mind-set towards them. On the other hand, the PWDs at "Cheers Gallery" progressively grew more and more confident, as they became better equipped with social skills and manners through daily contact with the community as a whole.

Build "Cheers Gallery" as a distinctive retail brand operated by PWDs. The brand "Cheers Gallery", by its very meaning, was first conceived as a place where the disabled could learn and work happily, as well as a place to share their work with the community. Its Chinese name, 卓思廊, translated literally into English, means "showing the superb job performance of the disabled".

In March 1998, the first "Cheers Gallery" held a grand opening function, inviting a popular singer to hold an autograph-signing ceremony, in order to draw public attention to its work. This ceremony also served as an introduction for the Hong Kong media to the concept of "Cheers Gallery" and how PWDs run the store thoroughly and efficiently.

"Cheers Gallery" achieved break-even during the first year. "Cheers Gallery" began trial operations in December 1997. Continuous improvement in product and service quality was made from the time of inception, right up until the time it was put into formal operation in March 1998. The operation strategy during the commencement phase of "Cheers Gallery" placed emphasis on the enterprise as "a place for pre-vocational training for the disabled".

Indeed, "Cheers Gallery" was a clean and elegant café for customers, the likes of which had seldom been seen previously in Kwun Tong district. Furthermore, the gift shop and the printing service demonstrated the competence of the disabled staff members.

253

Since products and services offered by "Cheers Gallery" were competitively priced and of a high quality and standard, it served as an incentive to attract the local community. For instance, teachers and students from schools, the staff of a home for the elderly, as well as the residents of the home, visited "Cheers Gallery" for shopping on a regular basis. It was filled with customers during lunch hour each day, and the impressive efforts of the staff resulted in a monthly average turnover of over HK$30,000 in 1998. This income was sufficient to pay for trainees' allowances, management fees and depreciation as well as all daily operation expenses. At present, the monthly average turnover of the original Cheers Gallery reaches HK$60,000.

Development Stage (1999–2002)

New shops opened to increase open employment and training opportunities for disabled. The Marketing Consultancy Office (Rehabilitation) established by the Social Welfare Department in 1999 acted as an agent to help the MHAHK win the contract to operate the convenience store of the North District Hospital by means of bidding in a restricted tender. Since the concept, operation structure, product variety and quantity, as well as store opening hours, contained in its bid best met the hospital's requirements, the MHAHK was awarded the contract to operate a "Cheers Gallery" in North District Hospital. Apart from the shop supervisor, seven other staff members were rehabilitants. In February 2002, the MHAHK received permission to set up a rehabilitation shop in the new Tseung Kwan O Hospital. Besides the shop supervisor, two other staff members were both rehabilitants.

Experience of operating Cheers Gallery a powerful tool in combating competition. Although the MHAHK acquired the contracts for the North District Hospital and the Tseung Kwan O Hospital by restricted tender, there was still vigorous competition. Apart from a well-documented business plan, MHAHK had to give presentations to the hospital management and staff, explaining and elaborating on the business features of "Cheers Gallery", how it aimed to build a strong working partnership with the hospitals, the benefits to the hospitals in terms of rental income and the hospital's public image, as well as purchase discounts offered to staff and patients of the hospitals.

Besides a comprehensive plan that served client needs and requirements, the most important factor in securing the contract for MHAHK was the track record of "Cheers Gallery". The presentations enabled the hospital management to have a better understanding of the enterprise, for instance, participation of PWDs in the daily working of the original "Cheers Gallery", the sustainable support mechanism of the parent organisation (the MHAHK), standardised and systematised operations in "Cheers Gallery", and last but not the least, its self-financing ability.

Sheltered workshop products (sympathy cards and artificial silk flowers made for the hospital market by workers in sheltered workshops) together with rehabilitation products sold in "Cheers Gallery" shops generated good turnover, which directly increased the income of the sheltered workshop workers. Moreover, these products were widely accepted by the market.

Build a small integrated community within the hospitals. The MHAHK greatly values its relationship with hospitals. Therefore, its business plan presented to the hospitals while bidding for the tenders stated that MHAHK would offer training opportunities for in-patients. Once in operation, it also solicited opinions, advice and comments from hospital administration departments and/or therapeutic departments on a regular basis, on ways of improving operations in the "Cheers Gallery" outlets within hospital premises. This feedback enabled it to vastly improve product and service quality, besides responding with immediate feedback to hospital complaints.

As an indication of its efforts to integrate into the hospital environment, MHAHK invited the Hospital Chief Executive to officiate at the opening ceremony of the new "Cheers Gallery" store. Efforts at assimilating into the hospital culture, in order to cement a secure working relationship, went further, with the MHAHK staff greatly supporting hospital activities by participating in anti-smoking campaigns and similar sponsored hospital activities.

New shops achieve break-even point. With proper management techniques and governance, two of the businesses achieved break-even point during the first year of operation. By the end of

2002, the annual turnover of the two "Cheers Gallery" outlets reached HK$4 million. This income was sufficient to cover all expenses, including employees' salaries, trainees' allowances, concession fees as well as daily expenditure.

Golden Age of "Social Enterprise" (2002–present)

In this stage, the MHAHK envisaged further business expansion under the brand name of "Cheers Gallery", thereby creating more job opportunities for the disabled. To this end, MHAHK injected the North District Hospital "Cheers Gallery" convenience store and Tseung Kwan O Hospital "Cheers Gallery" rehabilitation shop and made them answerable to its newly set-up subsidiary, MCC, in order to strengthen the scale of operations. In the golden age of social enterprise, MHAHK developed a wider vision of scale – it aimed to advocate the development of SEs in Hong Kong, thus making it an integral part of the fabric of our socio-economic system. It aspired to accomplish this goal by working towards reducing the public stigma attached to people with various disabilities in society, and encouraging them to be their own masters in new or existing business ventures. MCC worked slowly yet steadily towards these aims, strengthening collaborations with business sectors, building up partnerships and achieving self-financing through profits gained from business expansion activities.

MHAHK set up MCC as its subsidiary with government aid. In 2002, the MHAHK set up MCC as its subsidiary, and was granted over HK$1.4 million from the Social Welfare Department project, "Enhancing Employment of People with Disabilities through Small Enterprise" for launching three businesses. These were: cleansing services, primarily bus cleaning services for Kowloon Motor Bus Co. Ltd, which was their major client; a franchised household products shop; and Ruttonjee Hospital "Cheers Gallery" convenience store, which opened in 2002.

Gaining experience in open bidding. The Ruttonjee Hospital "Cheers Gallery" convenience store was different from other existing "Cheers Gallery" enterprises in that bidding for the store was not by restricted tender. Rather, MCC bid in the open market along with other large chains of convenience stores. A consistent track record, sound operational direction and business practices, ultimately succeeded in securing the bid for "Cheers Gallery" to operate the store in Ruttonjee Hospital.

In order to achieve the objectives of economy of scale and business diversification, the MHAHK handed over the operations of the North District Hospital "Cheers Gallery" convenience store and Tseung Kwan O Hospital "Cheers Gallery" rehabilitation shop to MCC in late 2003. This helped MCC to attain a leading position in the market. After MCC took over these two "Cheers Gallery" stores, one more "Cheers Gallery" outlet was opened in 2004. Through business integration, MCC gained crucial experience and an impressive track record in operating rehabilitation shops, which significantly facilitated future business development.

Accelerated growth. During 2002-03, MCC worked hard on consolidation of the businesses funded by the "Enhancing Employment of People with Disabilities through Small Enterprise" project, as well as integration of the newly set up "Cheers Gallery" stores. In mid-2004, MCC obtained the tender for Pok Oi Hospital convenience store on the open market. It was a small shop and turnover was not high. Nevertheless, as it was predicted that Pok Oi Hospital would develop over time into a large-scale hospital, the acquisition by MCC of the Pok Oi Hospital store at that time laid the foundation for future business development.

In November 2004, an agreement was signed between the Marketing Consultancy Office (Rehabilitation) and West Rail, in which West Rail leased out shops in Siu Hong and Tin Shui Wai Railway Stations, without rental for the first year and with 5% of the shop turnover as rent for the second year. Traffic and customer flow on the West Rail is relatively low, and this led MCC to make a decision to operate the one and only railway rehabilitation shop in Siu Hong Station. This decision was also prompted by the fact that the station is close to Tuen Mun Hospital and thus it was convenient for patients and the community to buy rehabilitation products at better prices.

The success of the Tseung Kwan O Hospital "Cheers Gallery" rehabilitation shop acted as a stimulus for several hospitals in Hong

Kong to plan similar rehabilitation shops, specialising in retail of rehab products, on their premises. From 2005 to 2006, MCC successfully opened three more rehabilitation shops at Kowloon Hospital, Pok Oi Hospital and Queen Elizabeth Hospital, thus bringing the total of "Cheers Gallery" rehabilitation shops to five. This expansion of business sites created opportunities for PWDs to maximise their work potential, to further advance their career development and even to be promoted to positions in supervisory and managerial capacities, by taking up leadership and training roles.

Disabled staff benefit from service expansion. All staff members of "Cheers Gallery" receive competitive remuneration packages and labour benefits, according to prevalent market rates. They are also members of the Mandatory Provident Fund (MPF) scheme. The monthly salary for general sales staff is in the bracket between HK$4500 and 5500, whereas the salary of the store supervisor ranges from HK$5500 to 10,000.

Rapid expansion of its businesses enabled MCC to promote hard-working and competent disabled employees to posts of shop supervisors and supervisory posts. In fact, disabled staff members came to occupy key management positions in "Cheers Gallery" shops in Pok Oi Hospital, Ruttonjee Hospital, West Rail Siu Hong Station, Kowloon Hospital and Queen Elizabeth Hospital. This serves to motivate the more junior disabled staff members to improve their job performance, by demonstrating an eagerness to work and grow with the company.

Building up social capital promotes socio-economic development. "Cheers Gallery" shops actively create employment opportunities for disabled and disadvantaged people. A large portion of their income is earned from their retail and cleansing services. The profits thus generated are reinvested in future business expansion. The annual turnover of nine "Cheers Gallery" shops is expected to reach HK$12 million and provide 35 open job opportunities. It is estimated that 40 per cent of the staff were receiving social security benefits, under Comprehensive Social Security Assistance Scheme (CSSA) of the Social Welfare Department, before joining "Cheers Gallery". MCC has successfully utilised its business income to help both the unemployed and recipients under the CSSA Scheme to return to the workforce. After gaining employment at "Cheers Gallery" shops, some of the recipients have been able to withdraw from the CSSA Scheme or turned their status to one of "low income group".

This positive outcome directly reduces the social security burden on the government, increases productivity, and helps in building social capital, thereby fostering economic growth in society. Therefore, we can conclude that the development of social enterprise is indeed a process of social capital construction, which promotes socio-economic development.

Partnership benefits. With the establishment of more businesses over the years, MCC has witnessed a surge in its business partnerships; with suppliers, hospitals, the West Rail and even customers. In recent years, more and more hospitals have approached MCC to explore the feasibility of setting up rehabilitation shops on their premises. The enhancement of relationships with suppliers and business partners and the success of the new shops have been achieved through the concerted and determined efforts and hard work of a strong cohesive team.

Summary

The triumphant success of the chain of "Cheers Gallery" outlets in Hong Kong can be summarised by noting that initial funding for the project came from the Hong Kong Jockey Club Charities Trust and further financial support was obtained from "Enhancing Employment of People with Disabilities through Small Enterprise" project. This start-up funding was invested on shop renovation, equipment installation, stock and initial operation costs. Using the brand name "Cheers Gallery", as of March 2007, MCC operated nine stores and outlets (including four convenience stores and five outlets selling rehabilitation products), with most of the shops located within public hospitals. The enterprise employed 96 staff members, over 60 of them being disabled people. The combined business turnover is projected to reach HK$16 million in 2006-07. It is anticipated that "Cheers Gallery" as a whole can practically achieve break-even by the year 2006-07, and therefore further business expansion plans are on the anvil.

IV. Implications
for Cross-Sector/Service Collaboration

A strong synergistic bond is created between vocational rehabilitation services and SE, as we observed in this paper. Sheltered workshops (workplaces that provide a supportive environment where physically or mentally challenged persons can acquire job skills and vocational experience) and the supported employment service help train staff members and prepare them for the experience of working in a SE. Staff members who are referred from the supported employment service to MCC enjoy continuous support from the service. A monthly meeting between a vocational counsellor and the shop supervisor of every "Cheers Gallery" outlet further ensures that all possible support is extended to staff members. Besides, products from the MHAHK sheltered workshops are sold in "Cheers Gallery" stores, thereby increasing the income of workshop workers.

By working closely and cooperating directly with the public sector, the SE can attain numerous benefits that would not be possible under normal conditions. It is a widespread practice for a SE to turn to government departments for some resources support. This especially holds true in the nascent stages of setting up the enterprise. As we have seen, this holds true in the case of the "Cheers Gallery" hospital shops, and where West Rail agreed to adopt a restricted tender bid, in order to give higher credit for higher disabled staff ratio. This gave "Cheers Gallery" a superior edge, enabling it to win the tender. Public sector organisations could also consider giving more flexible rental packages to SE outfits, such as accepting a certain percentage of turnover, in lieu of a standard rental payment. This agreement would to a great extent help reduce the rental burden of the SE and could also reduce the risk to which the SE is exposed in case of adverse business conditions such as those prevalent during the SARS epidemic in Hong Kong in 2003. In fact, five of the "Cheers Gallery" outlets reap the benefits of a flexible rental system.

As MCC is committed to providing job placement opportunities for rehabilitation departments of hospitals, this practice helps reinforce the relationship between "Cheers Gallery" and the various hospital departments, with which MCC staff interact personally. The Social Welfare Department's Marketing Consultancy Office (MCO) acts as an advisory body to give consultancy services to SEs that are in the process of being set up through the "Enhancing Employment of People with Disabilities through Small Enterprise" project. Accordingly, MCC obtained funding from this project for its diversified businesses that include cleansing services, a franchised household products shop and seven of its "Cheers Gallery" stores. The value of the funding was the highest amount ever secured by a social service organisation in Hong Kong.

MCC has also built up a distinct and powerful partnership with the business sector in Hong Kong because of its diversified businesses, which enhance its collaboration and cooperation with this sector. Among its service and products suppliers, many are small and medium-sized enterprises (SMEs). Through continued collaboration and dealings with MCC, these SMEs gain flexible and knowledge about MCC's services. This very often induces them to offer better prices for their products and also easier payment terms. The business sector can in many ways contribute to the setting up and continued operation of SEs by offering donations, providing volunteers, extending their expertise and even sharing their business acumen and vision. In such an atmosphere, all parties would gain more knowledge about the business and benefit from the mutual relationship. Thus tripartite relationships involving the government, business sector and the third sector, or the SEs, are a critical success factor for a sustainable social enterprise. Due to the rapid growth of MCC, frequently there arises a situation where there may be insufficient disabled staff at the MHAHK Vocational Rehabilitation Service to fill the vacancies in MCC. In these circumstances, MCC welcomes referrals from other social service organisations to fill those vacancies. These exchanges serve to boost and encourage cooperation between MCC and other social service organisations.

As we have seen through this paper, the success of SEs in Hong Kong is to a great degree dependent on the partnership between non-governmental organisations (NGOs), the government, and the business sector. The diagram below depicts the significance of the

Business Sectors

1. Share business experience.
2. Open up sales channels for products of Social Enterprise that can be sold in the market.
3. Product and service suppliers offer discounts to Social Enterprises.
4. Franchisor provides preferential offers.
5. More flexible and privileged shop rental packages.
6. Strategic alliances.
7. Sponsorships.
8. Use services and products of Social Enterprises.

Social Enterprise

1. Develop a diversity of businesses to create job and training opportunities for disabled and underprivileged through tripartite cooperation.
2. Create social capital for the socio-economic system.
3. Re-invest profit for new business.
4. Provide superb products and quality services with a market and customer-driven strategy.
5. Social Enterprises to act as sales channels for sheltered workshops products.
6. Promote social harmony

Non-Governmental Organizations

1. Develop Social Enterprise proposals to apply for seed money from Government.
2. Encourage staff with business sense and service mission to develop business plan.
3. Monitor the development of Social Enterprise for the proper use of cross-sectoral resources and the protection of employees' benefits.
4. Ensure a balance between the profit requirements and social objectives of the Social Enterprise.

Government / Public Sector

1. Provide seed money/ start-up funding.
2. Provide sustainable developing fund/ resources for Social Enterprise development.
3. Provide Social Enterprise training opportunity to non-governmental organizations.
4. Provide favourable business environment to Social Enterprises by amending company ordinance and favourable taxation procedures.
5. Inter-departmental cooperation within Government to enhance Social Enterprise development.
6. Let out shops/ venues to Social Enterprises on more flexible and preferential terms.
7. Promote Social Enterprise in support of social capital as part of socio-economic development.
8. Services and products of Social Enterprises to be used by government on preferential basis.

roles enacted by each of these groups and how the synergy between them can be synthesised to achieve a harmonious blend of social missions.

V. Obstacles and Solutions

MCC encountered some hurdles through various stages of setting up its chain of "Cheers Gallery" stores, from which the SE learned some fundamental lessons. SEs by definition tend to be small, as their principal goal is integration of the disadvantaged groups working for them into the community. Thus, their size acts as a hindrance in terms of economy of scale in production and services. MCC sought to overcome this difficulty by opening more stores in various hospitals in Hong Kong. MCC envisaged that more jobs would automatically be created, which would also lower operation costs for the stores. However, the company did not contend with the fact that this would also lead to an increase in rent payments, increase in central administration costs and difficulties in maintaining service quality. The solution was to set up a complete operation and monitoring mechanism. The company sought to improve shop monitors by installing a modern IT system and making constant and consistent improvements in store management guidelines. MCC also proposed to provide standardised training to staff, in order to maintain a high standard and quality of services.

In the business world, operational strategies and ways to cut costs are more flexible and decisive than in a SE. Businesses in the real world have less to consider when they shut down operations than does a SE, which, when it considers retreating from the market, has to keep in mind resettlement of disabled staff members, the organisation's image, as well as accountability to the funding bodies. As with any business entity, the sustainability of a SE depends on whether it provides products and services that are in demand in the market, that meet market needs, that the market can absorb and that correspond with current and prevalent social trends. The SE can still claim to be in a healthy condition when loss in individual businesses can be covered by profits from other businesses. However, if there are huge losses that cannot be borne by the SE, it is sound business logic to shut down the business and retreat from the market. The survival of the enterprise at such times is more important than "saving face". However, diversified business development helps greatly in avoiding the impact of adverse business conditions in a niche market.

As competition between SEs becomes more intense, it is noticed that there may be an overlap of business ventures among the SEs. Very often, SEs may enter the market through an exceptionally low bidding price, without looking at future feasibility considerations, such as an increase in operation costs, which in turn would affect the future viability of the project. Continuing communication and feedback is therefore recommended among SEs. A platform for exchange and sharing of ideas and views of management and staff would go a long way in ensuring that all SEs can co-exist peacefully and conduct their businesses without impinging into each other's territory. Regular experience-sharing sessions, where SEs can exchange operation tips, business opportunities, market change and human resources demand etc., would be some of the techniques for ensuring peaceful co-existence between various social enterprises.

Retail industry is for the most part monopolised by large business groups, and many SEs struggle for survival in such a hostile environment. With their economies of scale, bargaining power, shop rental privileges, product variety and promotion strategies, large business groups have a better opportunity to cope in a harsh and unforgiving business environment, than most SEs operated by social service organisations. One method of combating this difficulty would be for SEs to consider operating small shops in marginal communities, with an emphasis on "relationship sales". They would do well if they operated as convenience stores or groceries which focus on selling consumables in smaller communities. Moreover, collaboration between SEs should be reinforced, in that similar businesses could consider forming strategic alliances, in order to bargain for better offers from traders and suppliers. The government could consider an alleviation of high rental burdens on SEs, by providing low-rent premises to SEs. This would in turn enable SEs to compete with large business groups.

The availability of satisfactory financial support is crucial to the survival of SEs. As most grants are of a short duration of one year, however, further funding becomes an imminent cause of concern, owing to the fact that a viable business enterprise may take a longer period of time to nurture and flourish. In this situation, the government can aid SEs by following the overseas model and setting up a SE financing organisation. When the SE requires capital for service expansion or faces a severe cash crunch, it can apply to such a permanent funding organisation for funds. The government can also offer incentive payments to SEs based on the number of disabled staff they employ annually, which, in turn, would serve to enhance the income of the SE.

VI. Conclusions

What is a social enterprise (SE)? SE should be different from the traditional enterprise that only focuses on profit maximisation. A SE should have two objectives. The first objective for a SE is to generate enough profit to sustain its operation. The second is to achieve social objectives.

Like other business operations, a SE has to compete with other business in the open market. Thus, a SE needs to execute a business plan, keep costs down, promote its service/product and eventually sustain its operation. This chapter illustrates the development of a successful SE in Hong Kong.

It is equally important that a SE has to achieve social goals, such as job creation for disadvantaged people who could not easily find jobs in the job market. A SE can provide a mid-way station for the long-term unemployed to return to the job market. The distinctive advantage is that they could accumulate social capital in working for SEs and gain experience of the work environment. Importantly, they can eventually find jobs in the open job market.

This job creation can relieve pressure on the government and the community in that that these long-term unemployed will no longer rely on social welfare payments. To illustrate the positive interactions between SE and social capital, we conducted a focus interview among employees of MCC. The results are summarised in the Appendix. Our findings confirm that the employees had positive working experiences in MCC. They all indicated that their involvement in MCC had a very positive effect on their overall well-being. Importantly, SE could provide a conducive working environment for the disadvantaged for social capital accumulation and eventually be able to become self-reliant.

Acknowledgements

The authors would like to thank Yvonne Yeung for providing information on Mental-Care Connect Company Limited (MCC) and to acknowledge the research support of Winne Chan, Joanna Mok, Roxana R. Shroff, Evian Wong and Doris Yeung.

Appendix

Focus Group

Summary

A quick overview of our paper confirms that the principal objective of any SE is to provide a supportive environment, and thereby aim to assist discharged mental patients to re-adjust to living in the community and to develop independent living skills. In order to have a more comprehensive and detailed understanding about the effectiveness of SEs and their impact on end-users, i.e., the disadvantaged groups, a focus group of seven staff members of Mental-Care Connect Company Limited (MCC) including both staff members who formerly suffered mental illness and those who have not, was organised for the purpose of this case study. The staff members interviewed were effusive in their praise for the significance of SEs, as they provide job opportunities to people with disabilities (PWD). These members focused on the fact that although PWD might find jobs in the open market, and thus slowly integrate themselves back into the mainstream of public life, the primary essence of a SE lay in the actual tangible reality, that the employer and other staff had a higher degree of acceptance of PWD, and were, on the whole, more considerate and accepting of these sections of society which were largely looked down upon by business and other service sectors. By virtue of the fact that the SE employer had an enhanced perception and insight of the problems faced by these groups, these employers had a heightened ability to value and appreciate their work and their efforts at succeeding in the work place. They were more willing to accommodate and allow concessions for the PWD group, and eager to make individual arrangements to account for their special needs, such as flexibility in their duty roster and working hours, helping them out if necessary at work in their assigned duties and also, by giving assistance in any other form, to the disadvantaged groups. SE employers thus succeeded in earning the admiration of the staff members, who in turn were indebted to the SE and were fervent supporters of all activities and tasks undertaken by the SE.

The staff members of Mental-Care Connect Company Limited (MCC) interviewed as a part of the focus group study, especially the ex-mentally ill staff members, had great job satisfaction, stemming from the fact that having a job created in them an attitude of pride, self-worth, self-esteem and self-respect. This led to them experiencing a sense of success and meaning in life, resulting in overall satisfaction and contentment with their way of life. Their families too were very happy with this transformation in their approach to living and the focused outlook of their disadvantaged family members – the families discovered that holding down a steady job and earning an income, and therefore becoming independent, bestowed upon their disadvantaged family members a feeling of confidence and identity, leading to fulfillment with their existence. Although, like all working people, the PWD encountered job pressures, a good and healthy working relationship with colleagues provided support and helped to overcome all obstacles and difficulties. Numerous opportunities provided in training junior staff/trainees further strengthened their confidence levels and went a long way in helping them to assimilate better into the work environment.

The interviews with the MCC staff members reveal that a social enterprise affirms its true value and worth when it reliably provides job opportunities for disadvantaged groups to re-enter the job market. These groups have an option to work either in a SE or in the business sector, but the predominant choice of the PWD when it comes to re-entering the job market is to work in a SE. At this juncture, it would be pertinent to ask why the PWD prefer to work in a social enterprise, for salary is definitely not a key consideration. As the interviews illustrate to us, the salaries in a SE are relatively low but still allow the employees to take care of their daily expenses. The crucial and most compelling determinant is the fact that the SE is more altruistic and humane in its approach and concern, compared with business and other service sectors, thus giving the PWD a sense of security and comfort when employed by a SE. The SE easily understands and empathises with their situation and is ready to offer higher flexibility in the job, as discussed above, keeping in mind their special needs. As business and service sectors operate with a profit motive in mind, the humanitarian and compassionate element is most often missing in these sectors.

Furthermore, the caring and supportive atmosphere prevalent in a SE greatly boosts the confidence levels and spirits of staff members. To a certain extent, this serves to ease the financial burden on the Comprehensive Social Security Assistance Scheme (CSSA) of the Social Welfare Department. This is because the staff members consider looking for other jobs when they are no longer working in the social enterprise, but they do not contemplate returning to the CSSA for their livelihood.

Although a SE provides positive experiences to disadvantaged groups, it faces its own unique problems.

Al though a SE has its own unique values and traits, there are not many SEs in the job market. Staff/trainees may thus face competition while job hunting in the open market. They may have hidden anxieties and worries about employers and colleagues accepting them and understanding their special needs as well as agonising about their own aptitude, skills and ability to adjust and adapt to a new and unfamiliar work environment. In light of this, it is suggested that the Social Welfare Department and/or other related organisations should offer training and assistance to business sectors, to enable them to have a more benevolent approach towards the disadvantaged groups. It is true that, if more incentives are provided to business sectors, more job opportunities in better working environments will then be provided to the disadvantaged groups. For the sustainability of the SE, it is not only financial subsidy from the government/Social Welfare Department that is essential, but additional assistance and/or training in areas of business operation and management should be encouraged in order to enhance the long-term sustainability of the SE. This can be achieved by establishing an effective platform for cross-sectoral co-operation between a SE and business sectors in the interest of all parties. In such a scenario, business sectors can provide technical consultation and their business expertise and acumen in areas of business operation, while the SE can provide training in areas like "understanding disadvantaged groups". Without due regard for sustainability, a SE would not be able to survive for a long period or achieve its goals. For the SE to meet the needs of its target group or groups, more attention should be paid to operational management procedures and training programmes, along with long-term co-coordinated planning in areas of immediate necessity and concern.

The case of MCC is an exemplification of a SE, which reveals that a successful blending of social missions and market opportunities hinges on implementing as much as identifying winning business ideas. It is understood that by applying an entrepreneurial spirit and management criteria to provide better and more enhanced social services to people with disabilities (PWD), a SE can mobilise more effectively and thereby reallocate its limited resources to serve a larger population.

Background information of focus group participants:

The following table gives a history of the staff members of MCC, who participated in our survey. We have deliberately avoided giving their names and identities, to enable them to be more forthcoming and transparent in their interviews with us.

Ms. A (Shop Supervisor)	Joined MCC in March 2006 through open recruitment.
Ms. B (Shop Supervisor)	Joined the MHAHK as a staff member in March 2004 through open recruitment. Later switched to MCC.
Ms. C (Rehabilitant)	Joined MCC in March 2005 as a staff member through Supported Employment Service (SES). Works in Direct Sales Team.
Ms. D (Rehabilitant)	Joined MCC in October 2006 as a staff member through SES. Had not worked for over 10 years.
Ms. E (Rehabilitant):	Joined MCC in July 2002 as a staff member through Supported Employment Service (SES). Had not worked for over 10 years.
Ms. F (Rehabilitant):	Joined MCC in February 2007 as a staff member through the "Sunny way – On the Job Training Programme". Had not worked for almost a year.
Mr. G (Rehabilitant):	Joined MCC in June 2006 as a staff member through Supported Employment Service (SES). Had not worked for about 5 years.

** None of the staff members were under Comprehensive Social Security Assistance Scheme (CSSA) before or after they joined MCC. **

A record of the interviews:

Reproduced below is a faithful interpretation of the interviews conducted for the purpose of this study. We have endeavoured to be as accurate as possible in our interpretation of the account given to us by the interviewees. The interviewer will hereafter be known as "I.".

I : **Would all of you share among us your feelings, job satisfaction about working in MCC, as well as your opinions on the differences between your previous job/jobs and present job?**

F : I worked as a sales lady before joining MCC about a year ago. However, a heavy workload in my previous workplace triggered the onset of my illness. In fact, I liked working as a sales lady. I am satisfied with my present job, the workload of which is bearable, and my relationship with other staff. Moreover with working at MCC, I am able to support myself though I work on a half-time basis, because I live close to where I work and I do not need to incur additional travel expenses or even pay for meals during my working hours.

G : I feel pressured at work and I have no channel or outlets to relieve such pressure. I think that by working in "Cheers Gallery", one acquires and gains more knowledge than by working in a "for-profit" organisation. This is because in "Cheers Gallery," we need to have sound knowledge of the rehabilitation products we sell, how to use the equipment, how to be friendly towards our customers and much more. We cannot afford to make any mistakes or errors, by giving wrong products to customers. Pressure mainly comes from customers and the medical staff in hospitals. At times, I even encounter irrational customers and have to instantly think of a solution, without any help from my supervisor. More frequently than not, I have to tackle the problem on my own, although I can seek help from my supervisor. In addition, I have to fulfil customers' needs, as well as comply with their irrational requests. For instance, there is the case of a customer who wanted to have a product exchange for a half-drunk carton of milk. As there was no problem with the product itself, the milk carton, I was not empowered to give him anything in exchange for the milk carton. All I could do was stand silently, while submitting to the customer's tirade, till he left. You ask me why I do not share my feelings or the numerous problems that I encounter with my colleagues. It is because I think they would not render any help whatsoever or even assist me to relieve my pressures. I also do not want to make others around me unhappy in any way, so I much prefer keeping my burden to myself, staying silent and not sharing even the complaints I often tend to receive from our customers.

A : I believe that if you have really done something wrong or made an erroneous judgment, you have to admit the fault and consider making improvements. We can always learn from our mistakes and must strive to better ourselves continually.

H : Yes, so you (G) must learn to speak up and we can think of solutions together. Don't always lay all the responsibility on yourself

I : What is that makes you all continue to work in "Cheers Gallery"?

G : The harmonious working relationship between colleagues, and good team spirit. All of us are very responsible and are always willing to help each other.

D : I am happy to utilise my professional knowledge in serving customers, because I think I can help them and make a difference. Cooperation with the medical staff of hospitals and fulfilling their needs leads to a high level of job satisfaction and thereby, also a sense of success. I know that there is job pressure but I feel I can increasingly manage it and view pressure as having a positive effect, in motivating me to work harder. My friends and relatives believe that I am happier and also more knowledgeable now, than before I started working here at MCC. More importantly, by working here, I gain invaluable working experience and my emotional well-being is much better and more stable now, than the time when I was out of a job.

Previously, I worked for the government in a clerical job but quit after the birth of my daughter, as I did not have any help to look after her. I took care of my daughter at home for many years and also supported us by working in a department store selling jeans, T-shirts and accessories. I am a half-time worker now, but I am able to support my living expenses and standards, because I also have maintenance from my ex-husband. My job here as a Supervisor is good and the company is considerate of my situation, and has permitted me to take leave for the period during which I have to go through the legal proceedings for my divorce to be finalised. I will try my best to find a full time job after all the necessary legal procedures and formalities of my divorce are complete. I do not care about my junior position in the company. I simply commit myself to the job without giving too much thought to the position. I prefer to go step-by-step in all my dealings in life. I have had this (mental) illness for many years and even been admitted twice to hospital. Life in hospital was so boring. Working provides me with the spiritual satisfaction and emotional strength to carry on. I am extremely satisfied with my work, as I also have a chance to train the trainees, when I myself was a trainee in the not so distant past. I also have the ability to get along well with them.

E : I am happy and satisfied with my job as I have learnt a lot from it, which I was not aware of before I started work. I have worked in the franchised Japan Home Centre in 2002-03 and at present work in the Rehab Shop.

A : I have no great expectations from my job but I have a mission in life now and therefore a commitment to the job. I was interested in working in a Rehab shop, as I was keen on working with people with disabilities. One major difference between my current job and the one I held in the past is, that here I have to train the trainees and staff. Additionally, they are not always intelligent enough to grasp what I teach them, and I end up teaching them the same task over and over again.

　I do not perceive myself gaining any benefit from this job, but I keep on working here because I believe it is God's will that I do so. I would like to serve in a social enterprise, just like my sisters, who are working in social service agencies. Another important factor is that this company does not lay stress on profit making. At first, I believed that the company lacked operational structures and procedures and was not serious about its goals. But now, I am happy working here and gain job satisfaction as I can help others, mainly people with disabilities. I have also come to realise that the company aims to provide more employment opportunities to people with disabilities, rather than lay stress solely on profit-making.

B : I have gained job satisfaction through helping people, especially elderly patients. They are able to learn from product introductions given by me. I am also happy in working with people with disabilities and helping them. I can share my true and genuine feelings with them, with no fear of betrayal by them. Whereas, while working for other professional organisations, one cannot share his or her true feelings with colleagues, for fear that they will turn against you.

　I have gained many friendships in the course of my work here too. Job pressure is not high and I can handle the workload. I keep working in this company not only for the money but also because I have a sense of belonging to this company. The working schedule also fits my needs as I am able to both take care of as well as devote sufficient time to my family. My friends and relatives have given me very positive feedback about my job. At first, I was worried about working with people with a history of mental illness. But now I find that I have changed my mind and outlook after working with them.

C : I have been working in the Direct Sales Team since September 2006. I am happy working in the team with an officer and a manager, and I am capable of handling the job. Before joining the company, I had worked in an accounting job for two to three years, but stopped after the onset of the (mental) illness. After that, I worked in part-time sales jobs in various shops continuously. Later, I received training from Supported Employment Service in the Mental Health Association of Hong Kong (MHAHK), from where I was placed in Ms B's shop. I had encountered various inter-personal problems in my previous job. But I get along well with my colleagues here and feel that they care about me, as well as other ex-mentally ill colleagues. They do not discriminate against us, and we feel no job pressure. Thank God I work in this company, because I am certain that other employers would stigmatise us because of our illness and then fire us from our jobs. Compared with working in other companies, I am happy about my situation.

(Starts crying and someone asks her why she is so agitated!) I don't know. I just feel unhappy that if I worked elsewhere, that company would fire me because I have this illness. But this company will not fire me.

A : Actually, I want to change my job but I do not want to attend job interviews. (Other interviewees claim that this is not possible).

D : Since it was diagnosed that I had recovered, I took the advice of the social worker from the Supported Employment Service. The social worker cautioned me to train myself step-by-step according to the demands of my situation and competencies, and not proceed too fast. Maybe I can find a junior post to prevent my illness recurring again due to job pressure. I plan to upgrade my computer skills so as to enhance my confidence in job hunting. I hope to find a full time clerical job in an NGO.

But, for now, I will concentrate on my current job. I love working as sales staff and hope to get a job promotion in the future.

E : I have gained job satisfaction because I now have a job. I am afraid I would be unable to get a job with other companies. This is my first job for four years, since I had the illness. I thank this company for their patience, though I may make mistakes in my work. I am happy working in this company since I can work with other colleagues with ex-mental illness problems. We show concern for and regard for each other. I am afraid my lack of qualifications would not help me get a job in other companies. Moreover, I am afraid that they would not accept me because of my illness. In this company, as they understand our situation and know that we have to meet our doctors periodically, I am able to take sick leave by making appropriate arrangements in the duty roster. As we share a close relationship with the company, we can talk about our situation frankly and confide in the management at all times.

I do have some pressure in working, in that I am very angry with a colleague because she/he is absent-minded. However, I am happy that I am also involved in training trainees.

I : What is your opinion about the job?

G : We have a mission, we are not for profit, and we can help others but do have pressures.

A : I can help people, which serves to enhance my job satisfaction.

B : My job satisfaction increases when a deal is complete.

A : I get further satisfaction from the fact that my customers recognise me as a Christian, because of my loving and caring attitude towards them. They claim they will pray for me, too. They also say that I look like a Christian and this makes me happy.

C : Have job satisfaction and value. I also enjoy more recognition from my family. I will do my best and hope to make more money, so that my family will be much happier. There is a higher degree of acceptance when working in MCC and we are treated like normal people. There is also the added benefit of more training and opportunities here, as compared with other companies. My family also perceives an improvement in my character – they feel I have a better attitude towards my job and have become more responsible, as I seldom take leave now without any reason.

E : I experience job pressure as I need to meet sales targets. But I also share a good working relationship with my colleagues and that makes me happy to be working here. It is very gratifying to train the trainees and see an improvement in them.

D : There is an increase in responsibility. I get along well with colleagues and mutual support goes a long way in enhancing job satisfaction.

B : Promotes sense of belonging, as I have worked for a long time in MCC. Nevertheless, I still expect an increase in salary, manpower as well as other fringe benefits.

A : Yes, an increase in salary but a cut in working hours.

G : More medical benefits too.

I : What is your point of view about social enterprise?

E : Good for helping disadvantaged groups.

G : Does not seem to be a serious, structured business enterprise, with well-laid out operational procedures, but it can really do a lot of good in society.

F : Good as it offers jobs to disadvantaged groups.

G : There is a positive feedback/return to society as rehabilitants have more job opportunities, which leads to a "life reborn", though the salary is low.

A : I think this is a transition period from low pay to high pay. If we can overcome the low pay stage, we will have a bright future.

G : It is worthwhile working here – it is much better than staying at home. I have not thought of my own self. I just think about whether social enterprise as a whole, is good for others or not. And help the company to fight for certain welfare and benefits. To me, mission is larger than money. I just aim to do my very best.

I : By the way, if you were out of a job and without CSSA coverage, would you apply for it?

All: No. Look for other jobs instead.

I : What kind of job?

F : I would take it step-by-step. I would equip myself first with the appropriate skills and then look for a sales job.

C : I would look for a job with a business firm, to see whether I am capable or not. But I would still be quite worried about it.

B : I would seek a job which has a mission and a sense of belonging. Also, a job which is flexible enough, so that I can also take care of my family.

G : If out of a job, I would prefer to stay at home. I am very flexible, so whether I have a job or not, I am fine. If I do hunt for another job, I may face bullying by people due to my illness. Therefore, if I do not get a similar job, I would prefer to stay at home even for some years. However, my present job is meaningful and I enjoy working here and love doing my job.

Interpretation of Staff Satisfaction Questionnaire

All staff members of the "Cheers Gallery" retail section, 34 in total, completed the questionnaire. The questionnaire was divided into three categories: working ability, mental health and inter-personal relationships as well as income and returns. There were 10 male and 24 female staff members at "Cheers Gallery". It was found that about 68% of them had acquired a senior secondary education, while two of the staff had even completed tertiary education. The study revealed that 70% of the staff worked as shop attendants in "Cheers Gallery," while the rest of them held managerial positions in the rehabilitation shops.

Based on the study, it was found that nearly 70% of staff thought they were capable enough to handle daily routine activities pertaining to their job profile, in addition to tackling and successfully overcoming the various difficulties and challenges that are innate to any job. These were the members (70%) who were satisfied with their job, as they were assured of various opportunities, like a steady income, job promotion, and a congenial and amiable working environment, among many other benefits.

About 62% of staff members were convinced that working in "Cheers Gallery" had a very positive effect on their overall mental health and well-being, which demonstrated immense improvement. This in turn cultivated in them a sense of peace and harmony, enabling them to deal objectively with all eventualities and untoward situations arising in the workplace. Around 82% of the staff admitted that the congenial working environment equipped them to handle job pressures better, while 85% agreed to the fact that the affable set-up of "Cheers Gallery" made it easier for them to get along agreeably with colleagues and supervisors. The vast majority (82%) of them accepted the fact that the positive effect of working at "Cheers Gallery" on their mental health also served to reinforce and strengthen their inter-personal relationships, whether in the workplace or at home.

Almost 88% (30) staff members loved their job in "Cheers Gallery". Around two-thirds of staff (68%), reflected on the reality that their friends and relatives gave them positive feedback and recognition for their jobs. More than two-thirds of the staff were of the opinion that it was better to have an income, instead of receiving assistance under the Comprehensive Social Security Assistance Scheme (CSSA). Although 76% of the staff considered their job to be a long-term job, it was noticed that less than half of the staff (47%), were in actuality satisfied with the workload and income gained.

"Cheers Gallery" has come a long way in helping people with disabilities (PWD) to adjust back to a normal, routine life. As the very name suggests, it has succeeded in providing a cheerful and positive working environment for its staff. It has aimed to empower PWD by providing different kinds of support, to enhance inter-personal relationships, and to engender public awareness, by publicising the social value of social enterprises. "Cheers Gallery", run by MCC, is the epitome of a Work Integration Social Enterprise (WISE) in the rehabilitation field and has become a spur in the development of social enterprises in Hong Kong. "Cheers Gallery" serves as a beacon of hope for people with disabilities in Hong Kong, by demonstrating that with the right mental attitude and approach, they can have the courage and fortitude to overcome all odds, and once again, become deserving and valuable members of society.

11

Social Enterprise as an Interactive Process between Entrepreneurs and the Community:

A Social Capital Perspective

Kevin Au
and Thomas A. Birtch

I. Introduction

The role of social entrepreneurship in the economy is receiving heightened attention. This is in no small part due to the fact that governments and scholars are now recognizing the range of potential benefits that social enterprises can offer. This chapter begins by delineating the key features of social enterprise and what makes this form of enterprise distinct from others. Next, a brief overview of relevant social capital research, as introduced earlier in this volume, and the Hong Kong context is provided. This sets the stage for the study of a case of social entrepreneurship in Hong Kong that follows. Our exploration is devoted to identifying emerging themes and relevant issues that influence the development of a social enterprise, City Greeny. In line with our main interest, we also attempt to offer insights into how the values (i.e., trust, mutuality, and reciprocity) and attributes (e.g., social relations and network access and interactions) that are viewed to underpin social capital at the mico-, meso-, and macro-levels are cultivated and maintained by a social entrepreneur.

II. Deconstructing Social Enterprise

Not unlike social capital, multiple definitions exist for social enterprise.[1] However, all share two central themes in common. First, a social enterprise is a profit-making entity. Second, its purpose is to provide some form of social impact or benefit to the community, the so-called double or triple bottom lines. That is, a social enterprise aims to create two types of value – economic and social. Economic objectives vary according to the business model and funding requirements range from cost recovery strategies for the provision of a social service or programme to self-financing social purpose ventures. Social objectives also vary widely according to the enterprise's mission and the social problem or market failure that it has been created to address. Simply put, a social enterprise uses entrepreneurship, innovation, and creative solutions to address social problems; employs commercial practices and business tools to generate and diversify its income streams; adopts socially responsible approaches to buying and selling products and services; and measures both financial performance and social impact. Business success and social impact are interdependent.

Figure 1:
An Enterprise Continuum (Adapted from Reis, 1999)

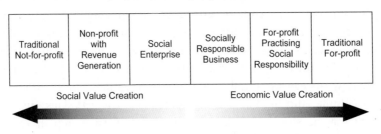

---

1   Social enterprise is defined by the Institute for Social Entrepreneurs (2008) as "any organisation, in any sector, that uses earned income strategies to pursue a double or triple bottom line, either alone (as a social sector business) or as part of a mixed revenue stream that includes charitable contributions and public sector subsidies." It is a business venture created for a social purpose that generates social value through adopting and applying private sector business practices.

As the continuum in Figure 1 suggests, a social enterprise can be viewed as lying at the intersection between traditional not-for-profit organisations and for-profit business. It can be structured within a larger organisation or as a separate legal entity. Distinctions can be made according to its duality of purpose. A social enterprise differs markedly from its for-profit counterparts or for-profit entities that practise social responsibility in that its purpose is social impact – social value creation. It also differs from a not-for-profit organisation, even those that generate income, with its added objective of economic value creation.

The benefits of social enterprise can be far-reaching. Examples include the alleviation of unemployment of disadvantaged groups or impoverished segments of society (e.g., youth, women and minority ethnic groups, the disabled, those with learning disabilities, and ex-offenders), education and worker retraining, helping to overcome limitations associated with more traditional working environments, and environmental and green movements.[2] Thus, in addition to generating the economic benefits similar to traditional business, the success of social enterprise is particularly important to government as it has the added potential to reduce fiscal pressures by either replacing or complimenting existing government-provided social programmes and activities. Today, consumers are also increasingly demanding goods and services that are socially oriented and of benefit to the community.

Building a social enterprise is a difficult task, however. Some would argue that it may even be more difficult than a traditional for-profit enterprise (Dees, Emerson, and Economy, 2001). Not only do social enterprises have to compete, attract customers in innovative ways, and face all the similar risks and challenges facing traditional business, but they must also satisfy their additional second bottom line – social value creation. At present, little is understood about how these types of enterprises develop or the different obstacles that social entrepreneurs encounter.

---

2   Many social enterprises operate in property development, maintenance and restoration, catering, consulting, call centres, and environmental management.

III. Understanding the Role
of Social Capital in Entrepreneurship

Apart from financial and human capital, social capital is viewed to be crucial to business and social activities (Aldrich, 1999). It has been defined in various ways. In the most general sense, social capital is defined as the norms (conventions) and networks that enable collective action. This encompasses the institutions, relationships, and customs that shape the quality and quantity of a society's social interactions (World Bank, 2002). From a management perspective, it is viewed as *the goodwill that is engendered by the fabric of social relations and that can be mobilized to facilitate action* (Adler and Kwon, 2002).

The source of social capital lies in the structure and content of the actor's social interactions, while its effects flow from the information, influence and solidarity it makes available to the actor (Adler and Kwon, 2002). Information refers to the access to broader sources of information which improve the quality, relevance, and timeliness of information. Influence refers to the extent of control, legitimacy and power possessed by an actor that enables him or her to achieve goals. Solidarity refers to the strength of social norms and beliefs that lead to a high degree of closure in the social network. Solidarity results in compliance with local rules and customs (rules of the game) and reduces the need for formal control mechanisms from outside authorities.[3]

Functionally, social capital fosters appropriability which is essential to entrepreneurship. That is, it facilitates using social ties of one kind to achieve other purposes (Coleman, 1988). For example, friendship ties may be used to mobilize the financial support necessary for establishing a new venture. Social capital enables entrepreneurs to gain, maintain or expand access to economic resources as well as reinforce their productivity (Aldrich, 1999;

---

3 Considerable evidence supports the notion that features of social capital lead to reduced transaction, search, monitoring, and agency costs, enhance learning, and provide a range of other benefits (Wallace, 1999). According to the learning perspective, interpersonal relations are important to learning and knowledge (Cooke, 2001).

Larson & Starr, 1993). Accordingly, the more social capital an entrepreneur possesses, the more likely he or she is to be able to benefit when establishing a new venture.

The benefits of social capital can be classified as occurring at the micro-, meso-, and macro- levels (Kimand and Aldrich, 2005). Micro-level benefits arise from the establishment of trust in relationships and enable the entrepreneur to access value chains, lower transaction costs, and develop competitiveness. Meso-level benefits, by contrast, relate to the depth of inter-firm networks and the institutional thickness of clusters. Deep networks and thick clusters enable groups of firms to engage in inclusive collective action, develop supportive localized networks, and generate spin-offs in terms of collective learning. Lastly, macro-level benefits entail the efficacy and efficiency of institutions and the relationships between state and the local community. They include generalized trust and shared norms that foster mutual collaboration and development in the community (Fukuyama, 1995).

IV. Gaps in Our Understanding

The above perspectives provide us with some important insights into the phenomenon of social entrepreneurship. To establish a social enterprise entrepreneurs must mobilize personal resources as well as those residing in the community (Haugh, 2005). While both government and community organisations are keen to help, the role of the entrepreneur entails identifying and acquiring the necessary resources and utilizing their own effort to establish the business (Austin, Stevenson, and Wei-Skillern, 2006). In the process, social entrepreneurs must overcome uncertainty and a lack of resources by utilizing, designing, building, and maintaining transactional networks, sometimes through deliberate planning and at other times accidentally or as an opportunity arises (Alder and Kwon, 2002; Pollock, Porac and Wade, 2004). Thus, this dynamic process requires the social entrepreneur to interact with a range of stakeholders and interested parties in society.

We also reveal that although these various perspectives provide important insights into different aspects and dimensions of the formation and evolution of social enterprise, they are incomplete. Our review suggests that research on social entrepreneurship is still in a nascent stage. A clear understanding about the dynamic nature of the social entrepreneurial process remains absent from the literature. More specifically, little is known about how social entrepreneurs utilize and create the various benefits associated with social capital, such as the values and attributes discussed at the outset. From a practical standpoint, even though many communities have a variety of resources at their disposal, our understanding about how prospective entrepreneurs collect and use these resources to establish their firm is limited. The need therefore arises for a more robust representation of how social capital plays a role in social entrepreneurship. These gaps in our understanding call for more in-depth analysis into social enterprise and how it co-evolves with the social capital inherent in a society (Aldrich and Martinez, 2003; Steier and Greenwood, 2000).

These types of questions, central to our interest, which are exploratory in nature, lend themselves to theory building as opposed to theory testing. This view arises from the fact that the various perspectives offered in the literature do not fully explain the phenomenon under investigation. The focus of theory building is not to verify established models and frameworks but rather to improve their substance (Flynn, 1990). Theory building represents a contextual method whereby the researcher is more interested in subjective experiences (Haslam and McGarty, 2003) and forming categories, and analysing interactions between those categories (Snape and Spencer, 2003). In the process of discovering and forming theory, the data collection and analysis are conducted simultaneously. The starting point is not to propose the theory and then provide evidence to support the theory. Instead the theory emerges during the process (Strauss and Corbin, 1998). Yin (1993: 3) proposed that the case study method is preferred "when the phenomenon under study is not readily distinguishable from its context". A focused examination of a case is therefore conducive to building an emerging theory (Eisenhardt and Graebner, 2007), as the discussion shall now turn.

V. The Emergence of a Social Enterprise in Hong Kong

The Hong Kong Context

Traditionally, the Hong Kong government took a positive non-interventionism or laissez-faire approach to voluntary, lineage, and self-help initiatives. However, this ideology has since changed dramatically. Several stimuli are apparent. First, a deep and prolonged recession in the late 1990s led to high unemployment, a significant increase in the number of disadvantaged people, and the associated socio-economic family problems. These demands combined with severe budget cuts placed formidable pressures on social service agencies to find new ways to reduce reliance on the government.[4]

Second, in the early 2000s, the Hong Kong government changed its funding policy for social service agencies, the primary objective being to control social welfare expenses while encouraging reform in the social welfare sector. One such initiative by the government was to provide grants to social service agencies that developed new ways to generate revenue. The result was that many agencies established not-for-profit social organisations (*HKEJ*, 2007b). However, many of these social organisations imitated existing businesses and lacked innovativeness. Social workers were asked haphazardly to become social entrepreneurs although they had limited exposure to business, technology and markets, and were not skilful in opportunity identification. Moreover, the government funding was targeted at increasing employment. Hence, many social organisations employed workers whose skills were low or had become obsolete with government subsidies. As public money subsidized the employees in these social organisations, small and medium-size enterprises subsequently complained about unfair competition. Also, other social missions, such as community rebuilding or alleviating gender inequality, were overlooked.

---

4   See the government website on the Enhancing Self-reliance through District Partnership Programme: www.had.gov.hk/tc/public_services/en_self_reli/index.htm.

A third stimulus, and in spite of the above shortcomings, emerged when both the Hong Kong government and community began to recognize the variety of benefits associated with social enterprise and in so doing played a more active role in its development (*HKEJ*, 2007a). For example, in a study by the Hong Kong Federation of Youth Groups (HKFYG, 2002), an examination of expert opinions (e.g., World Bank, 2001) on how business enterprises and community organisations could produce social capital enhanced awareness that paid holidays for employees to do voluntary work and mentorship and volunteer programmes aimed at knitting networks within a community were beneficial measures in creating social enterprises. The study also included a survey about the role of family, community, and government in social capital. The findings revealed that family support networks were relatively strong in comparison with community-based programmes. This is not surprising given the typically strong familial values found in Asian cultures, in particular Chinese societies (Yang, 1988). However, policy initiatives for solving community problems, such as local unemployment, were beginning to achieve some level of success, underscoring the viability and importance of socially oriented enterprise (*HKEJ*, 2007a).

Given the above economic and policy reform backdrop, supporting social enterprise in Hong Kong has now become a major policy initiative aimed at fostering the economic revitalisation of disadvantaged communities and mobilizing and retraining stranded labour.

The Case of City Greeny

City Greeny[5] is a landscape company that specializes in garden design and maintenance and the training of gardening and

---

5 Primary information relating to City Greeny (http://www.citygreeny.com) was obtained from interviews and communications with the founder, Kane Lui, over the period of July 2007 through March 2008. City Greeny was selected for the interesting examples it affords, not because it represents an exemplar model for the development of a social enterprise. The responsibility for any errors or omissions, if any, shall rest with the authors.

landscaping related skills. It was established by an enterprising individual, not by a social service agency. At the time of its inception, Kane Lui founded the company with both limited resources and a limited knowledge of gardening and landscaping. According to Kane, City Greeny came to fruition out of his desire to not only earn a living but also to assist unemployed workers. As we shall elaborate in the discussion that follows, City Greeny exemplifies the dynamic and interactive process a young entrepreneur faces in his attempt to establish the legitimacy of a social enterprise within the community.

City Greeny qualifies as a social enterprise for three reasons (Wallace, 1999). First, like creating any new for-profit venture, City Greeny combines opportunity recognition, innovative organisation creation, and profit-seeking (Hornaday, 1992). It differs from traditional for-profit ventures, however, in that it also pursues the creation of social value. City Greeny hires unemployed workers and trains them to provide gardening services to its clients, primarily schools. Building on its relationships with schools, it also runs gardening workshops to educate students about various life values. While Kane, like any entrepreneur, is innovative and keen to create a new business model, his concern is not limited to profit, but includes caring and social purpose.

Second, City Greeny's structural characteristics typify a social enterprise, including its reliance on a mixture of employees and volunteers, having multiple sources of income (as opposed to solely donations or grants), and business performance appraised according to both profit and the social value it creates (Dees et al., 2001; Wallace, 1999). City Greeny trains unemployed workers in new skills in gardening and then employs them as part-time workers. In doing so, the company has improved the design of school gardens, introduced new ideas to improve the environment, helped the unemployed, and enlightened students outside their normal spectrum of learning.

Third, social entrepreneurs have been described as "path breakers with powerful new ideas" who are "totally possessed" by their vision. They are change agents, pioneers who pay attention to market forces without losing sight of their social mission. Their motivation may take some form of altruism — achieving personal satisfaction from one's own act of charity, the "warm glow", or gaining satisfaction from the gratitude and affection of beneficiaries (DTI, 2005; Haugh, 2005). Kane embodies many of these characteristics. Although the nature of his business is not new, Kane identified a market niche, built a new venture to implement his ideas in innovative ways, and was motivated to act with social purpose. City Greeny therefore exemplifies an alternative development path for social entrepreneurship at a time when most other social enterprises in Hong Kong have charitable and non-profit origins.

A Dynamic Entrepreneurial Process

No matter how motivated the founder was, City Greeny would not have been possible if it were not for the benevolent support and resources from organisations in the community. It is an important string of events, some planned and some not, that led to the creation and development of City Greeny (see Table 1 for a summary of the relevant events and issues), as shall now be discussed.

After graduating from high school, Kane received a diploma in banking. His interests, personality, and desire to be independent led him in a different direction from a career in banking, however. One afternoon on a mundane bus ride he noticed several gardeners working. Captivated by the moment he thought to himself that this may provide a business opportunity (*SCMP*, 2007). An entrepreneurial instinct motivated him to learn the trade and with that the dynamic process of his entrepreneurial journey began, the different phases of which are illustrated in Figure 2.

Phase I. Kane's journey began when he joined a gardening course organized by Stewards, a Christian NGO charity.[6] At the time, Kane was in his early twenties and had little practical or life

---

6   Stewards originates from the Christian Brethren movement and was incorporated in 1962 as a charitable organisation. Its mission is to provide quality social services for the benefit of the Hong Kong community, and elsewhere, and to promote the evangelical Christian faith. In 2001, Stewards established ARM Services Co. Ltd. With the aim of offering seed funding to promote social enterprises in Hong Kong (see http://www.stewards.org.hk/about/history_en.php).

Table 1:
The Entrepreneurial Evolution of Kane (City Greeny)

Year	Activities	Purposes/Benefits or Problems
1998–2001	Secondary school; professional school (2-year banking diploma).	Education.
2002–2004	Insurance agent; part-time photographer.	To get by.
2003 May	Observed gardeners working in the field while on a bus ride.	Business idea stimulated.
2003	Attended gardening training at Stewards (an NGO), subsidized by the Self-Employment Plan of the Labour Department of the HKSAR Government.	Learning and practising gardening skills; learnt about the concept of Life Education from Stewards.
	Employed in a school gardening service.	Recognized schools as a potential market; opportunity recognition.
2005 June	Started City Greeny.	Seize opportunity as the incumbent firms were out-of-fashion / the wages offered for work in this industry were much too low to attract young people.
	Achieved second runner-up in a school gardening competition.	Gained reputation.
	Taught gardening to unemployed workers at one of the shelter workshops of Stewards.	To get by, but also recognized the potential of hiring the unemployed after training.
2006	Participated in Youth Business Hong Kong.	Borrowed money to set up a formal office/attracted new customers/ received advice
	Tried planting grass on roof using the office of a YBHK participant.	Testing new products for expansion.
	Hired a social worker.	Developed more and better gardening workshops for students.
	Met designers while doing jobs for private estates.	Entered garden design market.
2007	Diversified businesses.	Stuck in unfinished projects.

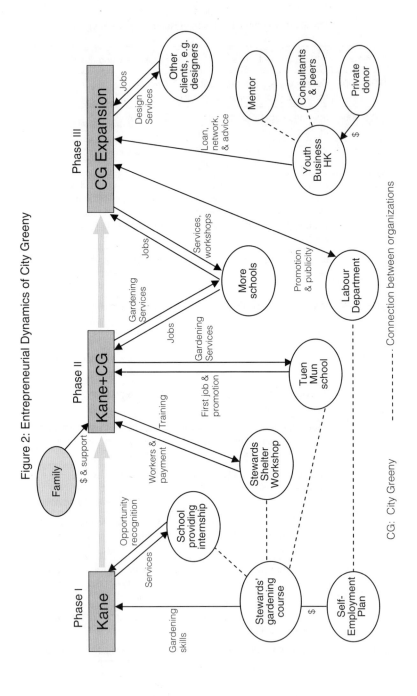

Figure 2: Entrepreneurial Dynamics of City Greeny

CG: City Greeny

experience. Stewards provided re-training to unemployed young-sters, so that they could learn a trade skill for setting up their own business or become more marketable in the job market. Due to its religious affiliation, emphasis is placed on "Life Education". Students are taught to appreciate the value of life.[7] The Self-Employed Support Fund administered by the Labour Department provided funding to support the course.

A defining moment for Kane occurred during an internship that formed part of his course. Stewards arranged an internship in a school within the same charity group. In this way students could practise their new skills and earn stipends to support themselves. Noticing the school's garden and a potential opportunity to improve it, Kane spoke to school administrators. He learned that due to a small budget, the school could only afford to hire one gardener. At the same time, gardeners at the schools within the Stewards group tended to be old and were often incapable of or unmotivated in keeping up the appearance of the gardens. Moreover, youngsters refused to join the profession due to limited prospects and low wages relative to other jobs.

Phase II. Recognizing this as a business opportunity, Kane decided with the support (financial and spiritual) of his family to set up City Greeny. His family members, including several relatives, ran small businesses and, we believe, served as role models. This may in part explain Kane's own drive to become an entrepreneur. His first customer was a school in Tuen Mun referred to him by the Stewards. Kane believed schools provided a good market niche for a start-up because they required simple garden design (and therefore required less investment), paid generously, and were part of a network that could help promote his work. After completing work for his first customer, Kane was able to gain a few more schools as customers and even won an award for his garden design at a school.

As City Greeny's reputation grew, Kane's relationship with Stewards led to another interesting opportunity. Stewards invited Kane to teach gardening to unemployed middle-aged workers.

---

7   Kane adopted this theme in the educational programmes that City Greeny offers.

Sympathetic towards their situation, Kane began to hire these workers when they had completed their training. He paid HK$30 per hour and allowed them to work flexible schedules. This was a win-win arrangement for both sides. Working outdoors was a demanding job. Nevertheless, workers gained a sense of purpose and felt less dependent on welfare. We think that these workers also proved instrumental in other ways. Given the workers' experience, they were able to learn quickly and to run the gardening projects with little supervision. This enabled Kane to free himself from routine work and focus on attracting new customers, ponder future directions, and expand the business.

Phase III. Eventually, a few housing estates became customers of City Greeny. As one project led to another, Kane embarked on more specialized projects that incorporate landscaping design. Design oriented projects were larger in size and consequently more profitable. Leveraging his relationships with schools, he also entered into the service market by providing gardening workshops to students. Income was generated from tuition fees and the sale of seeds for plants. The result was a more diversified and stable business. While teaching a workshop, Kane met a social worker who was eager to collaborate with him to provide more workshops on "Life Education". These developments meant that Kane required more resources and potentially an office to house employees and meet customers. They also meant more risk.

At this juncture, Kane discovered the service of another charity organisation, Youth Business Hong Kong (YBHK). YBHK assists disadvantaged youngsters in setting up their own businesses by providing them with loans, training, mentorship, and public exposure (see Appendix for further details).[8] Kane's motivation, track record, and need convinced YBHK to lend him $50,000 for the purpose of business expansion (*SCMP*, 2007).

Despite this funding,[9] business expansion proved difficult. For example, difficulties associated with his relationship with a mentor

---

8 Being a social enterprise was not a funding criterion.
9 The mentor assigned was a businessman in the gardening industry. However, Kane learnt little from him, apparently as a result of conflict of interest and a lack of rapport between them.

appointed by YBHK and Kane's lack of participation in gatherings of YBHK prevented him from expanding his skills and customer base. His networks (i.e., social workers and school administrators) were not as helpful as originally anticipated. In fact, paradoxically, they constrained his ability to pursue new business contacts and knowledge (Aldrich, 1999). And, although he was able to break into the landscape design and high-end services market, he was unable to manage the business and financial risk. For example, one large client took advantage of Kane's design, but did not pay for the service. Inexperienced and powerless, Kane was not able to resolve the issue. He also began to find himself under financial pressure to repay the YBHK loan. Kane recognized that he must learn quickly if he was to sustain his business.[10]

VI. Discussion

Based on the concept of social capital, we will now discuss whether and how the main actor used social relations and resources (information, influence, and solidarity) conferred upon him to facilitate his actions (Adler and Kwon, 2002). We categorize our observations relating to City Greeny's development according to the three levels of analysis introduced earlier (Kimand and Aldrich, 2005).

Micro-level. Our first observation relates to Kane being an enterprising free agent (Pollock et al., 2004). Although he possessed little social capital or other resources to begin with, he utilized resources (e.g., knowledge and networks) made available by NGOs and the government (Self-Employment Plan of the Labour Department). In doing so he developed his own social capital (Pollock et al., 2004). Kane was able to "appropriate" his social relations (Coleman, 1988). For example, he opened training workshops for unemployed workers and in turn converted these training relationships into employment relationships. He was also able to convert service relationships with schools into partnership

---

10 Kane was able to weather the storm and later on restored a good relationship with YBHK.

relationships when he began to offer educational workshops for the schools. His success was subsequently showcased by the Labour Department and recognized as a successful outcome of their youth service programmes.

Kane's experience was starkly different from others who studied with him in the gardening course. They lacked the drive necessary to become entrepreneurs or establish a business. In contrast, Kane was entrepreneurial in the sense that he decided to pursue the opportunity regardless of the resources in hand (Stevenson, 1983). As Figure 2 illustrates, a lack of connection or complementarity between social organisations (e.g., between Stewards and YBHK) could prove to be a barrier to most individuals. However, through his own efforts Kane bridged these gaps to obtain needed resources. His dynamic behaviour also demonstrated how social capital at the micro-level can foster the development of trusting relationships essential for accessing resources, lowering transaction costs and developing competitiveness (Kimand and Aldrich, 2005).

Meso-level. Our second observation relates to inter-organisational networks and social capital. The case revealed both favourable and unfavourable dimensions. Cohesive relations should enable groups of organisations to engage in collective action, develop supportive networks, and generate spin-offs for collective learning (Kimand and Aldrich, 2005). Stewards, using its internal network, was able to mobilize branch units, such as schools and shelter workshops, to share information, for referral, and resource sharing. City Greeny profited from and may have also helped to strengthen such inter-unit supportive networks.[11] The solidarity or shared norm within Stewards is likely to have made these benefits realizable for City Greeny (Coleman, 1988). However, the reach of this network was confined to affiliates of the Stewards organisation. In City Greeny's case, an unfavourable outcome occurred when a network gap between NGOs became apparent, such as the lack of linkage witnessed between YBHK and Stewards.

---

11 For example, the founder of another new company, who originally met Kane in the Self-Employment Plan, told us that he also applied to YBHK in part due to his encouragement. This company, New Verdure Painting & Design Co. (www.newverdure.com), was supported by YBHK.

City Greeny had to bridge this gap in order to access different kinds of essential resources. A determined mind and diverse skills were required. An entrepreneurial spirit is therefore vital, so that when marketable knowledge is acquired, such as gardening, from one social entity, that resources can be obtained, such as a loan and advice, from another entity as the venture develops. This involves not just the discovery of resources but also the ability to undo old ties and nurture new ones. As we witnessed in this case, this is no easy task. Kane could not establish a trusting relationship with his mentor, or engage consultants or other incubatees from the YBHK. Ties with these parties could have enriched his financial or business know-how, ultimately helping him to avoid subsequent trouble. Moreover, when the business demanded that he established connections with a new group of individuals and organisations (networks), Kane was overwhelmed by his current networks comprised of social workers and school administrators. His capability to overcome such a predicament is certainly subject to debate, but so too is the question of how inter-organisational gaps act as a barrier and what might be done to help minimize this dynamic.

Macro-level. Our third category of observations relates to the efficacy and efficiency of institutions and the relationship between the state and local community (Kimand and Aldrich, 2005). The presence of generalized trust and shared norms were evident in the case. It is evident that the representatives of the NGOs showed concern for youth in Hong Kong and went to some length to provide support and assistance. The government and the community (e.g., private donors) were less visible, yet both contributed funding to make the programmes of the NGOs possible. Social enterprise in Hong Kong is therefore benefiting in two key respects. A sense of belonging and trust is emerging in society (Fukuyama, 1995), compelling individuals to do social good. This atmosphere is apparent in Kane's case, especially his sympathetic view toward the unemployed. Moreover, these institutions collectively reduce the risk of being a social entrepreneur by providing essential resources to budding entrepreneurs. In the case of Kane, Stewards (with the assistance of government sponsorship) offered training, market information, opportunity exposure, and job referrals, while YBHK provided financial assistance, advice, and business mentoring.

What is interesting about these laudable efforts is that the respective institutions were not fully aware of the collective good they produce. While NGOs and the government communicate with each other, they were not cognizant of the outcomes of each others' programmes (e.g., who was trained and what was the content). To a certain extent, this is understandable as each institution has its own mandate and scope of operations. Governmental units also contend that they should focus on executing policies without interfering in the affairs of NGOs. In this respect, social institutions work independently and autonomously in Hong Kong. Excessive brokerage and zealous cohesion has been acknowledged to stifle innovativeness (Adler and Kwon, 2002). Overly strong solidarity within institutions may inhibit collaboration and collective learning. The lesson from City Greeny is therefore that enough room must remain between institutions for enterprising individuals to maneuver and combine resources in new ways, so that novel ideas and platforms can become possible (Pollock et al., 2004).

VII. Recommendations
for Promoting Social Entrepreneurship

Our first recommendation relates to the fact that Kane was the only entrepreneur to emerge from the gardening class. [12] Social organisations must identify those individuals who are inspired to become entrepreneurs versus those who merely wish to re-enter the workforce. Social entrepreneurs must be opportunity-driven, flexible in their networking to acquire resources, passionate about doing social good, capable of connecting diverse groups in building their own networks, and satisfied by the gratitude and affection of beneficiaries (Haugh, 2005). Tests and personal observations are needed to spot entrepreneurs (Timmons, 1999), for instance, when they are involved in training programmes or other social purpose activities. Special attention and resources, based on the social capital

---

12 The founder of New Verdure also said that he was the only entrepreneur from his design and printing class in the Self-Employment Plan.

framework (Alder and Kwon, 2002), are also needed to cultivate ability and opportunity networks and motivate individuals to become social entrepreneurs.

The second recommendation relates to increasing the success rate of social entrepreneurs. Hong Kong is well endowed with resources for enterprising individuals. The challenge then becomes how to lower or share risk in the entrepreneurial process and to provide essential resources in a timely fashion. One dimension of this need that surfaced in the case of City Greeny had to do with the quality and transparency of information. Our study revealed that the information possessed by different institutions was fragmented and disconnected. Stakeholders in social enterprises can therefore benefit from designating "brokers", who are trustworthy and informative, to identify gaps and connect otherwise disconnected parties (Pollock et al., 2005). The establishment of a platform to provide information about the locations and providers of training, jobs, market information, advice, and loans is also important.[13] These measures, barring excessive brokerage (Alder and Kwon, 2002), can facilitate dialogue as well as the sharing of lessons among different parties (e.g., see *HKEJ*, 2007c). The key then becomes identifying and serving the specific needs of entrepreneurs at the right time and building policies essential to existing local and regional initiatives (Cooke, 2001). Organisations in the community should remain independent whilst at the same time continuing to be creative in their approach, as exemplified by YBHK in the case of new start-ups. Organisations that provide other much needed resources, such as early stage and growth financing (Emerson, Freundlich, Fruchterman, Berlin and Stevenson, 2006), should also be established.

VIII. Conclusions

In this chapter we explored the nuances of a social enterprise's development. Our investigation of City Greeny demonstrated that

---

13 Note the newsletter edited by K. K. Tse and the platform established by HKCSS.

community organisations and social capital play a central role in the emergence of social entrepreneurs and social enterprise in Hong Kong. It is hoped that social organisations can glean lessons from this study in their quest to develop innovative programmes and initiatives that stimulate social entrepreneurship. At the same time, the study also offers scholars some guidance about possible directions for future investigations into social capital and social entrepreneurship (Aldrich and Martinez, 2003; Kimand and Aldrich, 2005).

Acknowledgements

The authors would like to thank Mingles Tsoi and Louisa Lau (YBHK) for their assistance in the preparation of case materials. The authors would also like to extend their gratitude to the editors for their helpful comments and suggestions on earlier drafts of this chapter. This chapter is partially supported by a research grant from the Hong Kong UGC (CUHK 440008) and NSF China (70732004) awarded to the first author.

References

Adler, P. S., and Kwon, S.-W. (2002). Social capital: Prospects for a new concept. *Academy of Management Review*, 27, 17–40.

Aldrich, H. (1999). *Organisations evolving*. London: Sage.

Aldrich, H., and Martinez, M. (2003). Entrepreneurship as social construction: A multi-level evolutionary approach. In Z. J. Acs and D. B. Audretsch (Eds.), *Handbook of entrepreneurship research: An interdisciplinary survey and introduction* (pp. 359–400). Boston MA: Kluwer Academic.

Austin, J., Stevenson, H., and Wei-Skillern, J. (2006). Social and commercial entrepreneurship: Same, different, or both? *Entrepreneurship Theory and Practice*, 30, 1–22.

Coleman, J. S. (1988). Social capital in the creation of human capital. *American Journal of Sociology*, 94(Supplement), s95–s120.

Cooke, P. (2001). *Knowledge economies: Clusters, learning and cooperative advantage*. London: Routledge.

Dees, J. G., Emerson, J., and Economy, P. (2001). *Enterprising nonprofits: A toolkit for social entrepreneurs*. New York: John Wiley and Sons.

DTI (2002). *Social enterprise –A strategy for success*. The Department of Trade and Industry, UK, available online at www.dti.gov.uk.

Eisenhardt, K. M., and Graebner, M. E. (2007). Theory building from cases:

Opportunities and challenges. *Academy of Management Journal, 50,* 25–32.

Emerson, J., Freundlich, T., Fruchterman, J., Berlin, L., and Stevenson, K. (2006). *Nothing ventured, nothing gained: Addressing the critical gap in risk-taking capital in social enterprise.* Working Paper, Skoll Centre for Social Entrepreneurship, University of Oxford.

Flynn, G. L. (1990). Physicochemical determinants of skin absorption. In T. R., Gerrity and C. J. Henry (Eds.), *Principles of route to route extrapolation for risk assessment.* New York: Elsevier.

Fukuyama, F. (1995). *Trust: The social virtues and the creation of prosperity.* London: Penguin.

Haslam, S. A. and McGarty, C. (2003). *Research methods and statistics in psychology.* Thousand Oaks, CA: Sage.

Haugh, H. (2005). Nonprofit social entrepreneurship. In S.C. Parker (Ed.), *The life cycle of entrepreneurial ventures* (pp.401–436). New York: Springer.

HKEJ (2007a). 曾蔭權呼籲商界更多支持社企 (The Chief Executive of Hong Kong asked for more support from the business community to support social enterprises), *Hong Kong Economic Journal,* 2 June 2007 (in Chinese).

HKEJ (2007b). 何謂社會企業 (What is social enterprise), *Hong Kong Economic Journal,* 23 August 2007 (in Chinese).

HKEJ (2007c). 曾德成稱年底公佈協助社企措施 (The Minister of Home Affairs Bureau will announce measures to support social enterprises), *Hong Kong Economic Journal,* 6 November 2007 (in Chinese).

HKFYG (2002). *A study on social capital with regard to social networks, trust and reciprocity.* Hong Kong Federation of Youth Groups, Hong Kong, available online at www.hkfyg.org.hk.

Hornaday, R. W. (1992). Thinking about entrepreneurship: A fuzzy set approach. *Journal of Small Business Management, 30,* 12–23.

Kimand, P. H., and Aldrich, H. E. (2005). *Social capital and entrepreneurship.* Boston, MA: Now.

Larson, A., and Starr, J. A. (1993). A network model of organization formation. *Entrepreneurship Theory and Practice, 17*(2), 5–15.

Pollock, T. G., Porac, J. F., and Wade, J. B. (2004). Constructing deal networks: Brokers as network "architects" in the US. IPO market and other examples. *Academy of Management Review, 29,* 50–72.

Reis, T., (1999). *Unleashing new resources and entrepreneurship for the common good: A scan, synthesis, and scenario for action.* Report for the W.K. Kellogg Foundation, January 1999. Available online at, http://www.wkkf.org/Pubs/ PhilVol/Pub592.pdf.

SCMP (2007). Sowing the seeds of social awareness. *South China Morning Post,* 5 September 2007.

Snape, D. and Spencer, L. (2003). The foundation of qualitative research. Ritchie, J. and Lewis, J. (Eds.), *Qualitative research practice: A guide for social science students and researchers* (pp.1–23). London & Thousand Oaks: Sage.

Steier, L., and Greenwood, R. (2000). Entrepreneurship and the evolution of angel financial networks. *Organization Studies, 21*(1), 163–192.

Stevenson, H. H. (1983). A perspective on entrepreneurship. *Harvard Business School Working Paper* No. 9-384-131. Boston, MA: Harvard Business School.

Strauss, A. and Corbin, J. (1998). *Basics of qualitative research*. Thousands Oaks, CA: Sage Publications.

Wallace, S. L. (1999). Social entrepreneurship: The role of social purpose enterprises in facilitating community economic development. *Journal of Developmental Entrepreneurship, 4*, 153–174.

Timmons, J. A. (1999). *New venture creation: Entrepreneurship for the 21st century.* 5th edition, Boston, MA: Irwin/McGraw Hill.

World Bank (2002). The Wolrd Bank. *What is social capital?.* Available online at, www.worldbank.org/poverty/scapital/whatsc.htm.

Yang, C.-F. (1988). Familism and development: An examination of the role of family in contemporary China mainland, Hong Kong, and Taiwan. In D. Sinha and H.S.R. Kao (Eds.), *Social values and development: Asian perspectives*. New Delhi: Sage.

Yin, R. (1993). *Applications of case study research*. Beverly Hills, CA: Sage Publishing.

Appendix

Youth Business Hong Kong

Adapted from http://www.yen.org.hk/ybhk/new/index_e.htm

By working in partnership with the local business communities, YBHK provides access to finance for business start-ups and supports young people through an intensive and extensive programme of business mentoring. It helps to encourage involvement in the local community, by inviting established business executives and experts to coach young business starters not only in the area of business, but also by sharing with them gleaned wisdom on developing the right attitude towards life. YBHK provides four core services:

- **Seed Money:** A maximum of up to HK$100,000 will be provided as an interest-free business start-up loan. This will be determined by the Vetting Panel who approve of a viable business plan.
- **Business Mentorship and Professional Consultancy:** *Business mentors* will be drawn from amongst fellow entrepreneurs, senior executives in corporations and industry, consultants and other professionals.
- **Business Support:** YBHK will provide or liaise with partners for suitable business hardware and resources support as well as business networks as required for business start-ups.
- **Information and Networks:** YBHK will provide business information while providing young people with access to local business networks.

Note that the Chinese University of Hong Kong Centre for Entrepreneurship (www.cuhk.edu.hk/centre/entrepreneur) is a research partner of YBHK.

12

Capturing Business Value Out of Corporate Social Responsibility and Social Capital

Edward Tse

Behaving in a socially and ethically responsible manner is increasingly a powerful way of transforming corporations to become preferred employers, business partners and suppliers. As many leading corporations have found to their great cost, perceived or actual failure to behave responsibly can prove to be extremely damaging.

During recent years, many frameworks have been developed to align business management with "ethical" behaviour, e.g., the well-discussed Sarbanes-Oxley Act [1] and the Foreign Corrupt Practices Act,[2] to just name two regulations originating from the United States. However, forcing companies to do "something ethical" in general to meet compliance standards is not the answer to the quest for more companies to behave in a socially responsible way. Instead, companies undertaking any corporate social responsibility (CSR) initiative need to analyse in detail and understand the value the initiative will deliver to the society, the company itself and the company's other stakeholders.

---

1 The full text of the law is available online at, http://frwebgate.access.gpo.gov/cgibin/getdoc.cgi?dbname=107_cong_bills&docid=f:h3763enr.tst.pdf.
2 Please see http://www.usdoj.gov/criminal/fraud/fcpa/ for details.

In this chapter, I propose that corporations should assume a more strategic perspective on corporate social responsibilities and ways to leverage social capital in a business context. Based on my experience of working as a management consultant for nearly 20 years, advising senior executives of Chinese and multinational companies on their entry and growth strategies, corporate transformations and merger and acquisition activities, I am of the belief that companies with stronger understanding and bonds to their key stakeholders, including government and society, will also become more successful in competing on the global scene and reaching their long-term sustainable objectives.

I. Strategic CSR, Social Capital and Soft Power

The concept of CSR has increasingly become the focus of international corporations and is now widely supported by senior executives and company boards. Although we are seeing signs of more sophisticated and strategic approaches to CSR, many corporations remain at a stage where CSR is mainly evolving in the areas of marketing, public relationships or corporate philanthropy. Seemingly few corporations have developed the right relationships with their surrounding stakeholders and therefore have insufficient understanding of which CSR initiatives to prioritise and which ones will have the most impact on both the company itself and society in general. Following an unstructured set of guidelines and criteria and starting unrelated CSR initiatives is no longer enough to generate long-lasting trust of the market, investors, employees, business partners or regulators. Consider, the example of Enron, which has become a byword for corporate irresponsibility. However, before its failure, Enron was doing the whole "social responsibility thing" with CSR reporting, and environmental and community programmes.

To reach a more advanced "social responsibility level", corporations need to start viewing themselves as interdependent with society rather than being independent, and with the obligation to "give something back" to society. CSR is seldom a zero-sum game where one needs to trade between corporate success and community welfare. The most influential and sustainable CSR initiatives offer "win-win" results for the company as well as the stakeholders specifically being targeted.

Based on my observations, leading CSR companies typically possess the following two mutually dependent mindsets:

1. View management of CSR as a strategic initiative in a similar manner as critical business decisions are analysed and made.

2. Emphasis on establishing the right connections with communities and key stakeholders.

These mindsets also coincide well with the definition of CSR by the World Bank Group's Corporate Social Responsibility Practice[3]: "Corporate social responsibility is the commitment of businesses to contribute to sustainable economic development by working with employees, their families, the local community and society at large to improve their lives in ways that are good for business and for development".

II. Looking at CSR Strategically

For companies with even the slightest ambitions of becoming, or remaining, successful, their business strategies must go beyond competitive benchmarking and best practices. As the famous Harvard Business School professor, Michael Porter, argues, strategy is about choosing a competitive positioning – doing things differently from competitors in a way that lowers costs or better serves a particular set of customer needs. This mindset can easily be broadened to include a company's relationship to society by the former investing in identifying and developing innovations that makes a positive social impact and at the same time strengthen the company's competitiveness. Famous examples include Toyota's hybrid electric/petrol engine vehicle Prius, Starbucks' brand value

---

3   The World Bank's definition of CSR is set out in a document, available online at, http://web.worldbank.org/WBSITE/EXTERNAL/WBI/WBIPROGRAMS/ CGCSRLP/0,,contentMDK:20279365~pagePK:64156158~piPK:64152884~theSite PK:460861,00.html.

developed in cohesion with it portraying itself as a socially responsible citizen, General Electrics' "ecoimagination" strategy of developing environmentally-friendlier technologies, and The Body Shop's policy of not accepting tests on animals by any of its suppliers. These come easily to mind to illustrate unfulfilled, though highly valued, social needs or consumer preferences.

Commonly for the leading companies, both performance-wise and acting as respectable corporate citizens, they treat CSR strategically:

- Including social issues and emerging social forces into the strategic development process to be discussed and evaluated by the senior executives (and board of directors).
- Understanding and choosing on which social issues it can have a significant impact and at the same time generate a competitive advantage.
- Developing broad metrics or summaries for the social issues and forces in a similar fashion as industry and customer trends are analysed and tracked.
- Going beyond stakeholder "dialogues" to more pro-active conduct, detailed stakeholder analysis based on the known agendas and interests of these groups (e.g., governments, consumer groups, lawyers and media) and taking "preemptive" actions when required (e.g., by increasing company transparency, educating and lobbying, shifting R&D/asset focus etc.).

In general, the more closely tied a social issue is to the corporation's business and vision, the greater is the opportunity to leverage the company's resources and capabilities to benefit society as well as itself.

Shifting from ad hoc and fragmented CSR to a strategic mindset emphasising selection, pro-activity and social and business impact will require dramatically different thinking for many corporations. Booz & Company offers its clients a four-step methodology to help them integrate and align business modelling with shareholder analysis:

1. Integrated business modelling and stakeholder analysis: the business is modelled so as to highlight all relevant

stakeholders, their relationships, and their possible impact (mid- and long-term) on the company's operations and strategies.

2. Evaluation of company positioning with respect to its stakeholders: threats and opportunities from each stakeholder group are analysed and compared with the company's capabilities.

3. Strategic options generation and evaluation: options for managing the company's value proposition to each stakeholder group are generated and evaluated both qualitatively and quantitatively when applicable.

4. Investment monitoring panel: the chosen strategy implementation is detailed in a set of performance indicators to be used for tracking and following-up on investments returns (both tangible and intangible).

The essence of the recommended approach, and strategic CSR in general, is to include social/stakeholder contexts naturally into the company's business strategy development process and managing CSR initiatives as longer-time strategic investments, just like any R&D or product development. Throughout this approach, differentiation comes from gaining stakeholder insight and understanding what needs are currently unfulfilled.

III. Using Social Capital to Connect with Key Stakeholders

Historically, companies have developed great expertise in, and elaborate processes for, managing physical assets. As vertically integrated companies refocus on their core businesses, they become increasingly reliant on their ties to critical stakeholders – involving customers in product/solution development, sharing more information with vendors, building wider and longer bridges with alliance partners, and demonstrating these same behaviours within their own organisations, at every level.

The importance for companies of connecting to their surroundings was also confirmed in a study in 2001 by Booz &

Company and Northwestern University's Kellogg School of Management. The research comprised surveying 113 executives at a representative sample of Fortune 1000 companies, and found that winning companies define and deploy relationships in a consistent, specific, and multifaceted manner. Although some companies will dub any concluded business deal a relationship, top-performing companies focus extraordinary, enterprise-wide energy on moving beyond a transactional mindset as they develop trust-based, mutually beneficial, and long-term associations, specifically with four key constituencies; customers, suppliers, alliance partners, and their own employees. Starbucks, although it has recently experienced a fair amount of performance issues, exemplifies this model of the relationship-centric organisation by its "partnerships" with employees and suppliers, innovative long-term alliances with business partners and one-to-one connections with customers (or "one cup at a time" as referred to by the founder and CEO Howard Schultz).

One way for corporations to connect with their key stake-holders is by accumulating social capital. According to the World Bank, social capital includes institutions, relationships and standards which shape social interactive capability and quality. Social capital not only pools each institution in the society together but also works as glue integrating each institution into unity. Generally, the concept is considered to include the following main elements:

- Network – the collection of all communication channels; contact and sustainable development between individuals and institutions.
- Trust and care – the trust and care between individuals and institutions.
- Mutual assistance and benefits – individuals or organisations willing to contribute to help others.
- Participation in social affairs – individuals participating in social and community affairs and volunteer issues; the way civilians' recognition and sense of belonging to the community can be strengthened.

Why is social capital important also in a business context? Start by first considering a metaphor from society, the so-called prisoners' dilemma. In this game theory-based model, two criminals have been arrested and are about to be questioned independently of each other. Each criminal has the choice – to stick with his partner and at the end be released without any charges or to betray his partner and earn a chance to reduce the penalty (on another criminal charge) while the betrayed party will be sentenced severely. To the criminals, the best scenario would be if they both insisted to ally and stick to the same story, while worst case would be if they betray each other at the same time and both receive severe penalties. From a self-centered perspective, the best case would be to betray his partner because there is an obvious possibility that he will himself be betrayed. Given that most people would consider their own benefit first, one would argue that criminals would betray their partners and prioritise their own benefits over the potential group benefits.

However, research reveals that as long as the two criminals are able to communicate, the probability for them to betray each other is largely reduced. Communication enables individuals to learn about each other's preferences and strengthens the trust between the parties. The process of communication may also stimulate shared value concepts or a sense of group belonging that serve to prevent mutual betrayals. In other words, amongst a group of people, if there is an institution that facilitates more communication, the mutual understanding within the group is likely to increase, potentially to a stage where a common belief and a sense of group belonging are established.

What does this tell us about social capital in a business environment and CSR context? In the previous section, I argued that strategic CSR requires corporations to be as selective with CSR initiatives as with business critical strategic decisions. The means to understand what opportunities to pursue increasingly come from sources outside of the company, i.e., from its key stakeholders. However, to create (or recreate) the necessary trust for stakeholders to openly discuss their preferences and priorities, as well as to get their positive influences, corporations need first to accumulate sufficient social capital. This can be achieved by the corporations increasingly making pro-active efforts to listen and understand the stakeholders and creating environments where interaction and communication are stimulated and mutual trust created.

Once the stakeholders have been identified using the methodology outlined previously, it is easy to see the benefits for corporations, and the society in general, of maintaining trust-based connections. For example, externally, outside of the corporation, if a company has developed trust-based relationships with its business partners and relevant regulators/policy makers, it is likely that the company will save valuable time and resources in information collection/analyses, negotiations, controls and reporting etc. Similarly, the same arguments are applicable to the internal functioning within a company, i.e., benefits from social capital include strengthening internal communication and collaboration and effectively improving the productivity of the organisation.

Not only is social capital a key enabler for strategic CSR, it provides significant benefits for company executives in realising their business strategies and managing day-to-day operations. In the next section, I will propose that social capital also has a key enabling role to play in companies' quest for what we call soft power.

IV. Leveraging Social Capital
to Increase Soft Power

What is soft power? Originally, the two concepts of soft power and hard power were applied to countries and the ways in which they gained influence internationally. Hard power refers to countries' use of military and financial might to impose their will. Soft power refers to the ability to gain influence based on culture and aspirational dimensions; e.g., American culture has historically had broad global appeal. This concept was originally developed by the former Dean of Harvard University's Kennedy School of Government, Joseph Nye, in 1990.[4]

Applied to a business context, hard power compels people to do

---

4   See Joseph Nye, *Bound to lead: The changing nature of American power* (1990) and the subsequent *Soft power: The means to success in world politics* (2004).

business with a particular company through sheer economic logic (e.g., financial ability, low cost position, technological superiority etc.), while soft power attracts stakeholders to the company and allows the company to gain influence – whether through a seductive brand, a heroic mission, or its willingness to be a genuine part of the community.

Although hard power is indispensable at any time, enduring success can hardly be assured by hard power alone. A sustainable top-performing corporation also needs soft power. This proposition is crucial, especially for companies that want to grow in the global marketplace. Consumers, for example, do not just buy the technically superior or cheapest products; they seek out brands that offer emotional or aspirational connections as well. Similarly, hiring the best, most committed, and most entrepreneurial managers is not just a question of compensation. These individuals want to work with the best people, enjoy personal development, and be part of a grander design. Furthermore, communities do not always welcome the company that is willing to invest the most money locally and create the most jobs, because they may be more concerned about environmental issues or the impact on existing businesses. Regulators and governmental officials look at businesses not simply for their profit-making potential, but for the contribution they can make to national and local policy objectives, such as the development of local infrastructure, the creation of new jobs, or the development of "national champions". Finally, even hard-nosed financial investors are increasingly incorporating perspectives such as corporate social responsibility into their investment decisions.

The history of multinational development over the past century shows that companies proceed through four stages in their acquisition of soft power; unknown, new arrival, corporate citizen, and global attractor.

Stage 1: Unknown – In the first stage, whether the company is large or small, it lacks soft power and has a low profile with the global stakeholders that it is seeking to influence. Many Chinese companies find themselves in this category today as they move their operations overseas. Some of them have developed soft power at home in China through familiar branding and good governmental relationships, but others face the same soft power challenge domestically or abroad, when they seek to develop beyond merely a low cost position.

Stage 2: New arrival – In the second stage, the company takes the first steps towards establishing a distinct profile among its target stakeholders. As with newcomers in any arena, this is the stage when things can go wrong; on the other hand, well-planned moves can provide a strong positive platform for future expansion. For example, a company may fail to take into account the role of non-governmental organisations in its chosen market or disregard norms on gender roles in the workplace. Although the new community may initially welcome the company's investment, there could be a backlash against the company later for not respecting local customs. This is a critical stage that can shape the direction and pace of a company's future development of soft power.

Stage 3: Corporate citizen – Most established multinationals fall into this category, with operations in many countries and a track record of success in global markets. They understand how to operate effectively and enjoy some degree of soft power. They do not, however, exploit their full potential, as they neither shape their business environment nor project a distinctive influence on the world. For example, engagement with community groups, regulators, and policymakers is mainly a "box-ticking" exercise done for compliance reasons rather than as a way to advance the company's business success. Opportunities to hire some of the best people are missed as the company lacks a distinct profile with potential employees.

Stage 4: Global attractor – Companies that are able to realise the full potential of soft power become global attractors. They are the true global leaders. In the past, most global attractors came from the USA and Europe, but the past few decades have seen the rapid rise first of Japanese and then of Korean companies. Chinese companies are just starting the race to become global attractors, and they want to reach this stage more quickly than anyone before them.

What, then, are the dimensions of soft power? How do companies attract, persuade, and influence the various stakeholders in their business – customers; employees; shareholders; government officials; and broader civil society, including NGOs, unions, and community groups – to align goals and drive business success? We have identified four dimensions of soft power and one common platform that provide the route to becoming a global attractor (see Figure 1).

Figure 1. Dimensions of Soft Power

- Market leader at the forefront of technology
- Standard-setting and influencing
- Prominent communication of R&D success

Technology & Innovation Leader

- Superior value proposition with clear brand image
- Aspirational and emotional connections that transcends product
- Often linked to power of home country's "brand"

Customer Aspiration & Inspiration

Management & Leadership Mystique

- Known as a leader in management best practices
- A training ground for managers
- Chairman/CEO a well-known public figure, with a distinctive character

Responsible & Influential Citizen

- Sensitive to society's needs; not just focused on profit; a track record of corporate social responsibility
- A credible influencer and discussion partner on related governmental policy issues

Values-based management and leadership

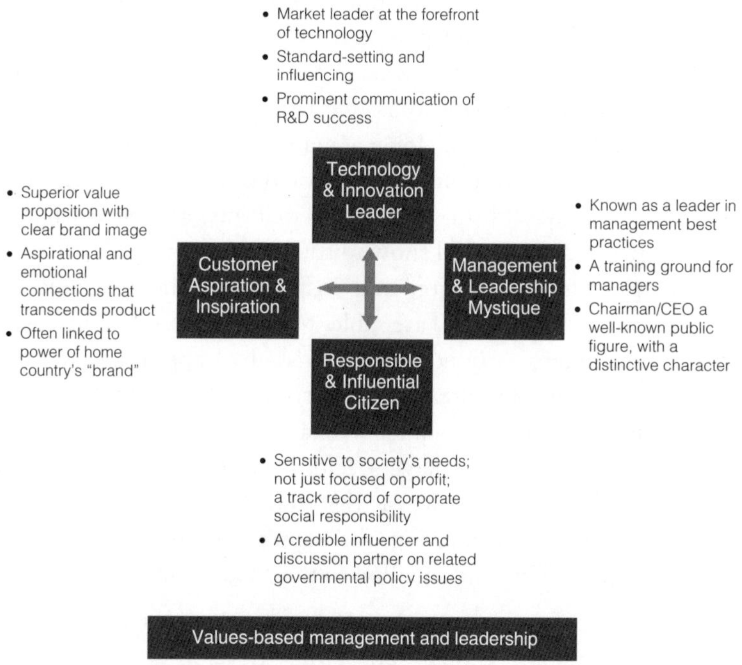

1. Technology and innovation leader: For many companies, technology and innovation are at the core of their soft power. These leaders do more than simply offer superior products; they leverage their innovation capabilities to build further strength. This can take the form of enhanced branding, a superior ability to attract key talent, and an active role in shaping industry standards and future research directions.

2. Management and leadership mystique: Companies such as GE, Apple, and Toyota have built their soft power in part on a management and leadership mystique. The basis can be a distinctive management process, for example, the "Toyota Way" of manufacturing and GE's application of

Six Sigma methodologies. Soft power can also arise from the character of the company's leader. One good example is Steve Jobs at Apple, whose track record and persona have successfully reinvigorated that company's internal effectiveness and consumer appeal.

3. Responsible and influential citizen: Increasingly, companies realising their full potential of soft power are staking out positions as good citizens in the public arena. One example mentioned previously is the case of Toyota and its hybrid car Prius. Toyota, long a management innovator, moved rapidly to position itself as an environmentally friendly car company with the promotion of Prius, at a time when US manufacturers had shown little interest in this issue.

4. Customer aspiration and inspiration: Many leading soft power companies are able to connect with and inspire customers around the world by appealing to their self-image and dreams. The very act of owning the product becomes aspirational. For example, when Apple launched the iPod, MP3 players had been marketed already for several years, but it was the iPod that became a must-have icon – reinvigorating the Apple brand in a way that extended beyond the iPod to the Mac computer.

• Common platform – Values-based management and leadership: Global attractors develop a culture and leadership style that is effective in aligning, inspiring, and engaging employees around the world from many diverse cultures and backgrounds with different aspirations.

As one intuitively understands, social capital is an important enabler to a company reaching for soft power. For example, innovation leadership and customer inspiration typically come from a detailed understanding of market and customers trends and supported by a company culture that stimulates cross-team collaboration, networking and tolerance for "innovation failures". Similarly, values-based leadership and management mystique are largely based on trust from employees, business partners, investors etc. in the company's management, culture and business model for operating the company.

Soft power is today an indispensable part of success as a world-class company, sheer scale and financial might alone are not enough. The route from unknown company to global attractor demands vision and strategic and relentless implementation. Soft power is also based on a deep understanding of what different stakeholders value and how the company can fulfil those needs – whether through a seductive and aspirational brand, a heroic mission, a distinctive talent development approach and company culture, or a willingness to be a genuine part of the community. Accumulating sufficient social capital is therefore one of the important first steps for a company with a desire to expand its soft power and eventually reach sustainable high-performance on a global scale.

Resources

Edward Tse, Magic power of collaboration, Speech at Community Investment & Inclusion Fund meeting, Hong Kong, 2007.

Edward Tse and Andrew Cainey, Attracting global interest: How Chinese companies can leverage "soft power" in the international marketplace, Booz & Company white paper, August 2007. Available online at, www.boozallen.cn/media/ file/AttractingGlobalInterest.pdf.

Booz & Company, *Intellectual capital: Strategic corporate social responsibility: A pragmatic approach to strategic choices in the "ethical" market*, 2004.

Michael E. Porter, Strategy and society: The link between competitive advantage and corporate social responsibility, *Harvard Business Review*, December 2006.

Ian Davis, The biggest contract, *The Economist*, May 2005.

Ranjay Gutati, Sarah Huffman and Gary Neilson, The barista principle: Starbucks and the rise of relational capital, in *Transformation cases. A strategy+business reader*, Booz, Allen Hamilton 2004.

Index

collective social capital, 105
community
    concept of, 123
    entrepreneur, 251
community activism, 145
community-based social capital
    intervention programmes –
    Sham Shui Po Child-Friendly
    Network, 67
community building, 37, 91, 96,
    122–124, 126–129, 131, 134,
    137, 139, 141, 148
    Hong Kong, 133
community capacity building, 123,
    129–130, 156
community cohesion, 134–135,
    138–139, 147
community development, 69, 76,
    122, 124, 132, 140, 169, 238
community empowerment, 123, 246
community engagement, 91,
    124–126, 128, 131, 134–135,
    139, 143, 147–148, 207
community groups, 16, 104, 108,
    123, 125–126, 130, 133, 141,
    148, 239, 312
Community Investment and
    Inclusion Fund (CIIF), 22,
    24–25, 27, 67, 77–80, 86–91,
    95–98, 105–109, 113–114, 145,
    228, 236, 240
    background, 95
    CIIF Evaluation Consortium, 79,
    96
community organisations, 66–67,
    106, 124–126, 129–130,
    133–135, 139, 142, 145,
    147–148, 247, 283, 286, 298
community safety net, 90
community self-help, 130
Comprehensive Social Security
    Assistance Scheme (CSSAS), 258,
    268, 270, 278
connectivities, 23–24

corporate management, 27
corporate social responsibility (CSR),
    27, 125, 246, 303–307,
    309–310–311, 313
    definition, 305
    strategic CSR, 307, 309–310
Creativity Index (CI), 106

D

dark sides of social capital, 181
definition of social work, 223
democratisation, 102, 128, 145–146
demography, 25, 199, 228
determinants of health, 25, 76, 155–
    156, 158, 165–167, 170–171
disadvantaged groups, 67, 97,
    102, 105, 165–166, 247, 263,
    267–269, 276, 281
District Administration, 142–143
District Council, 96, 142, 169–170

E

early stage and growth financing,
    297
economic capital, 38, 158, 175
economic development, 1, 3, 8–9, 13,
    16, 18, 28, 39, 81, 104, 127,
    131, 160, 225, 236–237, 251,
    258–259, 262, 305
eco-system, 156
Elder Shop, 87, 98
empowerment, 91–92, 123, 224, 248
enterprise continuum, 280
ethical behaviour, 303

F

family, 4, 12, 26, 46, 50–51, 55–56,
    67, 80, 82–84, 87–88, 133,
    145,156–157, 163–164, 170,
    186–188, 190–191, 204–207,
    213, 215, 224, 226, 230–232,

social value creation, 281
social welfare, 54–56, 59, 139–140, 145, 222, 250, 265, 285
social work, 24, 26, 38, 43, 56–66, 68–69, 76, 83, 91, 124, 140, 142, 146, 221–227, 229–240, 274, 285, 289, 292–293, 295
  emergent model 237
  paradigms, 222
  social capital, and 221, 225, 232
social work groups with secondary school students – the building of social capital among secondary school students in Hong Kong, 65
social workers, 24, 56–65, 68–69, 76, 91, 140, 142, 224, 226, 235–240, 285, 293, 295
  contribution of, 59
socio-
  demographic characteristics, 159
  demographic covariates, 163
  demographic variables, 155
  economic background, 58, 88, 90
  economic determinants of health, 185
  economic development, 251, 258
  economic family problems, 285
  economic groups, 166
  economic status, 82
  economic status, experiences, or needs, 82
  economic system, 251, 256, 262
  economically disadvantaged people, 175
  political determinants, 155
  psychological needs, 101
soft power, 27, 304, 310–315
solidarity, 3–4, 44, 55, 76, 81, 83, 86, 109–110, 186, 188–189, 191, 282, 293–294, 296
"Stewards" (an NGO), 288–291, 294–295

structural social capital, 101, 109–111, 182, 186
successful ageing, 200, 202, 204
superordinate goals, 85
sustainability, 3, 21, 79–80, 96–97, 164, 175, 186, 188, 247, 249, 263, 269
sustainable, 7, 28, 67, 105–106, 113, 130, 136–137, 155, 158, 165, 239, 245, 255, 261–262, 304–305, 308, 311, 315
sustainable communities, 136–137
sustainable development, 7, 113, 308
sustainable social development, 106
systems theory, 227

T

The Big Issue, 234–236, 240
theory and practice, 61, 113, 224
theory building, 284
transaction costs, 9, 40, 283, 294
trend, 37, 41–43, 48, 105, 124
Triad, 180, 183–186, 192–194
tripartite partnerships, 77, 95
trust, 2–8, 11, 18, 22, 28, 39–41, 43–46, 48–50, 59, 64–69, 75–76, 82–84, 88, 91, 97, 102, 104–105, 108–110, 124, 126–127, 134, 139, 142, 147, 159, 173, 183, 187, 189–192, 194–195, 201, 229–230, 259, 279, 283, 295, 304, 308–310, 314

U

United Kingdom, 134, 147, 223, 226
urban renewal, 104, 137

V

vertical communities, 88
voluntary work, 102, 209, 286